Cheechakoes in Wonderland

A Southeast Alaskan Odyssey

By Willard E. Andrews

DORRANCE
PUBLISHING CO
EST. 1920
PITTSBURGH, PENNSYLVANIA 15238

Dorrance Publishing Co
585 Alpha Drive
Suite 103
Pittsburgh, PA 15238
Visit our website at *www.dorrancebookstore.com*

ISBN: 979-8-8868-3183-2
eISBN: 979-8-8868-3756-8

Cheechakoes in Wonderland

A SOUTHEAST ALASKAN ODYSSEY

Dedication

For Linda, who shared the journey. And for all of those friends, colleagues, and neighbors who touched our lives throughout those years in Southeast Alaska, and made them richer.

Author's Note

This book had its genesis in the Southeast Alaskan cruises we took with National Geographic/Lindblad in the summers of 2019 and 2021, as part of revisitations—pilgrimages, if you will—to a place we had lived and loved for so many years. These one-week cruises hosted only sixty-five or so passengers, and it was possible to get to know and chat with many over meals and at cocktail hour. They were by and large interesting, curious people, interested in and curious about a land that most were seeing for the first time. They were fascinated to learn that we had actually lived in this place and experienced in depth many of the wonders they were witnessing, and many others that they would not be able to in so short a span. They devoured information and antidotes; even those who neither fished nor hunted were eager to hear about these activities in Alaska, and we found ourselves filling in gaps even amongst the superb naturalists of the expeditions' staffs (we learned even more from them). Toward the end of the second expedition, one of our fellow passengers said to me, "You should write a book." And so I did.

This book essentially wrote itself. Other than the inevitable tinkering, rewording, and rearranging, which did go on forever, the basic text was written, start to finish, over a period of less than three months.

My only outside sources of information, suggestions, and fact-checking were my wife and immediate family, those who lived this adventure with me most intimately. I intentionally avoided consulting those mentioned in the book that I remain in contact with; I wanted this book to be grounded in my—our family's—own, unfiltered memories.

The book is based entirely on recollections of places, people, and events that began more than fifty years ago. Over the time we spent in Alaska I took no notes, kept no diaries. I, and we, were living in the moment. Being well aware of what time can do to memories, I take full responsibility for any errors of fact, and for any exaggerations or distortions created by the imperfect lens of time. I've done my best with dates and times, and have tried to honor the sometimes wobbly line between fact and opinion.

This odyssey took place over the course of forty years, although we actually made our home in Southeast Alaska for just over half of those. The narrative does not lend itself to a precise chronological telling; our years and experiences in Southeast did not follow an arc. Bear with me as I move back and forth between the years and decades.

Writing this book has allowed me to relive many treasured memories of a magical time and place. It is my hope that the reader will find pleasure in experiencing them with me.

Introduction

"Cheechako" is Alaskan for tenderfoot, or greenhorn. According to Webster the term was first used circa 1897, and derived from a Native-American expression that quite literally translates into "newbie." I first encountered it when, early in our Alaskan experience, we borrowed and read a book entitled *The Cheechakoes*, by Wayne Short—a true account of a family that homesteaded in the wilderness of Southeast Alaska shortly after WWII.

Everyone who arrives in Alaska from somewhere else is, by definition, a cheechako—but some arrive less clueless than others, farther along some of the many learning curves. Once arrived, some progress along those curves at a faster rate—based on both intensity of effort and innate aptitude. A few never progress at all, and of those some don't really want to.

The opposite of cheechako is "sourdough," a grizzled old-timer who has seen and done it all, and is at home in the Alaskan outback as we are in our own living rooms. In theory there is a path leading from cheechako to sourdough, something like accumulating enough merit badges to become an Eagle Scout. But in fact very few make it to the top of the mountain. As pilgrims on the road find out, each of the many essential learning curves eventually begins to flatten into infinity. The chosen ones who make it all the way have incredible aptitude, and the ranks are limited almost entirely to those who have devoted their lives to the Alaskan outdoors. During my tenure in Southeast Alaska it has been my privilege to know a few.

This is the story of one pilgrim who, like most others, never made it to the promised land—but had one hell of a grand time along the way. Any regrets about falling short of the top? It was never really about the destination. It was always about the journey.

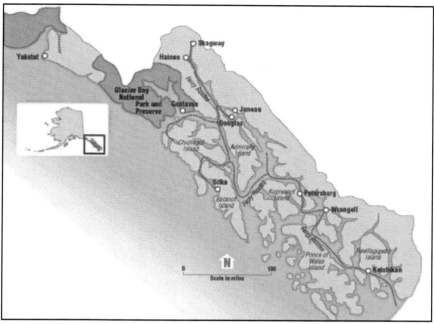

Southeast Alaska

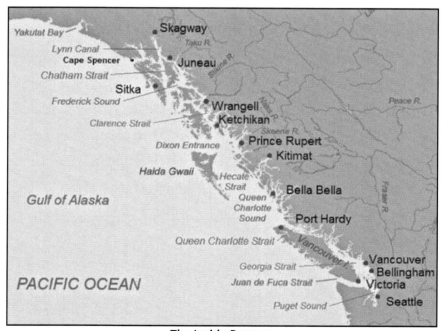

The Inside Passage

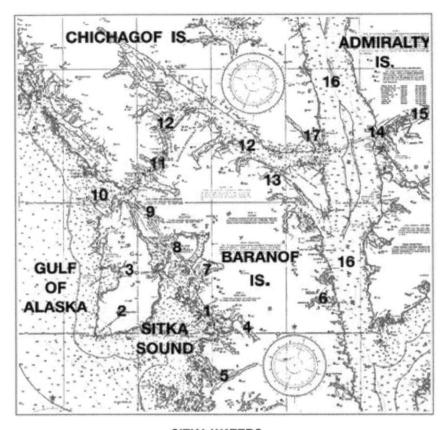

SITKA WATERS

1 - Sitka
2 - Mt. Edgecumbe Volcano
3 - Kruzof Is.
4 - Silver Bay
5 - Redoubt Bay
6 - Baranof Warm Springs
7 - Katlian Bay
8 - Olga Strait
9 - Neva Strait
10 - Salisbury Sound

11 - Sergius Narrows
12 - Peril Strait
13 - Hanus Bay/Eva Creek
14 - Angoon
15 - Mitchell Bay
16 - Chatham Strait
17 - Sitkoh Bay

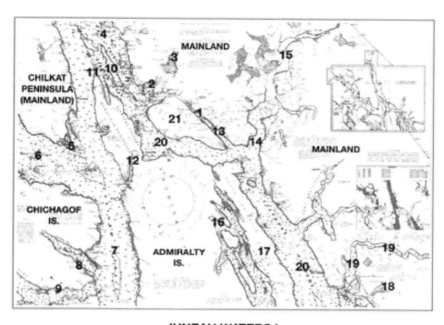

JUNEAU WATERS I

1 - Juneau
2 - Auke Bay
3 - Mendenhall Glacier
4 - Lynn Canal
5 - Pt. Couverden/Swanson Harbor
6 - Icy Strait
7 - Chatham Strait
8 - Pavlov Harbor
9 - Tenakee Springs
10 - Shelter Is.
11 - Pt. Retreat
12 - Hawk Inlet
13 - Gastineau Channel
14 - Taku Inlet
15 - Taku River
16 - Pack Creek
17 - Glass Peninsula
18 - Sumdum Glacier
19 - Tracy Arm
20 - Stephens Passage

21 - Douglas Is.

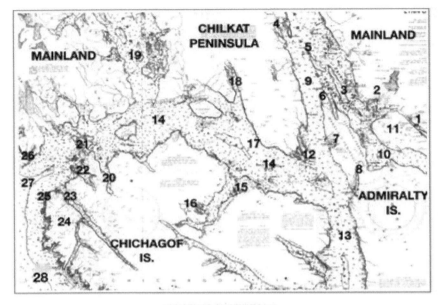

JUNEAU WATERS II

1 - Juneau
2 - Mendenhall Glacier
3 - Shelter Is.
4 - St. James Bay
5 - Ralston Is.
6 - Pt. Retreat
7 - Funter Bay
8 - Hawk Inlet
9 - Lynn Canal
10 - Stephens Passage
11 - Douglas Is.
12 - Pt. Couverden/Swanson Harbor
13 - Chatham Strait
14 - Icy Strait
15 Hoonah
16 - Neka Bay
17 - Homeshore
18 - Excursion Inlet
19 - Glacier Bay
20 - Idaho Inlet

21 - Inian Islands
22 - Elfin Cove, Port Althorp
23 - Lisianski Strait
24 - Yakobi Is.
25 - Cape Bingham
26 - Cape Spencer
27 - Cross Sound
28 - Gulf of Alaska

Tracy Arm Fjord

Mendenhall Towers and Glacier, from Glacier Hwy. north of Juneau

7

The Missing Paperwork
(Or, The Dog Ate My Homework)

Until the phone call from Washington, D.C., came sometime in April of 1969, thoughts of visiting, traveling to, or, perish the thought, moving to and living in Alaska had never crossed my mind. I was but a month or two from completing a residency in general surgery at the Medical Center Hospitals of Vermont in Burlington, and my wife and I were increasingly concerned that we had not heard from the U.S. Public Health Service. I'd known for over four years that the U.S.P.H.S. had a claim on my services for my first two post-residency years, and had been anticipating hearing what and where my assignment would be.

The mid-sixties had marked the height of the Vietnam era, and newly minted medical school graduates could expect, with near 100% certainty, to be drafted into the armed forces as GMOs—general medical officers, the military equivalent of general practitioners—after having completed one postgraduate year of internship (now morphed into the first year of residency). This was brought home to me in no uncertain terms as I began my final year of medical school in July 1963, with a rotation on the GYN service: Of the new OB/GYN residents expected to begin their specialty training in the Columbia-Presbyterian program, none showed up. All had been drafted, conscripted to spend two years as GMOs with Uncle Sam before they would be able to get back on the career track they had chosen.

For my classmates and myself, in another two years this would be us. Unlike many others of our generation, we were by and large apolitical and uninvolved in this time of activism and the counterculture, having spent the turbulent early sixties with our noses to the grindstone in medical school. No protests, no vigils, no pot for us. Most of us had no feelings one way or the other about the war in progress—the *raison d'etre* for the doctor draft—or about the military, but virtually all of us had by that time identified the field in which we hoped to specialize, and saw the conflict as an impediment barring the way, albeit temporarily, to our career goals. As it was, college, medical school, and the long period of postgraduate specialty training took a big bite out of a physician's youth and productive years, so what we most dreaded was the prospect of marking time for two or more of those precious years while our professional aspirations were put on hold.

We went into our internship year knowing that a fortunate few of us would get the opportunity to do our obligatory military service time as specialists later rather than generalists now. A small percentage, based on a lottery, would receive deferments for the duration of their specialty training, after which they would called to active duty by the particular service that had granted the deferment. This program, which involved all branches of the armed forces, was called the Berry Plan; everyone knew about it, and every one of my intern contemporaries at the University of Minnesota Hospitals signed up for the lottery.

What I saw that apparently none of my fellow surgical interns did was an inconspicuous notice posted outside one of the hospital elevators, asking for applicants to the C.O.R.D.—commissioned officer residency deferment—program...a U.S. Public Health Service equivalent of the Berry Plan. I almost couldn't believe what I was looking at. I hadn't even known that the U.S.P.H.S. was at that time a uniformed service, equivalent to the military and complete with military ranks and pay scales. It had a far-flung network of hospitals and healthcare mandates, including the staffing and administration of VA hospitals and the provision of medical care to Native Americans both on and off reservations—the Indian Health Service. Selection for the C.O.R.D. program was not based on a lottery—I don't know how the selection process worked—but I signed up for consideration, completed a required interview, and did not share the information with my colleagues. If any of them did see that notice, they didn't tell me either.

I was not selected for the Berry Plan (and haven't bought a lottery ticket since). As I recall, neither were any of my thirteen surgical intern/first-year resident colleagues at the University of Minnesota Hospitals. But I did receive a deferment through the C.O.R.D. plan, and now, four years later, it was time to pay the piper.

———

At least four months earlier we had received from the U.S.P.H.S. a packet in the mail containing a reminder of my upcoming two-year obligation, and a lengthy list of potential duty assignments. I was asked to list my preferences for assignment and return the form to Washington ASAP, as preferences would be honored on a first-come-first-served basis. The obvious choices for a surgeon just out of residency were those offering, presumably, the most rewarding and challenging professional experience, and I vividly recall checking the boxes for the big hospitals in Seattle, San Francisco, and Staten Island.

The caller from Washington wanted to know why I hadn't submitted my preferences months ago. Whoa! *Wait a minute!* It was unthinkable that Linda and I had neglected to put in the mail something with such a profound bearing on our future (just how profound we were yet to find out). It had to have been a postal service glitch. Or, our precious document had been swallowed up and digested deep in the bowels of the government bureaucracy. Did our dog eat it on its way to the mailbox? We'll never know, but it really didn't matter: We were last in line for a surgical assignment, and all the choice postings had long since been taken.

It happened that there were three more postings than there were surgeons to fill them, so we were given a short list to choose from: the leprosarium at Carville, Louisiana, and Indian Health Service hospitals at Shiprock, New Mexico, Tuba City, Arizona, and Mt. Edgecumbe, Alaska. The man on the phone gave us a week to scope them out, make a choice, and get back to him.

We got out our world atlas and located each on the map. Carville we eliminated quickly—neither leprosy nor Louisiana had much appeal. We were totally unfamiliar with the high desert country of New Mexico and Arizona and knew of no one who was, but neither Linda nor I could get enthusiastic about living there (it was not until decades later that we would be able to see and appreciate firsthand the uniqueness and beauty of the American Southwest's high desert country—but we would still not choose to live there). Mt. Edgecumbe turned out to be an appendage of the town of Sitka, on the outer coast midway along Alaska's southeast panhandle. We'd at least heard of Sitka. We knew less than nothing about it, only that it was far to the North and West of where we were, and by thousands of miles. We had visions of igloos and dogsleds. But we did have some sources of information to explore.

I recalled that an intern who had been on my service two years before in Burlington had been assigned there as a GMO, and would be on the home stretch of his two-year P.H.S. hitch. I managed to track him down on the phone one evening. The call lasted an hour, and he went on like a revival preacher selling salvation. The superlatives kept coming: the wildness, the scenery, the boating, the fishing, the hunting (after finishing at Mt. Edgecumbe he would do an ophthalmology residency "down south" and return to Alaska to open a practice in Soldotna, on the Kenai peninsula).

I also knew that a first-year ENT resident at the University of Vermont had, the year before, completed a two-year stint as a GMO at the Indian

Health Service clinic at Juneau, only a long stone's throw from Sitka. He and his wife came over for coffee one evening, bringing with them a bunch of slides and more glowing stories of life on the Last Frontier.

———

I'd grown up during the 1940s and '50s in Fort Lee, New Jersey, a mixed blue- and white-collar community within spitting distance of the George Washington Bridge and with a view of the Manhattan skyline from the Palisades only blocks away. Thanks to frugal, hard-working parents who valued education, I'd gone to college in a toney Philadelphia Main Line suburb, and medical school at Columbia University's College of Physicians & Surgeons in New York City. No one in my family, nor anyone we knew, hunted, and only a great-grandfather, who passed away when I was three, had fished. We did not have a gun in the house, or know of anyone who did (my mother's father had apparently owned a pistol, but when he died my grandmother buried it in their backyard). A middle-class-plus East Coast suburban pedigree—not a promising resumé for one considering casting off for a wilderness at the far end of the earth. If the earth were flat, one step further would take us over the edge.

In 1969, that was not an exaggeration. Alaska had been a state for only ten years, and other than the two P.H.S. physicians mentioned, no one we knew had so much as visited there. It may be difficult for Americans of today, accustomed to travel in an age where everyone has been everywhere, to grasp that at this point in time hardly anyone had been anywhere. Alaska might as well have been on the moon. For us and everyone else, Alaska was more an abstraction than a reality—"Seward's Folly" and "Seward's Icebox," it had been called when purchased by the U.S. from Russia only 102 years before, a vast expanse of wilderness with lots of trees, wild animals, snow, ice, and very few people, not even attached to the continental United States. What people there were we vaguely imagined to be either natives—maybe Eskimos—or not much

13

different from those hardy folk who had ventured beyond the American frontier in colonial times. Think Daniel Boone. Could this be us?

But there's more.

I had liked to fish for as long as I can remember, possibly inheriting that unlikely itch from my great-grandfather, from whom I also inherited some second-tier tackle (his grown-up nephew got the good stuff). From the age of three or four my grandmother would take me to nearby Hudson County Park in North Bergen, N.J., on the first day of trout season. The Park had an artificial concrete-bordered impoundment of about 3 acres, far better suited to the ducks that people came to feed in summer than to the 1000 or so trout that had the misfortune to be dumped in by the New Jersey Department of Fish & Game a few days before every April opening day (those trout were probably grateful to be caught). Opening day drew a huge crowd with anglers lining the bank elbow to elbow, as it was the only trout-fishing venue for miles around. After each troutless opener we'd walk back to Grandmother's house, stopping at a fish market along the way where she'd buy a proxy trophy that would be cooked for lunch.

My father, good sport that he was, took up where Grandmother left off. By that time I was convinced that preserved, bottled salmon eggs were far better bait for trout than the worms that Grandmother (wearing gloves) had dutifully threaded on my hook. Not about to spend money on such nonsense, he dug out a bottle of maraschino cherries from the kitchen fridge. His argument was that they were bigger, redder, and therefore better than salmon eggs—but of course I continued to catch no trout (Dad could be very creative when it came to devising ways to avoid the fuss and bother involved with catching fish. This was but one of his successful ploys.). The succession of fishless years only made me more determined that, *someday*, I would get the skunk off the deck and actually catch one.

The universe of most families in the WWII and immediate postwar eras was small. Ours was slightly larger than most, as from earliest childhood I'd spent summer weekends, and at least part of every summer, at a small family vacation cottage in Gloucester, Massachusetts—250 miles and an 8-hour drive from our home in New Jersey. For us children growing up it seemed light years from New Jersey, as far from civilization as it was possible to get. The cottage had been built by my grandfather in 1933 and was surrounded by acres of upland woods, out of sight of the road and with no nearby neighbors. A short hike down through the woods took my brother and I to a swimming hole in a tidal creek that ran through the saltmarsh. The cottage was primitive in those days, uninsulated with only an open fireplace for heat, and totally unfinished inside—open ceiling, rooms separated by thin, eight-foot-high plywood partitions, and bare studs on the walls. No electricity—kerosene lamps and an icebox. Coleman stove for cooking. Outdoor plumbing, of course. We kids loved it (our mother, less so).

We had a Daisy BB gun at the cottage, and for one season a single-shot .22 rifle that was stolen by vandals during a winter break-in. These we plinked tin cans with on our isolated property, and I found it fun.

As our cottage was not far from saltwater, Dad owned a succession of outboard-powered skiffs in the years after WWII. I finally caught my first fish when I was about nine—mackerel—with a handline and spinner trolled behind the boat as we traversed the waters of Ipswich Bay. Even Dad couldn't keep those mackerel off the hook. My brother and I developed an enduring affinity for saltwater and boats, thrived on learning the essentials of small boat seamanship through our childhood and teen years, and learned to be comfortable on the water.

I had been a member of our local Boy Scout troop in my early teens, until participation was eventually preempted by high school basketball. I particularly enjoyed the day and overnight hikes, and learning the woodcraft skills that went hand in hand. These I did not forget.

As I progressed through my teen years I began, along with a like-minded high school friend, to experience some very modest fishing success. However, my most impressive trophies were fantasy ones, my imagination fueled by stories in *Outdoor Life* and *Field & Stream* magazines, both of which I had subscriptions to and which were avidly devoured cover to cover—including the features that dealt with hunting and hunting firearms. There were sometimes features about hunting or fishing in exotic faraway places, like Alaska.

Fishing, hunting, and the out-of-doors, real or fancied, were put out of sight and out of mind for the combined eight years of college and medical school, and the first year of postgraduate medical training—but I was fortunate to do the final four years of surgical residency at an institution that not only offered superb preparation for a professional life to come, but also proximity to Lake Champlain and the forests and streams of Vermont's Green Mountains. Despite the rigors of the program, I found just enough time to sample some of the outdoor opportunities at our doorstep, including teaching myself the bare rudiments of fly-fishing—with bargain-basement equipment, all I could afford—and actually catching an occasional trout and smallmouth bass.

What all this is leading up to is that P. T. Barnum himself could not have picked a better mark for a pitch on Southeast Alaska. We called the guy in Washington and told him that Mt. Edgecumbe it would be.

——

My spouse was a bit more circumspect. If anything, hers had been an even more conventional suburban upbringing than mine; for her, roughing it had consisted of one week of one summer at a Girl Scout camp, which she'd detested (leeches in the lake water! Uggh!). But neither of us aspired to a life in suburban New Jersey where we grew up, nor were we drawn, as some are, to the energy and pulsing vitality of a large city, New York or otherwise. We'd had a taste of different and better—for us, anyway—and my profession should give us the latitude to eventually make that happen. As products of middle-class suburbia, at that point in our lives neither could envision anything more outside the civilization box than a New England country house with a white picket fence. Alaska was to be a two-year interlude, possibly the adventure of a lifetime, prior to settling down and practicing surgery somewhere in New England.

There were preparations to be made, and at this late hour time was of the essence. We had been advised—by the government, as I recall—that many staple food items might be difficult or impossible to obtain in Sitka, so we bought $2000 worth of soups and other canned foods, sugar, flour, coffee, even powdered milk, just as the pioneers would have loaded their covered wagon with staples before heading west. Since we were headed west of even the wild west, I went all in and also purchased a second-hand 30/06 rifle from a local gun shop, along with a new .357 magnum revolver. I learned the ABCs of ammunition handloading at the gun shop, a sagacious move on my part and also on the part of the proprietor, as he then sold me basic reloading equipment and lots of components—cases, bullets, primers, powder. Every spare moment when not at the hospital or on call was spent practicing and gaining a head start on proficiency with these new toys.

We were able to afford all this thanks to a bank loan, and a doubling of my salary that had gone into effect at the beginning of my final year of residency (during the prior four years we had probably lived well below the poverty line, although we didn't really know where that was. Linda, an R.N., had worked nights at the hospital part-time and fed our growing family on a food budget of $8 a week). Our move would be paid for by Uncle Sam.

One of the last orders of business took me by surprise, although it shouldn't have. Linda was expecting our third child in late December. I received a call at the hospital from her obstetrician one late June morning, who asked, in the unlikely event Linda required delivery by C-section, who would perform it (he had asked Linda that question on her last prenatal visit, and her answer prompted the call). It was one of those "duh" moments when it dawned that the answer was...well, me. We knew there would be no obstetrician at the Mt. Edgecumbe hospital—obstetric care and deliveries would be the province of the GMOs, fresh from a one-year rotating internship, with two to three months of that time spent on an OB service. Sufficient (we and they hoped) for dealing with routine prenatal care and deliveries, to recognize complications when they arose, but unequipped with the surgical skills to do deliveries via C-section. My familiarity with the procedure had been limited to observing a few from the back row during my obstetrics rotation years before in med school, but five years of training in the performance of surgical procedures far more complex had provided me the necessary tools. Linda's obstetrician knew this, and took me through a C-section step by step on the phone while I took notes. As it turned out, Linda's delivery was routine, but a number of others during my tenure at Mt. Edgecumbe were not. The combination of the obstetric expertise of our very capable GMOs, and my technical facility, managed to keep everything on the rails during the course of a half-dozen or so C-section deliveries. Little did I realize at the time that, over the course of a career in Alaska, C-sections would rank among my single most commonly performed procedures.

Circling the Wagons

Since my residency officially ended on the last day in June 1969, D-day was July 1 or very soon after. We certainly felt like pioneers, even if we weren't real ones, as we loaded the family into our version of a covered wagon, a green '64 VW Bug; Susan and Betsy, ages four and two, in the back seat wearing seatbelts improvised by my dad, Linda riding shotgun in front along with who would be, six months later, son David. Taffy, our bloodle—a bloodhound-poodle mix that I'd rescued from the medical center's animal lab as a puppy—would be boarded and eventually fly up to join us. Unbeknownst to Taffy or to us, she would make not one but two more transcontinental flights, making her by far the family's most frequent flyer.

This would be an adventure from the start. With the exception of a surgical internship/first residency year at the University of Minnesota, where I crossed the Mississippi River each time I went the few miles from our apartment to the hospital or back, neither of us had been more than a couple of hundred miles from the Eastern Seaboard.

Late each afternoon we would circle the wagons around a Holiday Inn (we had visions of hostiles waiting until after dark to raid our wagon train, in places like South Bend, Indiana). Once west of the Mississippi, the country we encountered was like nothing we'd ever seen before:

South Dakota's badlands just west of Rapid City. The Bighorn Range of the Rockies, rising in the distance out of the barren high plains of Wyoming. The majestic Tetons marching out of Jackson Hole. Yellowstone Park. There were times I wished our Bug had an afterburner as it struggled up the long grades of the mountain west—or maybe just more oxen under the hood. The girls were good travelers, too young for "Are we there yet?" and entertained, as were the grownups, by stops at prairie dog colonies, the reptile gardens outside Rapid City (where Susan lost a tortoise race to her younger sister), and the wildlife and geysers as we swung through Yellowstone.

At Livingston, Montana, we made the obligatory stop at Dan Bailey's fly shop, at the time a mecca for fly-fishermen transiting the area. One area of the shop was given over to rows of tables where more than a dozen women were seated in front of fly-tying vises, knocking out flies to be sold in the shop or by mail order. Two-year-old Betsy, taking it all in, exclaimed in a loud voice, "My daddy can tie better flies than these." I wished at the moment I had a bag to slip over my head; each of these women were producing a dozen beautifully tied flies in the time it would have taken me to produce one crude, sloppy one (I would get better over time).

With the exception of throwing a wagon wheel (read alternator) in Jackson, Wyoming, which held us up a few days waiting for the part to come in, our wagon train made it to Seattle without attack by hostiles or further hardships. In Seattle we paid a visit to Noodleman's—a store near the waterfront that specialized in military uniforms and accoutrements. We had a list of the items to be purchased, supplied by the Public Health Service, as I would in a few days be a man in uniform—a commissioned officer (lieutenant commander, no less!) in the U.S.P.H.S. The particular item that stands out among all those purchased were the several pair of black socks, to be worn as part of the "winter" uniform (summer socks were khaki). Those socks exceeded their "use by" date by well over a decade, and I wore them for years after my days in uniform were over. They refused to wear out; we talked of their being made of cast iron—they felt like it—and referred to them as my "Noodleman socks." I think we ultimately gave them a decent burial while they were still serviceable.

———

Sitka is situated at about the midpoint of Alaska's southeastern panhandle, a narrow strip of mainland backing on British Columbia with an extensive north-south oriented chain of islands just offshore—the Alexander Archipelago. The islands vary in size from very small to very large, so large that they don't seem like islands at all until you realize that you can't drive to or from them. Most of Southeast Alaska's communities are on islands rather than the mainland; Sitka, on the outer coast of Baranof Island, had been the Russian capitol at the time the U.S. purchased Alaska from Russia in 1867. As implied, the only ways to reach Sitka were, and are, by water or by air. Our belongings had been containerized in Seattle and sent on by barge. Our VW Bug would also make the trip by barge. We would fly.

Sitka lies about 900 miles due north of Seattle, in the jet age only two hours by direct flight, and our first landing there was a memorable one. Actually, every landing at Sitka is memorable. As our 727 descended through an overcast (that we would find the rule rather than the exception) and circled on approach, the view from our window conjured images from an old WWII movie: John Wayne in the cockpit, gamely trying to nurse his shot-up fighter down on a pitching, bobbing carrier flight deck.

Sitka's airport is actually located on Japonski Island, a small, flat island separated from Baranof Island and Sitka by a narrow channel (on all but the largest-scale maps they appear as one and the same). It was chosen for the airport because it was the only nearby place flat enough, yet far enough from the towering peaks of Baranof that in places came almost to the water's edge. The comparison of the airport's runway to a carrier flight deck is not an exaggeration. The flight deck—er, run-way—was hard against the seaward edge of the island, and extended out from it at each end—much more so on the south end, where the runway had been extended out into Sitka Sound on rock fill to satisfy FAA landing and takeoff requirements for the 727. It was said to be the nation's shortest runway so certified. On the seaward side, breaking waves almost reached the tarmac when the wind was right. The flight deck/runway didn't actually pitch and bob, but the combination of whitecaps in Sitka Sound and air turbulence that commonly buffets air-craft landing there made it seem that way. Just after touchdown, the harsh deceleration and roar associated with the full reverse thrust needed to stop on the truncated runway must have felt similar to what a carrier aviator experiences when his tail hook grabs the arrest wire (after a number of close calls and the introduction of the larger 737, the runway was lengthened yet again). When we finally came to a near-stop as the 727 made a U-turn at the end of the runway, all we could see, looking down out of our window, was water.

As we disembarked and walked across the tarmac to the small ter-minal, the realization hit: This was the end of the line. We were in Alaska, on the Last Frontier. Whether or not we were pioneer material we'd find out soon enough.

The Welcome Wagon that Wasn't,
and Chickens Wearing Turkey Suits

We didn't know quite what to expect after retrieving our luggage at the Sitka terminal, but the date and arrival time of our flight were well known to the Public Health Service, and we anticipated that someone from the hospital would be there to meet us. The terminal quickly cleared of other arriving passengers, leaving us quite alone. Our plane had departed for points north, and the airline counter personnel had vanished. Someone had even turned out the lights. After waiting 20 or 30 minutes, it became obvious that we were on our own; no taxis, no buses, no traffic, no people. We weren't in Kansas anymore.

Looking up and down the empty, unpaved road in front of the terminal, all I could see were dense conifer woods lining the opposite side in both directions, with craggy, snow-capped peaks in the distant background. Flipping an imaginary coin, I left Linda with the children and walked south.

Good choice, as twenty minutes later I arrived at the imposing but bland edifice of the Mt. Edgecumbe Alaska Native Hospital. Once inside I was directed to the office of the service unit director—the hospital administrator and overseer of the entire Southeast Alaska Native health program—and shortly after was driven by Jon Gove, one of the veteran

GMOs (one who had already served there a year) to the house that was to be our home for the next two years. He stopped at the airport to pick up Linda and the children on the way, and kindly invited us to dinner that night.

Turns out we were supposed to have been met at the airport by the wife of the hospital's internist, the ranking officer on the medical staff, but she had dropped the ball and totally forgot. This was a source of great amusement to the rest of the staff, for as we learned at dinner, the woman had lobbied haughtily and hard, as the ranking wife, to be the one to greet us as well as host us that evening—and had blown it. She was well known among the staff veterans—as we would soon find out for ourselves—for being every bit as status-conscious as the rest of the wives were not. She'd have made an ideal career military wife. She and her husband lived next door to us, and it wasn't long before she was carping to Linda about my wearing black winter socks in summer with brown loafers, and sometimes passing her house on the way to the hospital at 8:05 when the official daily "report for duty" time was 8:00. Linda replied that if these things bothered her, she should tell her husband, my immediate superior (although equal in rank, he had seniority). "That's the trouble!" she exclaimed in frustration. "Tom doesn't care!"

And what a good thing that was. I have no knowledge of how military protocol and discipline played with physicians conscripted into the other uniformed services, but was thankful that Tom Keith's attitude prevailed in the U.S.P.H.S., at least at Mt. Edgecumbe. All of the physicians on the clinical staff were short-timers, two-year wonders like myself, having instantly acquired ranks that non-physician career officers in the military take years to attain. In the process, those officers become immersed and indoctrinated in the uniformed service culture as they made their way up the lengthy career ladder. We, on the other hand, were like chickens wearing turkey suits. We would get used to wearing a uniform to work every day, but despite the disguise had little idea of how to behave like proper turkeys. And up to a point we were permitted to act like the chickens we were. There was no social hierarchy, deference to rank, formality, or pecking order, amongst ourselves or our families. Other than my own and Tom's, I didn't even know what my colleagues' ranks were. Uniforms were never seen at social functions, parties and the like. There were no barriers between us and the "civilians," the non-uniformed people that we lived and worked alongside of all the time, such as there are between officers and enlisted personnel, or civilians, in other services. All of this must have greatly disappointed Tom's wife.

None of us had been taught how or when to salute, an omission that rendered us the lawful prey of some of the enlisted "coasties"— Coast Guardsmen—stationed there. The staff veterans warned us newbies of a particularly nasty prank they enjoyed at our expense: Well aware of our cluelessness, when they encountered one of our number shopping in town while in uniform, both arms filled with grocery bags, they'd snap a smart salute. Often as not the hapless, flustered officer would drop his bags to return the salute, spilling bag contents all over the street. Unbeknownst to the mark, returning the salute of an enlisted man was entirely unnecessary.

A welcome perk was finding that a lieutenant commander's pay grade was far above what I had made as a resident. And considering that our housing and home maintenance were free, it was also far above what I would make in my first two post-service years of group practice. We were finally able to afford a few extras, pay off our loan, and put a little money in the bank.

The good parts notwithstanding, I was happy to be just passing through. The few career P.H.S. officers stationed at Mt. Edgecumbe during my stay were specialty-trained physicians that had abandoned clinical medicine to climb the career ladder by becoming administrators. They were nice enough guys, but as a clinician I could not help but feel a certain—distain is a strong word but the only one that comes to mind—for colleagues who had chosen to become 8-to-5 bureaucrats, driving desks and shuffling papers. Maybe an unfair characterization; they may have been doing vital and important things, but in medicine an unbridgeable gap has always existed between clinicians and administrators, and probably always will.

In a bureaucracy such as the U.S.P.H.S. the clinical staff was subject to policies handed down from, and enforced by, the paper shufflers. It was a nagging reminder that despite our long leashes, at the end of the day our official status was still that of turkeys. We were expected to fall in line with whatever came down from the head gobblers, whether it made sense or not. Over my two years this was more a minor chronic annoyance than anything else, but I accumulated a few demerits when I pushed back against what I considered petty or faintly ridiculous regulations and policies that had nothing to do with professional performance. I never had a glance at my P.H.S. report card, but doubt that I got more than a C- when it came to "plays well with others." Who knows? For the same "infractions" in a military service, I might have wound up in the brig.

Looking back, this was not the fault of the U.S. Public Health Service. It was what it was, and it had been part of my job adapt and make it work for two years without making waves. I hadn't done that especially well. It appeared that my younger contemporaries on the medical staff did a uniformly better job of handling it than I did.

———

The Alaska Native Hospital at Mt. Edgecumbe was an impressively large but aging structure that began existence as a tuberculosis sanitarium, I think somewhere around the end of WWII. TB was endemic throughout Alaska until the emergence of effective antituberculous drugs, and the facility had been used for the treatment of natives from all over the vast territory. Much TB surgery, both pulmonary and orthopedic, had been performed there. As the incidence of TB declined, the facility morphed into a regional general hospital serving the native population of Southeast Alaska (along with others who fell under the aegis of the U.S.P.H.S. healthcare umbrella: U.S. veterans, servicemen and their families, and merchant seamen regardless of nationality), and far less space and fewer beds would be needed in this new role. The impressive size of the structure belied the fact that well under half the ward space once needed to house patients was currently being used.

When I arrived the hospital staff consisted of an internist, a general surgeon (me), five GMOs, or generalists, two dentists, a physical therapist, two pharmacists, and the service unit director. There would be a pediatrician the following year, as well as a full-time administrator for outpatient services throughout the service unit. There was an ENT specialist, not in the P.H.S. but there on a one-year privately endowed program to attack the backlog of chronic ear infections and mastoiditis endemic in the native population of Southeast. He also did a lot of tonsillectomies, a common procedure I might have been otherwise pressured to do but had no training for, and wanted no part of.

As chief of surgery, an impressive title for one fresh out of residency, I was provided an office, a secretary, and one of the GMOs to assist at surgery and help in running the service. The surgical service was only moderately busy, a far cry from what I had been used to as chief resident—but that isn't really fair, as nothing in most surgical careers compares with that one year. I, like every other young surgeon, loved to operate—but not always having a ward full of postop patients recovering from major procedures gave me the breathing room needed to explore our new and marvelous environment outside the hospital.

I had no idea of what to expect when it came to operating room facilities and staff, but was pleased with what I found. The single O.R. suite was modern and well-equipped, and the small O.R. staff, including nurses, technicians, and nurse anesthetists, competent and well-run by the O.R. supervisor. We dealt with the usual general surgical staples—gastrointestinal surgery, hernia repairs, etc., with a disproportionate weighting toward biliary tract surgery. Gallbladder disease was endemic in the native population of Southeast Alaska, just as in the Native American populations of the American Southwest. It was most prone to surface in spring, almost like a seasonal epidemic after the herring egg harvest had taken place. A traditional native delicacy was herring eggs fried in seal oil; for those with gallstones, it was like throwing gasoline on a fire (herring roe was harvested by natives throughout Southeast by placing cut evergreen branches weighted with stones in the shallows of coves known to be preferred herring spawning areas. Roe was deposited on the branches, which were then retrieved by the natives. We saw this once, later in time, at a cove at the north end of Auke Bay.).

Volume brought with it some unusual manifestations and complications of biliary tract disease, including some seldom encountered by most surgeons over a career in practice.

I was the *de facto* orthopedist and GYN specialist. My training had included rotations in a few of the surgical subspecialties, and I felt just comfortable enough dealing with non-operative orthopedics—simple fractures and dislocations—and much more comfortable doing gynecologic surgery and even the occasional C-section. Through sheer good luck—mine and that of prospective patients—I was able to dodge bullets and run between the raindrops for the most part, never forced too far out of my comfort zone in having to wear multiple hats that didn't quite fit.

It came as a surprise to find my expertise challenged on occasion by—the local shaman. More than once, elective surgery—usually involving an elderly native patient—was cancelled at the eleventh hour because the shaman advised against it.

The hospital had no radiologist. The radiology department was run by a lone very capable technician, who nursed the medical staff (myself included) through doing our own gastrointestinal contrast studies on our patients—upper GI series and barium enemas. We read our own films; all were officially read by a contract radiologist who came up from Seattle every three months and went through the backlog, far too late to be of any use. By the time they've completed a residency, surgeons were pretty savvy when it came to interpreting films that fell within their bailiwick, so it was not too much of a handicap.

Despite my exalted rank, for the first year I was expected to participate in the regular on-call rotation with the GMOs, 24-hour shifts which meant spending that night at the hospital covering the house and the E.R. To me it seemed like some sort of unnecessary rite of initiation, as I was essentially on call all the time for things surgical. Fortune again favored me, for the most part. The Mt. Edgecumbe emergency room was a slow place, and I was seldom called upon to deal with anything more serious than colds, flu, or sore throats, and not too many of those. I was, early on, called late at night to see an individual who was loud, abusive, and who demanded admission to the hospital despite the fact that his only claim to illness was being shitfaced. Grossly and obnoxiously intoxicated. I was more than a little pissed at having to get out of bed to deal with this, and was in the process of telling him to get his pixilated buns out of there when the night shift nursing supervisor intervened and lectured me that it was policy to admit such folk at their request (or demand), and allow them to stay until they had slept it off, sobered up, and left voluntarily. I was to learn that this was a not-uncommon occurrence. Alcohol abuse was an endemic problem within the native population, and some of the outlying predominantly native villages had voted themselves "dry"; when residents did visit Sitka, the Big City, many fell off the wagon with a *thunk*. So, it was not the last time I was obliged to play desk sergeant, booking a drunk into a hospital holding tank. My reaction didn't earn me any points with the head gobblers. I didn't ask whether I was expected to do an admission history and physical, write orders, and order lab work on these "patients." I didn't, and was never called on it.

I knew I was fair game for having to play obstetrician when I was "it"—on call—and prayed it wouldn't happen. But of course it did. My exposure to obstetrics had been limited to a rather inadequate 4th-year rotation in med school, during which I did a lot of watching, and performed only parts of some routine vaginal deliveries under supervision—never an entire one. More of my knowledge came from our textbook than it did from hands-on experience, and I was terrified at the prospect of having to put that theoretical knowledge to use.

When I arrived at Mt. Edgecumbe, the normally somnolent obstetrics unit was filled to the brim. An outbreak of staph had closed the OB unit at the native hospital in Bethel, far off in western Alaska, and the conservative decision was made to ship out all of their expectant mothers 7 months along or more. The Mt. Edgecumbe hospital had been selected as their landing site precisely *because* its OB facilities were chronically underutilized. This did not go over well with the women so affected, and as a lot they were surly, resentful, and uncommunicative. Small wonder, as they were being involuntarily held for an indefinite period more than 1500 miles from home. I'd have been too. It was the rule among them that those whose water broke, or who went into labor, did not inform the nursing staff, but waited for the nurses to find out for themselves. Certainly an interesting form of revenge.

So it was that I was called to the OB floor during one of my "on call" shifts by an overexcited nurse who told me that one of her patients had just been discovered crowning (the fetal head starting to emerge) in bed. I arrived just in time to go through all the motions of a delivery with the patient still in bed—actually a good thing, as there was no chance of my fumbling and dropping the newborn infant on the floor. To my credit I did every bit as well as any policeman, fireman, or EMT could have done, and all ended well for mother, infant, and me. It would be the only vaginal delivery of my career, and I have no recollection of whether the infant was a girl or a boy.

———

We did not see that many surgical emergencies or much severe trauma at Mt. Edgecumbe, so after-hours and weekend work was far less than

I had been accustomed to in residency—or would experience later in private practice. Sitka-Mt. Edgecumbe had only a modest native population, and Native Americans elsewhere in Southeast who required urgent surgical (or other) care went to the nearest medical facility capable of treating them—often in Juneau to the north and Ketchikan to the south, where they were treated by private physicians or surgeons. Just as well. As the hospital's sole surgeon, it was neither expected nor possible that I be immediately available 24/7, week in and week out, although I was most of the time. The most dire emergency that occurred during one of my brief absences was when our daughter Betsy got a pinky finger caught in a door and partially avulsed a fingernail. I arrived home to find a daughter with a digit enveloped in a bulbous bandage. Linda had taken her to the E.R., where several of the GMOs had conferred over the finger, trying to decide: "What would Will do?" Betsy had the answer: "If my daddy were here, he would kiss it and make it better." Anyway, they got it right, and even without the kiss the "Magic Finger" healed just fine.

There was sometimes delay in the treatment of those emergencies that we did get, a consequence of transportation issues, weather, or a combination of both that I would find so common throughout Southeast. A few patients with appendicitis, even after early diagnosis on location, arrived days later after their appendix had ruptured. A woman in labor with a history of prior C-section arrived only after her uterus had ruptured; she would be all right after emergency surgery, but the infant was stillborn. Things such as this were not unique to our hospital, and happened just as often in Southeast Alaska's private sector. Such were the realities of medicine and life on the Last Frontier.

Of our relatively few surgical emergencies, one stood out. I was awakened by a call at perhaps 4 A.M. on a Saturday morning—one for which a fishing or hunting excursion had been planned—from a Coast Guardsman at the local station. He was relaying information from a radio transmission received from a Japanese fishing trawler offshore in the Gulf of Alaska. It had been a garbled transmission complicated by a near-total language barrier, but the gist was that the trawler was headed in to Sitka, the nearest port, at maximum speed, as the ship's captain was hemorrhaging.

Since there was no mention of trauma, I assumed it must be gastrointestinal bleeding—from one of any number of possible sources, all serious and potentially life-threatening. I called the hospital and asked them to contact volunteers from our O-negative donor pool (we didn't have a standing blood bank) to stand by if needed, and also arranged for plenty of saline solution, IV setups, and personnel to be at the ready in the emergency room, including a Japanese-American woman who lived on the island and graciously volunteered as a translator when needed. I received regular updates from the Coast Guard regarding ETA, and was there at the hospital when the ship pulled in and tied up at about 10 A.M.

The captain arrived at the hospital in a wheelchair, sitting on a rubber donut and wearing a big smile. Perplexing, to say the least. But the mystery cleared as soon as we had him on a gurney and over on his side. There I witnessed some of the worst prolapsed, edematous, and inflamed hemorrhoids I had ever seen, adorning his posterior like a crown of ripe plums. Hemorrhage. HEMMORHOIDS! For the life of me I could not see how that man was smiling.

After dismissing the excess personnel and making sure that the potential blood donors were called, thanked for standing by, and given the word to proceed about their Saturday business, the captain was duly admitted and, after a few days of conservative treatment to cool down and shrink his grotesque torturers to manageable proportions, he underwent a hemorrhoidectomy.

Since he would be returning to his ship where conditions for convalescence would not be optimal and follow-up unavailable, I kept him in the hospital a few days longer than usual. On discharge day he was a happy and grateful camper. I accompanied him down to his waiting vessel along with the translator, with him again in a wheelchair on the rubber donut, and still smiling. On the way she engaged him in a spirited one-way conversation, none of which I could understand. He kept smiling and nodding.

When we reached the ship, and after he had been helped aboard, the translator transformed into a drill sergeant, barking orders at a cowed young crewman standing on deck. She was pointing at the many green blown-glass balls of different sizes, wrapped in rope netting, that lined the rails. These were employed as floats for nets or lines on Japanese trawlers; they broke loose occasionally and washed up on the beaches along Alaska's outer coast. The smaller ones, 4" in diameter or so, sometimes survived intact, but the larger ones, up to 20" in diameter, were almost invariably smashed in the encounter between surf and beach. The small intact balls got high prices in Alaskan gift shops, and the rare large ones got really, really high prices. The ones our translator was targeting were trophies. She kept carping at the crewman until he had cut off and handed down four of the very largest, ones with completely intact rope netting, as the captain's expression of gratitude for his treatment. Had the hospital had a display case in the lobby, I suppose they might have been reposited there, like bowling trophies—but it didn't. Fifty years later, we still have those balls in our home.

———

My wife went into labor on the morning of January 15, 1970, shortly before I was to leave for the hospital, so we made the 5-minute drive together. On arrival there I left her at the OB ward and I hurried down to surgery so as not be unduly late to begin a major case—a gastric resection—scheduled for 8 A.M. Time passed while I scrubbed and waited impatiently for the GMO who was to assist me. At approximately 8:20 (ask Linda and she will tell you the exact time) I was paged to the phone. It was Linda, calling from the delivery suite to tell me that son David had arrived, two weeks late but none the worse for it.

He made up for the delay by coming in a big hurry when he was finally ready. The doc who delivered him, Ross Brudenell, was the GMO who had been seeing Linda for prenatal visits—and, was the one who was late in coming to assist on my case. Turns out he was still rushing into his scrubs when David began lift-off, and he completed the delivery with his pants around his ankles. Needless to say, Ross was given a free pass for his tardiness to the O.R. He went on to become an orthopedist and practice spine surgery in Anchorage, Alaska. Not everyone can boast of having been delivered by an orthopedist.

———

When my time was up at Mt. Edgecumbe I was happy enough to leave the turkey suit behind, but not Southeast Alaska. I was indebted to the U.S.P.H.S., and to the lost paperwork or the dog who ate it, for allowing us to experience this land for a brief two years; it wouldn't have happened any other way. Just how indebted we would be in the long run we were yet to find out.

I would later learn that the U.S.P.H.S. was a conduit, a regular pipeline for bringing physicians who had served in Alaska into the State's private sector.

Mt. Edgecumbe and Sitka: The Last Frontier

While I was occupied from the beginning with learning the ropes of my new job and the ways of the U.S.P.H.S., our whole family was taking stock of our new and very different surroundings.

One look at our new home and we knew we weren't going to be homesteading. Like the hospital, it was on Japonski Island. It was the northernmost of four spacious two-story frame houses that backed on the channel, plain but attractive, far from new, but perfectly maintained inside and out. These houses were reserved for those at the top of the government food chain; ours had been the admiral's residence during WWII, when Mt. Edgecumbe had been a naval air and fueling station and a key link along the coastal defense chain. There was a spacious backyard bordered by a dense band of salmonberry bushes that kept our youngsters from wandering to the edge of the channel or worse (we were to discover that salmonberries made delicious jam). The front and side yards were adorned with rhododendrons and roses. Beyond the barrier of shrubbery in back was a beach, where the kids could play and explore as long as Linda and/or I was with them.

The beach was not what most readers would recognize as one. No white sand at the edge of an inviting ocean, no warmth and sunshine. In Alaska, a beach is anywhere the land meets the sea that is not a rock cliff. It might be of gravel, pebbles, stones up to the size of softballs or even larger, squishy mud, coarse dark sand, hard glacial silt, or any combination thereof. Below the high tide line beaches were encrusted with barnacles and mussels, coated with slick seaweed, and lapped by frigid, forbidding ocean. Our beach was close by a larger one known as John Brown's Beach; Linda and the children would log lots of time there exploring the wonders of the intertidal zone.

We could see from our back windows all of the boat traffic traversing the channel, including impressively long rafts of logs being towed to the pulp mill at Silver Bay. The view of Sitka across the channel was spectacular, especially in winter when in late afternoon the alpenglow lit the snow-covered crag of Arrowhead in the background, or at night when a full moon illuminated the magical scene. Our view up the channel to the north was equally grand.

All this was ours for the next two years, and it was rent-free with all utilities and maintenance paid! (but in the admiral's day it had servants housed in quarters in the basement, and now it didn't).

———

The thing that made the most profound impression on everyone our first day(s) in Alaska was the fact that it seemingly never got dark. We had arrived just after the summer solstice, and although at latitude 57 we were far south of the arctic circle, it remained light enough to read outdoors until after 11 P.M. Total darkness lasted for a two-hour period between about 1 and 3 A.M., after which the sky progressively lightened into morning. The effect of this on our wake-sleep cycle took a while for both adults and children to adjust to. Of course the extra daylight we received in the summer was balanced by the lack of it in winter, but the effect seemed to us, and to most, to be far less impactful. Even in the northern tier of the lower 48 where we had always lived, it was dark when I left the house and dark when I came home.

We would find that overcast days outnumbered sunny ones here, and that it rained—a lot. It seldom rained hard. More common was on-and-off drizzle, or a soft, steady rainfall that could last for part of a day, all of a day, or days at a time. Fall brought with it the heaviest rainfall, as a continual succession of weather fronts, storms spawned in the Aleutians, came roaring eastward across the Gulf of Alaska. Spring and early summer were a bit calmer and drier. Given all the overcast and rain, there were virtually no electrical storms. Only twice in all our years in Southeast do I remember witnessing good old-fashioned thunder and lightning. For all the rain, one thing we never saw in either Sitka or Juneau were umbrellas.

Summer temperatures were cooler than we had been used to—mostly in the 60s, not infrequently dipping into the 50s, and sometimes rising into the 70s—and winter temperatures were not as cold as the high latitude would suggest, or what we had experienced in Vermont. Snow accumulation at sea level, where all the cities and villages were, varied greatly from winter to winter depending upon whether the fickle temperature gods chose to provide more time above or below the critical freezing mark. The snow line on nearby mountains might go up and down between zero and 500 feet several times a winter. At the highest elevations accumulations were commonly 20 feet or more, no matter what was going on at sea level. In years with heavy snowfall and a cool spring, considerable snow might remain on peaks above 2500-3000 feet well into the following fall. In places it might last from one year to the next, but none of the islands of the Alexander Archipelago were glaciated, as they had been during the last ice age. The glaciers for which Southeast Alaska is so well known are confined to the mainland, and we would see much of those later.

The climate so described is *maritime*—cool, wet, and temperate. It wasn't for everyone. But the totality of the Southeast Alaskan ecosystem—its flora, its fauna, its marine life, its rivers and streams, the land itself—was entirely dependent on that climate. Even the topography was in part shaped by it over time. For me, and for others who chose to stay or return, it was a most worthwhile tradeoff. And, as a cool weather and shade person, I actually enjoyed the climate—most of the time (October could be a long month). Linda wasn't always quite so sanguine about it, but seldom complained and learned to appreciate the value of the tradeoff. Our children, as children do, never missed a beat in adapting to it.

———

In addition to being home to the airport and the hospital, Japonski Island was also the site of the Bureau of Indian Affairs boarding high school, where children from all over the vast state were sent if their home villages were too small to support a high school. I don't recall the exact enrollment, but estimate that it must have been about 500 at that time. For most of the students the school was a long way from home, as much as 2000 miles in some cases, and going back for holidays or spring vacations was out of the question. Around Christmastime each year, a nauseating, incredibly rank odor would pervade the Mt. Edge-cumbe post office; on inquiring, Linda found its source to be a North Slope Alaska Native delicacy—"Eskimo ice cream"—a mix of blue-berries and whale blubber, or muktuk, that parents sent to their home-sick children. It was put up in glass jars, many of which broke in transit.

The School, the Hospital, a Coast Guard station, and the airport were all under the aegis of the federal government, and the staff and employees of all were supplied with government housing on the island. Much of the housing and many other structures on Japonski dated to the World War II era, and remnants of old fortifications and gun em-placements were still to be found if one looked for them.

Japonski had no infrastructure of its own—no stores, shops, or other commercial enterprises—although the federal government did operate a filling station for both official and private vehicles. Its road system con-sisted of an unpaved 2-3-mile loop that touched on the airport, school, post office, hospital, and small boat harbor, and along which was situated some of the government housing. There were several spurs on which were located additional housing. Depending on just where they lived, some residents had no need for a car, or if they had one they kept it across the channel in Sitka. We elected to keep our car on Japonski, as our house was at the far end of the island from the hospital, the elementary school, and the boat harbor where transportation to Sitka was to be had.

Japonski Island was, and is, invariably referred to as Mt. Edgecumbe; that is what we, the U.S. Postal Service, and everyone else called it, and what it will be called henceforth in this narrative. The *actual* Mount Edgecumbe was a long-dormant volcano that greatly resembled Japan's Mt. Fuji, located on Kruzof island several miles to the northwest in Sitka Sound. It was an impressive sight from either Sitka or Japonski, its height appearing far greater than its 3000 feet because it arose essentially out of the sea. On one of the two April Fools' Days we were there for, a few of the Sitka town rakes, well known for capers such as this, chartered a helicopter to take them, along with a cargo of old tire casings and diesel fuel, into the crater, their intent being to awaken the sleeping giant and scare the bejesus out of everyone. The prank fizzled, as most, including ourselves, never noticed and only found out about it days later in the Sitka newspaper.

———

The town of Sitka, directly across the channel, was as old as European civilization got in Alaska, and was the Russian capitol when "Seward's Folly" was purchased by the U.S. in 1867. It was where Mt. Edgecumbe residents shopped for groceries and everything else. On one early shopping expedition to Sitka Linda heard behind her a voice familiar from the silver screen: It was none other than John Wayne, who must have survived his precarious landing on the carrier deck. We later learned that the Duke was a frequent visitor to Southeast, gunkholing about the islands in his converted minesweeper *Wild Goose*.

Free transit between Sitka and Mt. Edgecumbe was available via a ferry consisting of a small fleet of "shore boats"—gray WWII-vintage wooden navy launches, which could comfortably transport around 30 passengers at a time. They ran back and forth every half-hour, every day all day, from early morning until midnight, making the short crossing in only a few minutes. Anyone who missed the last shore boat back to Mt. Edgecumbe would have to sleep it off in the waiting shed on the Sitka side. The shore boats could not accommodate vehicles. Mail was transported between Mt. Edgecumbe and Sitka in a WWII-era amphibious duck.

Fortunately for Linda and the other Mt. Edgecumbe wives, Sitka's only supermarket made twice-weekly deliveries to customers on Mt. Edgecumbe. She also found that it was absurdly easy to purchase there all the staples that we had bought and stockpiled in Vermont and moved across the country at Government expense—and, fresh milk. Very unlike Boonesboro, Sitka also had an ice cream parlor, drug store, movie theater, clothing, hardware, and sporting-goods stores. restaurants, bars, and marine-supply chandleries. In all, it seemed little different from small-town America in the lower 48.

A bridge linking Sitka and Mt. Edgecumbe was begun about the time we arrived, and had been virtually completed by the time we left; it was opened to traffic weeks after our departure, and we would not travel across it until 50 years later. In retrospect we are glad to have lived there during the primitive funkiness of the shoreboat era.

What to wear? We would find that the stores selling outdoor apparel in Sitka, and later Juneau, had the right stuff, and sold only the best. Heavy flannel chamois shirts. Light wool "halibut jackets." Tough, quality commercial-grade raingear. Heavy wool pants for hunting. Later, outerwear of Gore-Tex/fleece. Weatherproof float coats for boating. Down vests and jackets, for the coldest winter conditions.

And the ubiquitous B.F. Goodrich Xtratuff brown rubber pacs, the boots worn by almost every man, woman, and child year round for almost everything out-of-doors. They were at home in boats, on the beach, in the woods, and around town slogging through rain puddles or snow. Every outdoor store in Southeast sold them, in a number of permutations—insulated or uninsulated, different heights, etc. They were spendy but tough and built for abuse; even so we all went through several pair during our Alaskan sojourn. I still have my last ones. I wore them on appropriate occasions during our recent National Geographic cruises around Southeast, and they stood out from the courtesy loaner boots most were wearing; on noting them, one of the naturalists volunteered the observation that I must be an old hand in these parts.

As common as they were/are throughout Southeast Alaska, one did not and does not see these boots anywhere else on the planet. Out of curiosity I recently looked for them on Amazon, and indeed found them buried deep in the rear of the "boots" section—but apparently nobody else has. Some years after we moved from Juneau, Linda and I were putting on our ski boots in the day lodge at the Sun Valley (Idaho) ski area when I noticed a man coming in through the door wearing these very Xtratuffs. Curiosity overcame me, and I had to ask where he was from. "Why, Petersburg, Alaska." Haven't seen another pair in the lower 48, other than my own, since.

We were at first amazed, considering the modest population, at the number of small pleasure craft in the boat harbors of Sitka and Mt. Edgecumbe. It was almost as though the usual ratio of boats to automobiles had been turned on its head; here, boats seemed the necessity and cars the luxury. Marine-related businesses serving both the pleasure and commercial fleets thrived, and filled an important role in the local economy.

Sitka had at that time, a population of around 4500, give or take. The lynchpin of the economy was the large Japanese-owned pulp mill, located on Silver Bay several miles south of town—which in turn was dependent on large-scale logging in the Tongass National Forest. Logging was seasonal but the mill operated year round, as huge rafts of logs were stockpiled and stored in Silver Bay. Commercial fishing, mostly for salmon and halibut, was next down the list. Not to be overlooked was the impact of the federal government, with its multiple installations and government employees housed on Mt. Edgecumbe.

Tourism was so far down the list of economic drivers in the Sitka of 1969 as to be almost out of sight. There were a couple of hotels in town, catering more to folks there on business than to tourists. There were no rustic (read luxury) sportfishing or vacation lodges—they would come much later—and it would have been difficult to find a boat charter to take a visiting party for a day's fishing. The big cruise lines were only beginning to sense the pot of gold at the end of Alaska's inside passage, and Sitka was just far enough off the beaten track to lag behind places like Ketchikan and Juneau when that tide started to turn a few years later (and for the same reason, it would never catch up). I recall seeing only two cruise ships tied up across the channel each of the summers we were there; they were small and classic-looking steamers, real ships, compared to the 3000-passenger behemoths resembling floating wedding cakes that would eventually follow in great numbers.

The Sitka road system was a bit more extensive than that of Mt. Edgecumbe, and all of it was paved. "Downtown" was concentrated along the waterfront and back from it to where development was blocked by encroaching mountains rising to 5000 feet. The town was laid out without regard to geometry, and the small business district more or less radiated out from the iconic St. Michael's Russian Orthodox cathedral—which had burned to the ground the year before we arrived, and was then in the early phases of reconstruction. The restored, onion-domed St. Michael's that we saw on recent return visits is impressive indeed. Although the town's population has doubled since our time there, to roughly 9000, it still proudly boasts only two traffic lights.

To the north, the road ran out about 8 or 9 miles to end at the Alaska Marine Highway terminal. The "Alaska Marine Highway" consisted of a fleet of sizeable seagoing ferries owned and operated by the

State. Their routes connected the communities of Southeast Alaska with one another, and with Seattle (now Bellingham), Washington in the "lower 48." The ships accommodated passengers and vehicles of all sizes, and along with the Seattle-based seagoing barge lines were crucial lifelines in getting goods to places where roads didn't go—which was essentially everywhere in Southeast Alaska.

An unpaved spur wound its way to the summit of Harbor Mountain. On one occasion we borrowed a friend's 4 WD Land Rover and went to the top. It was above tree line, and the only time our family (other than myself) would experience the high alpine of Southeast Alaska.

To the south the road extended only as far as the pulp mill at Silver Bay. Wherever one was in Southeast Alaska, be it Sitka, Juneau, or anywhere else, where the road ended you were indeed at the Last Frontier.

We found that our relationship with the outside world was a little different here. We had been accustomed to television as it existed just about everywhere down south at this point in time, 1969—a choice of several network channels, regular scheduled programming, live nightly news, and live sporting events. Sitka TV was different. There was one local station, and what we saw was on film flown up in a can several days after it had aired everywhere else. This made no noticeable difference for most of the programming—TV series, movies, etc.—since it mattered not at all that we were out of sync with the rest of the TV universe. But—no film can, or no plane, equaled no programs. It did matter for sports and news. We didn't get to see Neil Armstrong walk on the moon until days after the fact, and there was no point in watching Super Bowls because the outcome had been known by everyone for days.

We did have live nightly news at six and ten. This featured a screen saver, and the reading of a prepared script in an expressionless monotone peppered with labored mispronunciations ("Chappaquiddick" was one that eluded mastery). It was accompanied by background noises—children crying, clanking dishes—that obviously emanated from someone's home. Better than three-day-old Walter Cronkite? Just barely.

———

Daughter Susan entered kindergarten the fall of our second year at Mt. Edgecumbe, and for the school Christmas party a Santa Claus was needed. Her teacher recruited *me*. The school had a Santa suit complete with beard and moustache, and with some pillows for padding and a few practice ho-ho-hos I was good to go. I looked and sounded like the real deal. I must have—neither Susan nor younger daughter Betsy recognized who Santa was, even when sitting on his lap. Years later when looking through our family photos, they still didn't have a clue. They were in high school or perhaps beyond when we finally told them.

———

When we arrived at Mt. Edgecumbe we knew virtually nothing of the indigenous population that would comprise the bulk of my surgical patients. We'd learn that there were no reservations anywhere in Alaska. The native population of Southeast coexisted with the non-native in the larger communities such as Sitka, and also occupied a number of much older, smaller, traditionally and predominantly native villages scattered throughout the Archipelago and mainland.

The natives of Southeast Alaska were Tlingit except in the southernmost reaches, where Haida and Tsimshian peoples resided (most of their territory was in contiguous coastal British Columbia). I cannot tell you even the approximate percentage of Tlingit in Sitka's (or Juneau's) population; intermarriage and integration had long since blurred the lines (I'd learn that in order to qualify for healthcare as an indigenous person one needed to be of 1/8 or more Native American blood). Many of the surnames were Russian, a reminder of that not-all-that-long ago occupation. The Tlingit language was not heard in public; it had been long suppressed by government policy, and most of the younger people didn't know it. It was spoken by the elders in the privacy of their homes. Many older people spoke English with a peculiar inflection that belied the fact that English had not been their first language.

By 1969 the indigenous citizens of Sitka-Mt. Edgecumbe had, to casual observers like ourselves, become part of the American mainstream—but over time we would realize that they retained their sense of ethnic and cultural identity. To the outsider it was mostly hidden from view, in cultural observances within homes, in organizations like the Alaska Native Brotherhood and Sisterhood, and among the elders. We will see that it became much more apparent later in the 1970s, after passage of the Alaska Native Land Claims Settlement Act.

An undercurrent of resentment still smoldered in some, seen more in residents of those predominantly native villages where cultural integration had made the least inroads and met the strongest resistance. We would always feel vaguely unwelcome in those places.

The Tlingit culture did manifest itself in its artistic heritage. We were exposed to Tlingit art and craft in local gift shops, expositions, and in the totems for which the natives of the Pacific Northwest are well known. Tlingit artistry and craftsmanship had become highly evolved over centuries—the bounteous resources with which their land was endowed had provided ample leisure for a class of skilled artisans to prosper and perpetuate. Their art was characterized by the stylized, almost grotesque renderings of the creatures they knew from nature—eagle, raven, bear, beaver, otter, orca. These had a somber, silent, brooding aspect entirely in keeping with the land, and one could easily see how the form had evolved in this place. We would only later learn something of Tlingit mythology and legend, passed down through oral tradition; much of it was based on the transformation of the animals represented in their art into human form and back again. As such, it seemed every bit as eerie as the representation of these creatures in their art.

Messing About in Boats I: Sitka-Mt. Edgecumbe

"Believe me, my young friend, there is nothing—absolutely nothing—half so much worth doing as simply messing about in boats."

—Kenneth Grahame, **The Wind in the Willows**

Travel on the water had been a vital and necessary part of Southeast Alaskan life and culture from antiquity, a reminder of which was the Tlingit dugout canoe stationed in front of Sitka's centennial hall. These graceful craft were hewn from Sitka spruce or red cedar, and the larger examples could hold upwards of fifty people. They were basic transportation, essential for commerce, socializing with neighboring tribes, exploring, establishing new settlements, hunting, fishing—and making war.

Boats remained as essential when we arrived as they had been a thousand years before. We learned almost immediately that pleasure craft were ubiquitous in Southeast; everybody seemed to have one, from Lund aluminum outboard skiffs or Boston Whalers to outboard or stern-drive cruisers, to larger inboard types. Both then and later in Juneau, few if any megayachts were seen other than those visiting from ports in the lower 48. Totally absent were open-cockpit speedboats.

Also absent for the most part were the big, fast sportfishermen so popular on both coasts in the lower 48, at their best for day-fishing far offshore and hosting cocktail parties at the dock; their limited berthing
and galley space given their size and cost, and absence of a lower helm
station protected from the weather, made them a poor choice for
Southeast Alaskan conditions. Of the smaller number of sailboats, most
were cruising types that operated under power much of the time.

It seemed one had to have a boat here, unless one was content to con-
fine his experience of the country he lived in to the miniscule sampling
accessible by road, or on foot. We would find that without boats Southeast
Alaska, despite its vast expanse of wilderness, was actually claustrophobic.

I was introduced to boats, boating, and the vistas boats could open
up in this country within a week of our arrival at Mt. Edgecumbe when
one of the staff dentists invited me, along with several other members
of the medical staff, out on his 23-foot outboard cruiser for a day-trip
to Katlian Bay north of Sitka, where we would go ashore and fish the
stream at the head of the bay. Fishing with light spinning tackle I landed
my first Alaskan fish, a dolly varden of almost four pounds. It was the
largest fish of my angling career, and a *trout* to boot! Wow. I had taken
along my .357 magnum revolver, and when I went to unload it at day's
end found that, in my excitement, I had forgotten to load it.

Only days later Linda and I were invited out by neighbor and internist Tom Keith for an evening spin on his boat, a 21-foot outboard
cruiser named (by a previous owner) *Ginger*. It was of plywood, a little
long in the tooth at 18 years old, and reputedly built by a local. It had
a graceful hull that smacked of good design and good craftsmanship, a
very basic no-frills interior, it didn't leak and, powered by a huge outboard, was really fast. A few days after the thoroughly enjoyable ride,
Tom informed me that his outboard had gone kaput. For kicking in half
the cost of a new 110 h.p. Mercury, Tom offered us a half-interest in
Ginger. Tom may as well have been the Godfather. It was an offer I
couldn't refuse.

I had always liked most anything to do with boats, and small boat seamanship was one category in which I was already well along on the learning curve. Fortunately, part of what I knew was to be aware of, and respect, what I didn't know. It was immediately obvious that boating in Southeast presented challenges encountered in few other places.

Few small boats were equipped with VHF or even CB radios in the years circa. 1970, and ours wasn't. Once out of sight of the local boat harbor you were on your own and out of touch; one might not see another boat until returning, and wouldn't encounter another settlement within 90 miles in any direction. Before leaving on a trip of any distance or duration, we knew to not only check the marine weather forecast, but also to leave with friends or family a "float plan"—destination, route, and ETA for returning. There was actually a bulletin board at the Mt. Edgecumbe small boat harbor for the posting of such information, that was regularly monitored by the Coast Guard.

The waters of Southeast Alaska are subject to enormous tides, with extremes differing from high to low by as much as 25 feet. The extreme tides created powerful currents, rips, eddies, and even whirlpools in the inside passages. While these presented hazard enough, high tides could also conceal barely submerged reefs or extensive flats beneath what appeared to be safe water. Marine charts were an absolute necessity and local knowledge was invaluable; I am indebted to the many locals who willingly provided it, and probably kept us out of worlds of hurt.

The waters along the outer coast in particular featured pinnacle rocks arising abruptly from the depths, many not marked on the charts (one charted but still notorious barely submerged rock lurking near the outer end of Icy Strait, had been dubbed "million-dollar rock" by locals, for all the megayachts from the lower 48 that had come to grief on it).

A plethora of small barrier islands protected inner Sitka Sound and the bays coming off it to the south and east to some extent, and the narrow straits to the north that we frequented were likewise sheltered from the worst of weather (not that they couldn't get nasty). Only occasionally did we venture outside of these areas. The ante would be upped a few years later when our home waters would become those around Juneau, where the major passages were wider, longer with more fetch, and less protected.

The very term "inside waters," which applies to all those of Southeast Alaska save the outer coast, is deceptive. These waters appear protected on marine charts, but short, forbiddingly steep seas could build quickly in the passages, the winds that produced them intensified by funneling between steep mountain walls on either side. Where and when strong winds and tides were in opposition, conditions could get ugly even for vessels of considerable size. Standing waves would develop; particularly nasty were points where major passages intersected, narrowed, or abruptly altered direction, and we learned to be wary of them. Even normally placid channels leading into protected anchorages could develop enormous, cresting standing waves that rendered them impassable. The winds that, under certain conditions, roared out of Taku inlet just south of Juneau could turn a few miles of Stephens Passage into a deathtrap. Mariners underestimated the "inside waters" at their peril; over time they have taken the lives of many. We knew of a number, and had known a few. Staying out of trouble in the long run required knowledge, good judgment, good seamanship—and sometimes good luck.

Floating debris was a constant hazard in Southeast waters. Storms and high tides carried flotsam and fallen trees, often complete with root systems, off the beaches, and these also washed out of the rivers and streams that entered the passages. Most dangerous were "deadheads," escapees from log rafts or storage areas which became waterlogged and floated barely submerged, occasionally bobbing to the surface. These were difficult or impossible to see as one approached, particularly in choppy conditions or at night, and could impale one's boat if they bobbed up beneath it.

———

Time flew by. Summer was almost gone by the time we had become co-owners of the *Ginger*, and we would use her little until the following spring. The most ambitious foray was one I took with co-owner Tom Keith just before Christmas, a day trip that combined hunting for deer with hunting for our Christmas trees. We returned with neither.

The following spring we began to expand our horizons, getting into fishing for salmon and halibut and going far enough afield to get a better look at the country that surrounded us. Six-month-old David was now old enough to be taken along on some day outings; on one such outing we set him in his bouncy-chair up forward just inside the entrance to the cabin. We hit an Alaska state ferry's wake going a little too fast and the bouncy-chair bounced, catapulting our son up and out to land on the cabin floor. Linda was sure he'd landed on his head— but he appeared none the worse for his aerial adventure. Many years later we came to believe that he had indeed landed on his head, and woke up speaking Japanese (he had become fluent in the language in college and graduate school, embarked on a career in translation, and has resided with his family in Japan for many years).

Tom's stint with the P.H.S. would end on June 30, and we bought out his share in *Ginger*. Late that summer I headed *Ginger* toward the native village of Angoon on Admiralty Island, 90 miles away, where I, along with two friends from the medical staff, would explore the Southeast Alaskan outback for the first time. This long-weekend venture had been proposed by Hood Franks, the GMO assigned to oversee health-care in Angoon (each GMO was assigned a village, where he held clinics every few months and communicated regularly with the village health aides, local women who had been trained to deal with healthcare needs on a daily basis. In my experience they were very good at what they did.). He'd been there on official business several times, had heard about the superb cutthroat trout fishing that nearby Mitchell Bay had to offer, and had arranged for Angoon's village schoolteacher to take us there in his skiff and serve as our guide for a day. It would be my first opportunity to flyfish in Southeast Alaska.

The fishing lived up to expectations; much more on the "sea run" trout that inhabited this and many other Southeast Alaskan ecosystems in a future chapter. While a great distance by boat from both Sitka and Juneau, Mitchell Bay would become one of our favorite getaway places. Being guided by a local the first time in was, in retrospect, invaluable.

On the way back the following day we made a stop at Hanus Bay at the mouth of Eva Creek, on Baranof Island at the entrance to Peril Strait, as we'd heard the Creek also offered great trout fishing. This time, no guide. As we walked a deeply worn trail through old-growth rainforest alongside the creek in search of fishable water, it occurred to me, and I'm sure to my companions as well, that this trail had not been made by people. The trail was pocked by occasional decaying, partially consumed salmon carcasses, and frequent humongous mountains of poop, some still steaming. None of us had yet seen a brown bear, but I imagined that any creature capable of authoring a poop like that must be at least eighteen feet high at the shoulder. And none of us wanted to wind up as part of a mound of poop.

Long story short, we saw no bears but did encounter another human, a researcher from Scripps Institute in California who was there studying the ecosystem while living alone in a forest service cabin at the lake above. He'd been there all summer, and with the exception of the floatplane pilot who occasionally arrived with food and supplies, had seldom seen another person. We three made a cameo appearance in a book he subsequently authored on his experiences, *Red Salmon, Brown Bear*. We also caught plenty of cutthroat, and I would return once with our family some years later to enjoy both the fishing and the place itself. I released the trout I caught, but Hood wanted to take some fish home with him and was using an oversized pocket in his rain parka as a creel. In his enthusiasm he never noticed the large hole in the bottom of that pocket, and no sooner had a cutthroat been deposited therein than it was scurrying off to freedom at his feet. Far be it from me to tell him about the hole.

On returning to the beach and *Ginger* in early afternoon, we discovered our craft high and dry on the flats through which the creek now trickled, left there by the outgoing tide. It would be hours before the tide would refloat us, and we were a long way from home—perhaps 60 miles—without a trace of civilization between us and there. In the meantime we had no way to contact our families, who expected us back well before dark.

The light of the fall solstice was already fading when *Ginger* finally had water beneath her again. A decision had to be made: play it safe and use the remaining light to find a decent anchorage, then proceed home on the morrow—or, make our way home through the dark. We of course had no radar, but had the appropriate marine charts and a flashlight to read them by, and knew the way through Peril Strait, Salisbury Sound, and Neva and Olga Straits to be well marked by lighted buoys and shore beacons. The wind was light and the water calm. We elected to go for it (I think it was I who did the electing, as my less experienced companions deferred to my judgment, for better or worse).

Off we went into the gloaming, making good time while the light lasted. When darkness did fall, it became pitch-black. I throttled back to a crawl; the greatest hazard was that of deadheads, all too common in the heyday of logging. If run into at even moderate speed, they could easily hole and sink one's boat. Our slow pace allowed us some possibility of seeing them ahead even in darkness, and minimized the chance of calamity if we had the misfortune to strike one. We didn't.

Navigation was the easiest part, as I thought it would be, and actually rather fun. I was concerned, however, about our passage through Sergius Narrows, the bottleneck separating Peril Strait from Salisbury Sound. Sergius had current velocities, rips, eddies, and a narrow channel that commanded the respect of vessels the size of the Alaska state ferries, and was best negotiated on a slack tide. The gods were with us that night: as we approached Sergius shortly before midnight, the clouds parted to reveal a bright moon that guided us through the narrows at slack water. Once through, the clouds closed over once again.

The sight confronting us as we approached Whitestone Narrows at the bottom of Neva Strait was that of a Christmas tree, brilliantly lit in red and green. As we approached, *Ginger* cautiously edged back and forth until, all of a sudden, the nav beacons lined up in straight columns, red on one side, green on the other, perfectly defining the slot through the narrow channel.

We pulled into our stall at Mt. Edgecumbe's small boat harbor somewhere around 2 A.M. Linda was of course awake, and alone in our living room. The wives of my two companions had since departed, having spent the evening there planning their husbands' funerals. Linda never had a doubt that I would bring us back safely.

———

New Year's Eve of 1970 was the final day of deer season, and I had still not gotten a deer. I would be gone before the opening of next season, so it was now or, maybe, never. Ross Brudenell, who would deliver son David two weeks later, had already taken a deer, but was anxious to get one with his .44 magnum revolver.

We had a plan. We'd use *Ginger's* speed to take us beyond the range of most day-hunters, up into Peril Strait perhaps as far as Sergius Narrows (on looking back, probably not necessary. All the skookum hunters had long since filled their quotas.). There was snow on the ground, and chances were good that some deer might be close to, or down on, the beaches.

The day broke calm, clear, and unseasonably warm. We were where we wanted to be by midmorning, some deer were where we were hoping they'd be, and by early afternoon the mighty hunters were basking in the glow of success. Both of us had taken deer, and with our S&W .44 magnum revolvers at that (I had no idea at the time just how much this would affect the trajectory of my hunting career). I also took a second, with my scoped 30/06 rifle, and had learned the ritual of field-dressing from Ross. It was time to pick up our chips and go.

No sooner had we started than there was an abrupt and ominous change in the weather. The sky clouded over, the wind shifted, and a brisk headwind sprung up; the temperature plummeted over twenty degrees in only a few minutes to below the freezing mark. A sense of urgency set in. We hadn't shortened the distance to home by much when our big engine sputtered, coughed, and died—and refused to restart. The sudden drop in temperature had caused balls of ice to form in the fuel line; we had plenty of gas and a perfectly good engine, but no way of clearing the line and getting gas from the tank to where it needed to go.

We did, however, have a separate, six-gallon tank for the "kicker"—the small auxiliary outboard used for trolling and emergencies—and it was full. It took Ross precious time to jury-rig the big Mercury's fuel intake fitting to the Johnson tank's fuel line, but he got it done and we were back in business—sort of. The weather had continued to deteriorate, and we were rapidly burning daylight. Some mental calculations on my part suggested that our meagre fuel supply might—just might—get us home if we used it in the most efficient way. *Ginger*'s planing hull was most efficient at speed. I planned to get *Ginger* up on a step, then back off to the point where she would just barely stay there. Speed would also be our ally in the race against both darkness and the elements.

Off we went through intermittent snow squalls, *Ginger* pounding into a stiff chop that rattled our fillings. The stretch of open water through Salisbury Sound was particularly nasty, but I dared not back off on the throttle.

Darkness had fallen by the time we reached calmer water closer to home. We knew we were now running on fumes, but it appeared we were going to make it. With the lights of the small boat harbor in sight less than a half-mile ahead, the last molecules of fuel were consumed and the engine expired. We were in the Sitka-Mt. Edgecumbe channel—and right behind our house. The lights were on in our living room.

We were dead in the water, but far from still. Wind and tide began pushing us back in the direction from which we had come; the harbor lights, and our house, began to recede as we were pushed northward out the channel. The water was too deep for our anchor to find bottom. We had no emergency flares, only a flashlight with which we continually sent out the SOS signal in hopes that someone on shore would see us—maybe even Linda, from our house.

Thankfully, someone did see us—I don't remember who—and we were shortly in tow back to our slip. We tied up about 7 P.M., just in time to hang our deer in a neighbor's garage, clean up a bit, and take our wives out for a New Year's Eve dinner at the airport restaurant.

A phone call New Year's morning brought bad news. *Ginger* was sinking at the dock. By the time we arrived at the scene, her cockpit had filled halfway to the gunwales. Ross and I bailed frantically, miraculously gaining on the water coming in to the point where a rescue operation could be contemplated. The temperature had risen overnight, our battery was somehow still dry, and when I cranked over the engine, it caught. With me running the boat and Ross bailing, we crossed the channel and ran the boat up on the beach in front of the Sitka Engine marine dealership.

On returning to Mt. Edgecumbe, we found that a large, unprincipled neighborhood dog had eaten the hindquarters out of one of my deer.

The verdict came in the next day. The gallant old *Ginger* was done, her fastenings loosened and bottom literally pounded out by her last wild ride.

———

Less than six months remained of our Mt. Edgecumbe tenure, but we—I, mostly—still had to have a boat. Bob Couch, the proprietor at Sitka Engine, just happened to have a used boat of the same size and basic plywood construction as *Ginger*, and it would be a good fit for our big outboard, which we had salvaged. The price was right, and we bought it.

Our new craft had been commercially built, by Sabre Craft if memory serves, and was of more recent vintage than *Ginger*—just as fast, and an even better sea boat. It had been recently painted, and the interior was cleaner, brighter, and more comfortable. Nothing about that boat gave us any trouble. It was unnamed when we bought it, and we didn't give it one. I regret that we didn't, as it certainly deserved a name. It was a fine craft that served us well in our brief time together.

We caught king salmon and halibut that spring—this boat proved "lucky" at fishing—and I made a weekend steelhead trip to distant Sitkoh Bay on Chichigoff Island with ENT doc Tom Stengl. I do not recall who we sold it to when it came time to do so, but I hope the new owner gave it the TLC it deserved—and a name.

The Tongass

The Tongass National Forest is the largest temperate rainforest on the North American Continent—and, with the exception of the scattered outposts of civilization within it (and now, land ceded to native corporations), the Tongass *is* Southeast Alaska. In both Sitka and later Juneau, it was all around us. With a few notable exceptions, for our first two years we viewed it more from the outside looking in. It was only after we had moved to Juneau, when our children were older and we had more latitude to explore, and I began hunting in earnest, that we would begin to know it more intimately.

This is a good place to emphasize that Southeast—the Tongass— is very much unlike the rest of Alaska. A look at the maps will show that Southeast encompasses a mere sliver of the vast state, isolated from the rest, as it is attached by a strip of land only a handful of miles deep. Not only is it geographically isolated, it is climatologically and topographically unique within the state.

The land was inseparable from the myriad waterways that traversed it, and from the maritime climate that made it what it was. Beneath craggy spires were endless swaths of dark green conifer forest, often shrouded in mist, comprised of towering Sitka spruce, western hemlock, and Alaska yellow cedar. Inspiring awe in any weather and season, in winter beneath a brooding overcast the land-marinescapes of Southeast were possessed of a monochromatic beauty unlike anything I'd ever seen.

Walking through stands of old-growth timber—areas of forest that had never been logged, with trees hundreds of years old—made one feel like Gulliver must have felt in the Land of the Giants. The topography and terrain were defined by precipitously steep slopes that sometimes plateaued at intervals in benches; knife-edged ridges; and gullies that became steep-sided ravines, creek beds, and streamlets as they descended. Common were deadfalls, fallen giants with upended root systems that towered 12 to15 feet; steep slide areas; and impenetrable blowdowns that had to be gone around rather than through. Over centuries nature had differentially aged and randomly thinned the forest canopy so that on clear days sunlight dappled the forest floor, providing conditions where wildlife-sustaining ground cover could flourish. The ground itself, where not rock, was mossy, moist, and spongy with decaying vegetation.

The forest was punctuated by muskegs—boggy, water-saturated meadows of straw-colored grass, themselves punctuated by water-filled potholes and stunted bull pine, and crisscrossed with deer and bear trails. Some were intimate, some vast and rolling, most in between. Muskegs were built upon layers of vegetation that had decomposed over eons—much the same as the peat bogs of Ireland and Scotland.

Above tree line—3000 feet or so, except on or near the outer coast, where it dropped to under 2000—were wide-open grassy bowls where patches of snow could be found through midsummer. Small high alpine lakes might remain frozen for most of the year.

Even when it wasn't raining everything in the forest looked, felt, and smelled moist and damp, pungent with evergreen and a hint of decomposing vegetation (I missed out on much of the smell part; a mild conifer allergy of some sort invariably clogged my nasal passages when in the woods). Spanish moss draped from branches. The only deciduous trees were bands of scraggly alder defining virtually every beach fringe. The forests contained thickets mostly of blueberry and devil's club, both ubiquitous in Southeast—one a welcome gift of nature, the other not so much.

One thing that both the bears and the people of Southeast Alaska could agree on were that blueberries were good. They grew in profusion along the road systems of both Sitka and Juneau as well as just about everywhere in the wild. In Juneau we had them in our backyard. Our entire family enjoyed harvesting them, and we always had plenty in the freezer for year-round consumption. Wild blueberries, no matter where from, should be soaked in water overnight before using or freezing; they harbor tiny worms which emerge and float to the surface after a night of soaking. The worms are harmless, but once you see them you'll agree that soaking is a good idea. We took my parents berrying on one of their visits to Juneau, and admonished them not to eat as they picked. My father, however, was of the "one for the bucket, one for me" school of berrying. When he saw the worms floating atop the soaking berries the next morning, he looked a little green around the gills. We cheered him up by pointing out that he'd gotten a bonus of protein with his berries that we'd missed out on.

Devil's club was another matter. Its appeal seemed limited to the indigenous peoples of Alaska and the Pacific Northwest, who utilized it in a multiplicity of ways, and to bears, who liked the fruit. Attractive white blooms notwithstanding, the stems and branches were armored with tiny, cactus-like spines that could penetrate the thickest gloves and clothing, lodge in the flesh on contact, and fester, producing burning and inflammation that lasted for days. Those wise in the ways of the Tongass gave thickets of devil's club a wide birth; cheechakoes who waded through them came away with a nasty affliction we locals, after we became such, called "devil's crotch." And only the uninitiated were tempted to use the plant's invitingly huge leaves—which were, like the stems and branches, covered in spines—as emergency toilet paper.

Water was omnipresent. Some streamlets remained little more than trickles until they reached the beach and saltwater; others coalesced to form streams small and large. Midsummer through fall all but the most trivial were, in their lower reaches, glutted with spawning salmon. The mouths of larger streams often interfaced with saltwater in estuaries called "saltchucks," and/or in expanses of wetlands or flat, grassy meadows; both had rich ecosystems all their own, the wetlands providing prime habitat for waterfowl. Juneau had miles of such wetlands along Gastineau Channel, stretching from downtown to the airport, and each fall the grammar schools held a "sea week" during which pupils, teachers, and volunteer parents donned hipboots and raingear and spent long mornings trekking through these wetlands and learning the secrets of the ecosystem. Linda, of course, volunteered every year for all three of our children, and by the time our youngest had gone on to middle school she had had more than enough of the cold and the wet and the misery. She still talks about it.

The grassy interfaces were good places for seeing deer or bear as they emerged from the timber and moseyed about looking for food. We'll have much more to say about the fauna of the Tongass in later chapters. We made an effort to learn something of the edible plants that grew in these areas adjacent to the beaches; fiddlehead ferns and goose tongue were actually pretty good. I don't recall the names of others, but wouldn't recommend them unless one were really hungry.

Few peaks on the islands of the Alexander Archipelago exceeded 5000 feet, but viewing (or climbing) them from the perspective of sea level made them effectively far higher. Many mountains of the mainland, the northern reaches of the Coast Range, exceeded that height, with those of the Fairweather Range behind Glacier Bay rising to 15,000 feet.

————

As we ventured farther by water, and at times by air, we saw for the first time the dark side of the Tongass of the 1970s: clearcuts, vast voids in the forest where trees had been removed en masse by logging. As new-comers we knew absolutely nothing about the timber industry in Southeast, but the aesthetics were awful; clearcuts appeared as gaping, open sores on the land.

We'd later learn that clearcuts were ecological as well as aesthetic disasters, dead zones filled with slash left behind by the loggers, impenetrable on foot and devoid of habitat for wildlife. When cut to the banks of streams (where the most valuable timber was), the resultant siltation and warming rendered the streams unfit for spawning salmon, or as trout habitat. The U.S. Forest Service, charged with overseeing the Tongass, had been acting as shills for the timber industry as mandated by the politics of the day. It was as though there were no rules constraining logging practices in the 1960s and 70s. The cheery propaganda espoused by the industry and the Forest Service alike told us that in only fifty years from cutting, a clearcut would again be mature virgin forest, ready to be reharvested. Maybe so in some climes, but the sobering truth, as determined by scientists, was that here the number was closer to 200 years at best—and in cases where steep slopes had been cut and surfaces laid bare by erosion, maybe never. The same held for stream rehabilitation. The resources being depleted were essentially not renewable.

What we were seeing was a relatively new phenomenon; the oldest of these clearcuts dated back to the 1950s. It was jaw-dropping to see just how much forest had been leveled in such a short span. Megascale logging in the Tongass had been part of a devil's bargain brokered by Alaska's political fathers in moving Alaska from territorial status on to statehood (which it achieved in 1959). The opening up of the Tongass to essentially unregulated, government-subsidized logging was done to justify statehood status by bringing people, industry, jobs, and a self-sustaining economy to what the folks in Washington perceived as a vast backwater—but one with untapped resources there to be exploited. All was orchestrated by the godfather of Alaskan politics of the day, Sen. Ted Stevens, joined later by sidekick Rep. Don Young.

As newbies, we took industrial-scale logging and clearcutting, as harshly unpleasant as they struck us, to be immutable facts of life here, as much a part of Southeast Alaska as the forest itself. Fortunately for us and for the land, there were activists even then that didn't see it that way, and the tide would begin to turn in the late seventies as an environmental lobby became a growing force. A pitched battle between logging interests and environmentalists was waged throughout the '80s; we followed it in the Juneau newspaper and even national media, rooting hard from the sidelines. The environmentalists, seemingly against all odds—money, politicians, lobbyists, entrenched interests—would gain the upper hand as public opinion rallied to the cause. We owe them much.

We were in Alaska during the time when the taken-for-granted freebies and subsidies long enjoyed by the timber industry were yanked from under. Profit-cutting environmental regulations were belatedly put in place and enforced. Timber sales/leases were first restricted (and realistically priced), then later halted. Logging in the Tongass would grind to a halt, forcing the closure of both of Southeast's pulp mills (Sitka and Ketchikan) and many of its sawmills.

Not all Alaskans were thrilled with this outcome. Logging had become a key economic driver in Southeast's economy, more so as the sun set on the salmon canneries. The closure of the mills were blows to the communities where they existed. It was also naive of us to think that everyone who emigrated to Alaska past or present did so for the same reasons, and had the same values, that we did. Many who came before us were like the pioneers who had moved the American frontier westward, tough and resourceful people who tamed, developed, and civilized as they went; they may have professed to love the wilderness and many probably did, but were at the same time laying waste to it in the name of progress and the almighty dollar. Many old-time Alaskans, and a number of established businesses in the larger communities, had made their fortune catering to logging interests, and were bitterly opposed to the "greenies" raining on their parade. I think some old-timers had been in the State so long they'd forgotten that Cleveland had once looked like Sitka. The loggers themselves of course didn't like it, but by and large they weren't Alaskans; when the camps closed for winter, they took their paychecks south with them.

Almost all logging now conducted in Southeast is on lands that had been ceded to native corporations in the native land claims settlement act of 1973. Some of those corporations have logged their allotments—and stripped them clean. Unfettered by environmental constraints on their "private" lands, their practices have been generally atrocious.

———

Almost everywhere we went throughout our Southeast sojourn we encountered evidence of what life in the Southeast Alaskan bush had been like in the first half of the twentieth century: old pilings, rusted pieces of machinery, and the rotting remnants of what must have been docks or piers, where salteries, herring reduction plants, salmon canneries, small mining operations, or sawmills once flourished. In more recent years the remains of logging operations have been added to the list.

Salmon canneries in particular had been ubiquitous in, and a hallmark of, the Southeast Alaska of that time, when there had been many more fish and fewer ways of getting them to market. There seemed to have been a cannery in every bay and cove, but one by one they disappeared as the second half of the century wore on. Only a handful remained in operation at the time of our arrival; they too would shut down and most would go to ruin, but the abandoned Chatham Cannery in Sitkoh Bay looked, at least when we saw it in 1977 and again in 1981, like it might be reopened for business again tomorrow.

In their heyday the canneries had been mini-cities from spring through early fall, frenetically busy 24/7 when fishing was good, and attracting seasonal workers from Native villages (often most of their population) as well as homesteaders and migrant labor from Southeast's larger communities and "down south." Workers lived in dorms and ate in communal dining halls. The canneries were a significant source of cash money for those living a subsistence lifestyle, and a major part of the regional economy.

There were the sagging remains of cabins hidden back in the beach fringes that had once sheltered trappers, hunters, and homesteaders. An occasional camp was of more recent vintage, built and still used by hunters. Most were probably illegal, but unlikely to be discovered. It was an unspoken rule of the outback that such cabins were never locked, and anyone in need of food or shelter could enter without considering themselves trespassers, as long as they eventually replenished what they took. Many of the small islands retained evidence of the fox farms that flourished in the heyday of fur-as-fashion.

A visit to Baranof Warm Springs in 1977 took us back in time, to a place in the wilderness that was still being homesteaded. It might as easily have been 1940 or 1950. Warm Springs lies on the East Coast of Baranof Island, directly opposite Sitka on the west. The journey between them was a short hop by float plane, but via land required a hard two-day trek of sixteen miles over the mountainous terrain that separated them. By boat, the distance was close to 100 miles. We never went there during our time at Mt. Edgecumbe, but Ross Brudenell, the GMO who delivered David, made the trek over the top with a local who had done it several times before.

Baranof Warm Springs had been, in the earliest days of the twentieth century, a bustling community centered about a sawmill and a saltery, complete with a couple of saloons and a bordello. The enterprises folded, the town petered out, and it was subsequently inhabited by a succession of homesteaders that came and went; some stayed quite a while. Among those were the Short family in the 1950s; Wayne Short would write two classic chronicles of homesteading in the Tongass, *The Cheechakoes* and *This Raw Land*. I recommend them highly.

The trip by water from Juneau was roughly 100 miles, and we did it twice. We found Warm Springs a stunningly beautiful place, situated at the head of a small and well-protected bay and at the foot of a high waterfall coming out of Baranof Lake above. At the time of our first visit, it was being homesteaded by a family of three: The wife tended a small general store serving transients, and homeschooled their daughter, about the same age as our own daughters. The husband we did not meet; he commercial fished throughout the summer and was thus seldom there, and trapped winters. Word had it that he was a Vietnam vet with a survivalist mentality, politically reactionary even in those times, possessor of an arsenal excessive even by Alaskan standards, and most at home in the absence of people. Years later an unsubstantiated rumor circulated that a handful of Vietnam veterans who had failed to reintegrate into society had been relocated to various remote places in Alaska by the government to pursue subsistence lifestyles, for their own and everyone else's good. If there was anything to the rumor, we wondered if this might have been one.

The homestead site was a collection of weathered wooden buildings clustered along the waterfront not far from the base of the falls, connected by boardwalks some of which were built up on pilings. It must have looked very much like it had twenty, thirty, forty years before, other than for a large and new-looking floating dock, incongruous in view of the condition of the buildings and smacking of government money. It connected to the boardwalk on shore by a long gangway. The dock was large enough to accommodate several sizeable boats, and also the float plane that came in weekly from Sitka carrying mail and supplies. In earlier days, the many canneries and small outposts such as this were provided that service by boats making the rounds from Juneau, about once a week when weather permitted.

In 1977 Warm Springs was a seasonally busy place, a waystation for commercial fishermen working lower Chatham strait and for large luxury yachts from "down south." Also for smaller pleasure craft such as ours with the range to make the trip from Sitka, Petersburg, or Juneau. In the off season, the isolation must have been intense. We imagined it might go many weeks at a time between visitors, save for the mail plane.

Warm Springs, as the name implies, was a geothermally active site, one of several in Southeast Alaska, and one of the buildings housed the baths. The hot springs had been tamed to provide hot water to bathtubs in several small rooms walled off for privacy. Taps had been installed for both the scalding water direct from the spring, and cold water from the lake above, so the bather could dial in his own temperature just like at home. Bath towels could be rented at the store, and the facilities were clean. The only downside was the sulphurous odor, but we all found the baths delightful.

Not everyone did. While we were there a family disembarked from a large luxury yacht complete with professional skipper, home-ported somewhere in California, and marched up the dock gangway toward the baths (the skipper was quite obviously not included in any of the family's activities or even conversation, and greatly enjoyed talking to us while his employers were absent). Minutes later they returned, wearing uniformly sour expressions with pinched noses, like they had been exposed to a bad smell. They had.

While there, we flyfished the fast water at the base of the falls and caught some small cutthroat. Rods in hand, we also hiked the half-mile from the top of the falls to the lake. The scenery was so spectacular that we forgot to fish.

Things looked the same when we returned four years later, but they weren't. There was nobody home. The family that had been living there had left and moved to Juneau, to provide their daughter access to both better schooling and more immediate medical care, as she had significant health issues; they would be the last of the homesteaders. A few years later a Juneau consortium would open and operate a sportfishing lodge there. In its most recent incarnation Warm Springs has become a part of the borough of Sitka, and is now a seasonal community with a number of new and well-kept private vacation homes and a lodge that offers meals, accommodations, and sportfishing charters—and the baths. It reverts to its isolated self in winter, with only a caretaker in residence.

Baranof Warm Springs then and now is a living reminder that the era of homesteading in Southeast Alaska has passed. The wilderness remains, but for many reasons it will never again be possible for adventurous souls to do what the Short family did in the years after WWII, and what many had done well before that. They were among the last of a colorful, eccentric breed that once included legendary bear man Allen Hasselborg of Mole Harbor, Stan Price of Pack Creek (who we'll meet in a later chapter), and Tiger Olson of Taku Harbor; the latter two both attained the age of ninety before passing on over thirty years ago, during our tenure in Juneau.

The imprint of civilization on the Tongass, past and present, is around the edges. Water has always provided the lifeblood—for the present inhabitants, for their Russian and then Anglo predecessors from the lower 48, and for the indigenous peoples who occupied those edges for thousands of years. The island and mainland interiors have been explored, and in places even exploited for timber and deposits of gold and silver, but for the most part are, and always have been, devoid of human habitation. The pattern is apparent from the water but even more revealing from the air, where we saw it in our numerous comings and goings over the years: evidence of human activity past and present—more past than present—all around the watery margins, but interiors with endless tracts of forest and muskeg, lake and mountain, ice and snowfield—none of which gave evidence of having been touched by the hand of man.

————

Eager to squeeze every last drop from our Alaskan experience before leaving Mt. Edgecumbe, and knowing that it might be our last chance ever to do so, we left our children with friends on two occasions during the last months of our tenure and took excursions north. The first was by boat with Sitka guide and charter captain Ben Forbes. Ben was about sixty at the time we met him. Short, balding, and bespectacled, with a cherubic visage, he looked more like an accountant than the Alaskan sourdough that spent much of his life outdoors in the bush and had once killed a brown bear at point-blank range with a .44 magnum revolver.

This trip we did along with two other Mt. Edgecumbe couples that we knew well. Our itinerary took us north along the outer coast of Chichagof and Yakobi Islands, close by a sea lion rookery on an islet of rock just off the coast. On shore we took in the ruins of what had once been a sizeable gold mine, and the bath at White Sulphur Springs, another geothermal feature miles from anywhere that the forest service had built an enclosure over. The outside waters were very different from the inside passages we'd done our boating in; the massive, widely spaced rollers, while imparting little perceptible motion, took us from the crests, where we could look down on either side to the bottomless chasms of the troughs, into those troughs, where all one could see on either side were great walls of water.

We entered the mouth of Icy Strait from Cross Sound, where we saw our first killer whales, and experienced the rips, chop, and whirlpools in the bottleneck of South Inian Pass. Stopped for fuel at the funky little village of Elfin Cove, built on elevated boardwalks and with the appearance of a ghost town in this month before the opening of the commercial salmon and halibut fisheries would bring it to life. Then on to Idaho Inlet, where we would see our first coastal brown bear on the flats at the head, foraging on newly emerging spring vegetation.

On the north, mainland side of Icy Strait was the face of Brady Glacier, backed by the towering, snow-covered peaks of the Fairweather Range. On into Glacier Bay to the head of Muir Inlet, where we got our first look at a massive tidewater glacier which put on a magnificent calving show for our benefit. Lower down in the Bay two of us ascended several hundred feet of talus slide at the base of Mt. Wright to come within 30 yards of two mountain goats—a nanny and kid. We saw puffin and all manner of sea birds and their nesting sites, species whose distribution in Southeast Alaska was limited to Glacier Bay and the outer coast. We also saw our first sea otters there, once prevalent throughout Southeast Alaska but hunted to near-extinction by Russian fur traders.

Ben Forbes was a superb guide and storyteller, a fount of knowledge on the Southeast Alaskan wilderness. Our short time with him was unforgettable.

Our second venture took us via an Alaska state ferry to Skagway at the head of Lynn Canal, gateway to the Klondike during the gold rush of 1898, and where the scoundrel Soapy Smith and deputy Frank Reid shot it out on Juneau Wharf that same year to the detriment of both. We were excited to be heading into the country of Jack London's *Call of the Wild*, and Robert Service's Sam McGee and Dangerous Dan McGrew.

We traveled the White Pass & Yukon Railway from Skagway to Whitehorse, Yukon Territory, in the single, mostly empty, passenger car amongst a long line of empty ore cars deadheading on the return back to Whitehorse. The trip out of Skagway up into the mountains was spectacular, featuring trestles over deep gorges and a right-of-way clinging to impossibly steep mountainsides. It was often possible to see out of our window our engine and the cars ahead and behind as the tight curves and switchbacks followed the mountain contours. Our route paralleled that taken by the hordes of miners headed for the Klondike along the Chilkoot Trail.

Once over the pass we left the maritime climate of Southeast Alaska, and the rainforest of the Tongass, behind. This was the Yukon, colder and drier; forest had given way to great expanses of tundra, and the length of Lake Bennett—which the gold-seekers had built boats to traverse. Although it was May Lake Bennett was still frozen, and the tundra and mountains from there to Whitehorse still blanketed in snow.

Near Whitehorse we got our first and only glimpse of the mighty Yukon River, third longest on the continent, and at one of the last of the paddle-wheel riverboats to have run the river in years past. We were now far from Southeast, and were surprised to learn that the headwaters of the Yukon River were at Atlin, B.C., only sixty miles from Juneau as the crow flies. The River first runs north from Atlin Lake, then gradually turns west to traverse the entire breadth of Alaska before discharging into the Bering Sea.

This trip was definitely about the journey and not the destination. We spent the night at a Whitehorse motel, and arrived back at the train station for our return trip well before the scheduled departure time of 9:00 A.M. the next morning. There was no train awaiting, and the station appeared empty! On entering the station we finally found the sole occupant, an elderly gent wearing an official-looking cap, puttering about in the station office. On inquiring as to the whereabouts of our train, he replied, "Oh, that left twenty minutes ago." How could that be when it was not yet 9 A.M.? "Oh, we decided to change the schedule."

A fine fix we were in: Should we miss our ferry at Skagway, the next one was days away. The old gent brightened: Hop in his car, he said, we might just be able to catch the train at the Carcross crossing, thirty miles south. In we hopped. Our chauffeur put the pedal to the metal, pounding over the mostly gravel road at a furious pace. We eventually pulled abreast the train, running neck and neck with it all the way to Carcross, where we inched ahead just enough for our man to jump out and flag it down.

———

Weeks later we were gone. My service obligation completed, we were going with Plan A; it was with reluctance that we left our trusty green Bug behind and flew back to the East Coast, where we would begin the life in New England we had envisioned years before. We had returned from our trip to the Yukon by way of Juneau, where we rented a car and spent a day looking around. We were tourists pure and simple, and had no inkling that in little more than two years' time we would be calling Juneau home.

Fishing Southeast I: Salmon and Halibut

There's no need to discuss separately the fishing that we did during our Sitka sojourn and that we did in our later and much longer stay in Juneau. The targeted species were the same, as were the tackle and strategies. Only the places changed. Saltwater fishing in Alaska was, as we found, all about salmon and halibut. First, salmon.

We would quickly learn the ABCs of pacific salmon, although the season was too far along when we first arrived to do anything but watch and learn.

Of the five species indigenous to North America, only two are of interest to saltwater sport fisherman—the king, or chinook, and the silver, or coho. The other three—the pink (humpback, or "humpie"), chum (dog, or calico), and sockeye (red)—are primarily filter-feeders and, while commercially valuable, are uninterested in otherwise tempting attractions at the end of a line.

Kings are, as their name implies, regal and handsome fish; they look like what every other fish wishes they could look like. They look like what *I* always thought a fish should look like. In size they range from around 12 to over 60 lbs., the average being in the low twenties. As size increases, so does scarcity: A king of over 30 lbs. is called a "Tyee" in the Campbell River area of British Columbia and is cause for a celebration ritual, and anything over 40 lbs., anywhere, is bragging class. The rarified air inhabited by 50-pounders and up is something salmon anglers may get to sample only a time or two in a fishing lifetime, if that (I would eventually and barely make it, once). The sportfishing record is now somewhere in the nineties, and for some time the title was held by Juneau acquaintance Howie Ryder. The largest king salmon taken by any means was a specimen caught in a fish trap near Petersburg, Alaska, in 1949 that weighed in at 126 lbs.

Although kings can be caught year round in Southeast waters, the peak time for fishing is late spring through early summer, when sexually mature kings are making their way toward the spawning rivers of their birth. Since kings spawn in only the largest river systems of Southeast, those caught around Sitka, the outer coast, and many of the inside waters at this time of year were bound for distant destinations in British Columbia and the Pacific Northwest. Those caught in the immediate vicinity of Juneau were headed to the nearby Taku and Chilkat river systems.

Within weeks of our arrival at Mt. Edgecumbe we were to witness, from the sidelines, the socio-cultural phenomenon that was the Sitka Salmon Derby. It was an early and graphic demonstration of the king salmon's pervasive hold on Sitka and all Southeast. On day one of the two-day weekend event, we watched from our living room window as what seemed like every small boat in Mt. Egecumbe and Sitka milled about in the channel, jockeying for position as they awaited the 8 A.M. starting gun. At the gun there ensued a pedal-to-the-metal free-for-all as the boats roared off down the channel in both directions, each headed for a favorite spot where they just knew the Big One lurked. One of them would be right.

We would learn that every community of any size—Sitka, Petersburg, Wrangell, Ketchikan, Juneau—held their own annual salmon derbies, and the towns virtually shut down for that weekend. Some ran three days rather than just two, and attracted not only locals but anglers from all over Southeast and beyond. The derbies weren't related in any way, and each had its own rules and format; in every case the proceeds from the sale of the fish entered, and entry fees, went toward one or more worthy causes such as scholarships, and the prizes donated by local merchants could be substantial. Juneau's Golden North Salmon Derby was the largest, and the value of the prize for the top fish could be eye-popping. We fished a few derbies, but were content to sit out most—just too much company on the water.

Although there are other ways of fishing for kings—mooching or strip-fishing—king salmon in Southeast are mostly sought by trolling. That's what we learned at Mt. Edgecumbe and what we did there and later, and thus we'll stick to that. We learned by watching and listening, but much was gleaned second-hand from ENT doc and sometime fishing companion Tom Stengl, who was more aggressive that I when it came to coaxing "how to do it" information out of the locals. We found there were almost as many variations in setting up for king salmon trolling as there are fishermen, and I eventually equated it with performing appendectomies: There are almost as many wrinkles to doing one as there are surgeons, each of whom is convinced their way is best, but at the end of the day they all work. The only way we'd know whether our mix-and-match, cobbled-together system was going to work was to try it; we did, and it did. The basics went as follows:

The almost-universal bait was herring. Twelve-packs of frozen bait herring were to be found in freezers in virtually every supermarket, tackle shop, and convenience store throughout Southeast. Double-hooked commercial leaders about five feet in length could be purchased in a variety of permutations; some purists insisted that only leaders hand-tied by themselves were any good. We used commercial "slip-tied" leaders with a sliding upper hook, and learned one of the many intricate and stylized rituals of rigging the herring on the hooks so it would make its way behind the moving boat in large, lazy spirals. Some threaded a "hoochie"—a soft-rubber imitation squid available in a variety of garish colors—on the leader just ahead of the herring, varying the color with light conditions, time of year, time of day, and the signs of the zodiac. We didn't bother with them. We also didn't bother with flashers—large strips of chromed metal some called "Ford fenders"—attached ahead of the leader, attractors which some thought were a must. Everyone used either a lead sinker of six oz. give-or-take, or one of several patented planing devices such as the pink lady, to get their herring down to where the fish were.

Downriggers—devices for getting trolled baits or lures down to far greater depths—had not yet been introduced to sportfishing in Southeast, and would only begin to take hold in the early 1980s. By the end of that decade they would be ubiquitous in the salmon sport fishery, and greatly increased the chances for success, especially in off-peak times of year when the kings were deeper. The downrigger allowed for precise control of the depth at which one placed their bait or lure, and when used in conjunction the sophisticated fishfinder-fathometers that came along at about the same time, allowed the angler to place his temptation right in front of the nose of his prey.

We never got into downriggers, even after they became popular. We preferred to fish kings only during the peak spring months when the fish ran larger, were more concentrated, and were commonly found at lesser depths. While at Sitka we did fish a little in the winter, after we saw boats trolling—and catching—in the channel right behind our house. We did take a nice-sized king in January only a stone's throw from our backyard, but fishing winter kings never became an addiction. Too much sitting and waiting in the raw and the cold, too much like ice-fishing without a shanty.

On with the ritual of trolling for kings: Once the herring has been rigged to one's own precise formula and the special sauce added, over the side it goes. You shut down the boat's big engine and start the "kicker"—a small outboard clamped on the stern bracket of every boat in Southeast under 30'—as kings prefer a slowly trolled meal. Check that your herring is rotating to your satisfaction, then strip from your reel your own secret number of hand-pulls of twenty- to thirty-pound test monofilament, maybe 16 or 18. Park your rod butt in a holder clamped to the gunwale. You are now in business.

King fishing, like real estate, was about location, location, location. Watch when and where the locals fish; some generous souls even told us where some of the hotspots were. We got to recognize the boats of some known to be skookum fishermen, and shamelessly set up shop in the same places they did. Kings tend to gather where the food is; unremarkable-looking stretches of shoreline can conceal the fact that bottom contours and tides along them are just right for producing the upwellings that stimulate the entire marine food chain.

Now that you're trolling, settle back and enjoy the scenery and the salt air. Maybe the drizzle. Open a thermos of coffee. Some prefer to crack a beer, but please, go slow. It could be a long wait.

Trolling for king salmon is not for those who require instant gratification. The time between strikes, except for those once-in-a-decade days, is measured in hours and sometimes days. During the peak season for kings the local newspaper would keep us up to date as to the current number of rod-hours required to land one king—it was seldom lower than eight. Depending on the comforts of your boat and the roughness of the water, you may get cold, wet, seasick, or all of the above. Linda and our kids never got seasick, but did, in our earlier boats, get cold and wet.

The strike, announced by the sudden shrieking of your reel's drag, makes it all worthwhile. Put the engine in neutral, grab your rod out of its holder, and the fight is on. King salmon rarely jump and seldom head deep for the bottom; their fight is characterized by a series of long, powerful runs (200 yards of line on your reel is a bare minimum). The runs become shorter, and the exhausted (you hope) king is finally brought to the surface at the side of the boat. This is the moment of high drama, and when your fish is most likely to break off. A sudden frenzy or run with the sinker out of water can snap the leader, or pull out the hooks. A clumsy effort with the long-handled salmon net can likewise spell disaster (and might have even been responsible for some divorces). Netting a big king is a two-person job. One can do it, but it's quite a stunt. A long-handled gaff is a better choice for one fishing solo.

Our children were a bit young for the rigors (?) of fishing for kings while we were at Mt. Edgecumbe, so mostly I fished solo or with friends. On one of my last outings for kings at Mt. Edgecumbe, shortly before our time there was up, I had along Hood Franks, whose tour there was also coming to an end. Hood had gone the entire two years without having caught a king salmon. Toward the end of a long and fishless day, we ran over a shallow spot and Hood's line hooked up on the bottom. His rod bent into a deepening arc, and before I could stop the boat's progress his rod, complete with rod holder, flew off the stern like it had been shot from a bow. He took it well. It was like he knew that this was how it had to turn out, and now he didn't have to worry about how to dispose of his trolling gear. Hood went on to become an internist and oncologist in his home state of Texas; whether or not he ever returned to Alaska to try again for his king I don't know. But I doubt it.

When we reached Juneau fishing for kings became a family affair. Our first foray, an early-evening outing in the spring of 1974 in our spanking-new 23' Bayliner, was to DuPont, on Gastineau Channel just a few miles south of downtown; it was the site of the old DuPont docks, abandoned but still standing, where shiploads of dynamite had been offloaded and stored during the heyday of hard-rock gold mining in Juneau. DuPont was just around the corner from Taku Inlet, and kings frequented the area to fatten up in the weeks before entering the Taku River on their spawning run.

Beginner's luck. A big king, later weighed at 36 lbs., fell for our herring and put on a show that featured a couple of rare jumps. After boating our prize I gave it the *coup de gras* with the "salmon konker"—which could be either a short, stout club, or a mallet with a head of hard rubber. Susan's immediate response was "Yum!" Betsy, age 6, burst into tears, totally in sympathy with the salmon. When I tried to cheer her up by saying how good it was going to taste, David, age 4, weighed in with a dubious "I'll have an egg."

A year later, Susan was old enough to be fishing her own rod, which she did with enthusiasm. We gave her the slot over the stern, directly in the boat's wake and prop wash—to my way of thinking a slight handicap, if anything. Lo and behold, she began out-fishing us! In an effort to figure out what she was doing that we weren't, I watched carefully as she put her herring off the back and stripped out the requisite number of pulls as instructed. The secret was out—her sixteen pulls were the equivalent of an adult's eight. Her herring was at times visible, swimming close behind in the prop wash. The kings loved it.

Over time we did pretty well with kings, as good as or maybe even a little better than most. As they got older, all of our kids would land some very respectable specimens. My best was a fifty-pounder, while Linda took two in the mid-forties; one of those is worth telling about. It happened in the late 1980s when our children were in college, and Linda and I went off on some weekends alone. On this spring weekend we planned to take it easy at Swanson Harbor and catch up on some of the routine spring boat maintenance. Anchoring up on a calm day off Point Couverden, just outside the Harbor, we started in on waxing the fiberglass of the cabin. A good tide was running, so we set up two salmon rods and let the herring work in the current off the stern while we waxed. We were working up forward, and were interrupted every few minutes by a twitching of one or the other rod tips and a tentative grunt of a drag; we were being harassed by an infestation of "shakers," kings of far below legal size—most likely jacks, salmon that mature sexually a year or two before they should.

Each time one of us had to go astern, reel in, release the pestiferous dwarf, and rebait. After having repeated the exercise multiple times, I didn't even glance up when Linda went aft to deal with yet another. A minute of silence, then "Will, you'd better come back here and look at this." I did, and was confronted with the sight of a silvery monster attached to Linda's leader, swimming in languid circles next to the boat right beneath the surface, like a goldfish in a bowl. We warily awaited the inevitable surge and powerful run—but it never came. There was nothing for it but to scoop it up in the net and horse it aboard, all 43 pounds of it. Only when it hit the deck did it wake up and create a ruckus. That otherwise-healthy fish must have been stoned on tranquilizers, or maybe a conscientious objector who preferred to be eaten rather than fight.

Linda's father had always loved to fish, but over the course of a lifetime spent largely in New Jersey, had little opportunity and even less success. When he and Linda's sisters visited us in Juneau in 1984, one of our goals was to get him a fish that would cap an otherwise undistinguished angling career.

Sure 'nuff he hooked a king, and it soon became a toss-up as to which was playing which. I maneuvered our boat to keep his line out of trouble while Linda and David, back in the cockpit, tried to keep things on the rails. Not easy. Linda's dad kept wanting to tighten down on the drag, which I'd carefully preset, and which is a no-no for any savvy angler playing a powerful fish. Then, the retaining nut holding his reel in place on the rod began backing off. Through all of this Linda and David were remanded to keep their hands off and their suggestions to themselves, as this was *his* fish. Despite all the advantages bestowed on the salmon, it eventually allowed itself to be netted. Just as it was hoisted aboard both hooks dislodged from its mouth, and at the same moment the reel freed itself from the rod and clattered to the deck; almost enough to make one believe some benevolent power up there was directing events. The king weighed 22 lbs. Frozen hard and well-wrapped in newspapers, it was hand-carried by the triumphant angler on the flight back to St. Pete, Florida.

Our "once in a fishing career" day—two days, actually—arrived in 1994 while we were hosting Susan and new husband Chip aboard our boat for part of their honeymoon. Again, the setting was Swanson Harbor and Point Couverden. Shortly before departing from Juneau I realized we were out of salmon leaders, and on short notice had to settle for a brand X, the only ones I could find, rather than our favored, trusted brand. During a day's trolling off Point Couverden we hooked up with ten, perhaps twelve, kings, most of them sizeable. We boated none. All were lost at some point during the fight because of leader failure.

We felt awful for Chip. This was his first, and might be his only, opportunity to fish for king salmon, and he was being done in by our equipment. During that evening in Swanson Harbor I rummaged around in the boat and finally found, buried deep in the corner of a storage locker, a couple of our old leaders. The next morning, as we were leaving Swanson for a last go at it, I noticed on our fish-finder fathometer a large ball of herring right at the harbor entrance—so close in that we didn't usually put our lines over until we were well past that point. We put the lines down in a hurry, and in the course of four passes over that ball of feed Chip and Susan hooked—and landed—four kings, a couple of which topped 30 lbs. We called it quits at that point, as our limit had been reached.

———

Silver, or coho, salmon look like scaled-down kings and run from six to over twenty pounds. Given the size overlap, it sometimes requires inspection of some minor features, such as the gum line, to determine if one's fish is a coho or a king. Silvers are far more numerous than kings, and their run occurs later—mid-July through early September. Also in contrast to kings, they spawn in most streams of respectable size in Southeast, and when hooked may jump repeatedly. Most are sought by trolling in exactly the same manner as for kings, but we trolled for coho only when hosting friends or family from the lower 48 and wanted to insure they caught fish. We are saving coho—Southeast's, and our, most popular sport fish—for another chapter, for reasons that will come clear then.

———

Halibut are nowhere near as glamorous as salmon, as homely as salmon are handsome, but every bit as tasty and sometimes much larger. They are the largest members of the flounder family—flat, with both eyes on a brownish, mottled top, white on the bottom, and can attain sizes of several hundred pounds. They live and feed in the benthic zone—near the bottom—on virtually everything: fish of all descriptions (including other halibut), crabs, carrion, beer cans and can openers. We've caught halibut containing all of those items; one contained chicken bones tossed over the side of our boat only minutes before. Monster specimens were rumored to lurk beneath the pilings supporting canneries and fish-processing plants; our friend Hank Bryson, a scuba diver, claimed to have seen a few scary ones beneath such docks on the Juneau waterfront, and Linda's fear of falling in the water was not so much about the cold and deep as about the possibility of being devoured by a halibut. I don't think she was kidding. At appropriate times halibut come into the shallows near the mouths of salmon-spawning streams, scarfing up salmon on their way in and salmon carcasses on their way out. On one occasion while fishing for halibut we left a line down near the bottom while we took a break for dinner. The bait was taken by a small trash fish, a pollock about a foot long. I reeled it up and, not wanting to interrupt our meal, lowered it back to the bottom without unhooking it. Moments later the rod tip bent into the water and the reel's drag squawked. A sixty-pound halibut had swallowed our "bait."

Halibut tackle is of necessity heavier than that for salmon—stubby, stiff rods, and line of 40-lb. test or better. Sinkers heavy enough to get you to the bottom, and keep you there even with a current running.

Most of us fished with monofilament line, although the most serious halibuters, who sometimes fished at depths of 300-400 feet, preferred braided dacron. Dacron doesn't stretch, while nylon monofilament does. Trying to winch up a big halibut from a depth of even one hundred feet with monofilament can be a break-even proposition; rather than having the fish come up a bit with every laborious pump of the rod, the pumping only succeeds in stretching the line. We preferred to do our halibuting in water no more than 60-80 feet deep.

Given the halibut's lack of preference when it comes to food, bait can be almost anything. We often used belly strips from salmon we had caught—free, durable, good for little else (although some liked to smoke them), and effective. As with salmon trolling, after everything was in place—your sinker having hit bottom and then reeled up several feet, you sat back, relaxed, and—waited. A more active alternative to bait was the halibut jig, a heavy, bright chunk of metal with large hook attached, which was worked up and down near the bottom.

As with salmon, success was all about location. Halibut have their preferences when it comes to the type of bottom they prefer, and some spots are better at funneling in food than others. Locals tend to be secretive about their favorite halibut holes; in the modern age of GPS, the logs in which their coordinates are written down are carefully guarded, maybe kept under pillows at night. Some folk are more charitable than others, though, and we were indebted to Tom Parke, the Juneau sourdough we'll meet in *The Deer Hunters*, for disclosing to us a spot within Holkham Bay, on the mainland well south of Juneau. Tom made sure we knew this was his *second*-best halibut spot, as he was not about to divulge the location of his best.

Tom's spot was inside the Bay's entrance, over a shallow bottom of hard glacial silt at the foot of Sumdum Glacier, where Tracy Arm takes off to the north and Endicott Arm to the south. Converging currents at certain phases of the tide concentrated food, and halibut. For years it remained our best producer of big halibut, several running close to

100 lbs.; David in particular enjoyed hauling them up. The only downside was having to be on constant lookout for floating icebergs, some of which towered over our boat. Lesser bergs could be fended off with the boat hook, but we had to get out of the way of the biggies. To maneuver readily when required, we drifted rather than anchored when fishing this spot.

Halibut strategy when hooked is to stay at the bottom, resisting the pull of the line with not only size and strength, but also its flat shape. Some make swift, long runs along the bottom. Battling a halibut is a tug-o-war; bring it up a ways and then down it goes. The repetitive process becomes grueling, can wear an angler down, and near the end the battle is nowhere near as much fun as the uninitiated might imagine.

Our largest halibut, caught by Linda, came out of Tom's spot in 1983. We were nowhere close to a scale that could handle it, but did have a table published by the Alaska Department of Fish & Game which equated length, tip of the nose to fork of the tail, with approximate weight. Her fish measured 75"—6'3"—which worked out to 220 lbs. It was hooked in only 30 feet of water, but it took Linda about 45 exhausting minutes to work that halibut to the surface alongside the boat. At that time, the accepted way to deal with over-large halibut when brought to the surface was to shoot them. If one were able to hit a pea-sized spot between and just behind the eyes, it was game over.

They were shot because no one of sound mind would take aboard his boat a really big halibut with any life left in it. The mayhem they were capable of could trash a boat, and in one instance of which we heard, a Petersburg fisherman, alone on his craft, sustained a broken femur which lacerated the femoral artery. With no help at hand, he bled out.

On with the story: I missed the brain with my revolver, and rather than game over, the game went into overtime. The properly pissed goliath got a second wind and dove back to the bottom. Linda, not at all happy with her husband at this point, gave him a withering glare as she handed him the rod and told him he could bring it back up himself. Twenty sweaty minutes later we had a shark hook in the subdued beastie, attached to a heavy line with a rubber snubber and thence to a cleat. This specimen was far too heavy to horse over the rail and onto the deck, so when all was at last quiet we towed it to the beach in the skiff, where it was filleted and cut into chunks for the cooler. Linda was grossed out by the fasciculations—quivering—of the chunks of meat, even as they were lowered into the cooler.

Shooting big halibut was not only a hit-or-miss proposition, but also could be hazardous to the health of one's boat. An antidote which we heard over and over involved fishermen who shot their halibut after, rather than before, boating them, putting large-caliber holes through the bottom of their boats. We heard so many permutations of this story that we wondered if it was even true—or whether it happened all the time. Obviously a better mousetrap was called for, and it came along in the late 1980s in form of the halibut harpoon. This simple but elegant piece of technology featured a detachable, pivoting harpoon head on a short shaft attached to a length of stout line with a snubber. The head would detach from the shaft after the latter-day Ahab had driven it through the halibut just forward of the gills, and its pivoting action prevented it from coming back out. It was a welcome alternative to shooting.

Halibut were occasional (but welcome) incidental catches when trolling for salmon, especially over fairly shallow areas; the habitual bottom-dwellers were not averse to coming up near the surface when an easy meal was in the offing. The largest Sitka halibut caught from our boat was a specimen of around 100 lbs., caught while salmon trolling and landed by the teenage son of our physical therapist, Hugh Moffatt. That same teenager, only days after, would catch a 47-lb. king salmon from the *Ginger*, by far the largest taken while we were at Mt. Edgecumbe.

Both of these fish were caught in the same place—Hayward Strait, not particularly known as a hotspot and one we hadn't fished before. The king was caught on the eve of the first salmon derby we would fish, and there were herring dimpling the surface everywhere, suggesting that more big kings lurked below. We vowed to head for Hayward Straight on the morrow, as soon as the starting gun went off. We knew something nobody else did, and were gloating like insider stock traders. So off we went—arriving in time to see two guys in our spot, fishing from a skiff which had been faster than we were, landing in rapid succession two kings that would have pushed 50 lbs. each. Word traveled fast—this seldom-fished place became cluttered with boats within a few hours. We didn't get a strike all day.

————

There were incidental catches landed while either halibut fishing or salmon trolling. Small members of the pollock family were a common nuisance, as were sculpins known as Irish Lords, or double-uglies. The most intriguing was the ling cod. We encountered them only while at Mt. Edgecumbe, as they were only found on or near the outer coast. The specimens we caught were in the range of 15-20 lbs., and in appearance must rank among nature's least-favored creatures: brownish, with huge heads out of proportion to the rest of their bodies, bulging eyes, and gaping, toothy jaws. We rated their size by the number of Olympia Beer cans we estimated their mouths could hold (five oly, seven oly, etc.). Their grotesque appearance proved a Darwinian gift, at least with us. In our ignorance, we released them and threw them back. We had no idea at the time that the ling cod was highly prized as table fare.

————

Our family ate lots of fish, salmon and halibut, during our years in Alaska—fresh, frozen, and smoked. I do not recall once buying it. Had we been interested in doing the math—which we absolutely weren't—our "free" fish would have been many times more expensive per pound than had we bought it, or what we pay for it now.

Our National Bird

In the latter half of the twentieth century Alaska was the only state (other than Hawaii, where it has never existed) in which the American bald eagle did not appear on the endangered species list. We had never seen one until a few days after we arrived at Mt. Edgecumbe, when one alighted in a tree next to our house at the level of our second floor. Our family was mesmerized by the sight of that huge, magnificent bird perched only feet from a bedroom window. It would not take long for us to realize that bald eagles in Southeast were about as common as crows everywhere else.

It would also not take us long to realize just how incongruous was the bird's wimpish, high-pitched squeak with its majestic appearance. Made us wonder whether Benjamin Franklin—who termed the eagle "a bird of ill character" (probably for cadging a living mostly as a scavenger)—was right when he lobbied for the turkey to be the new nation's national bird.

When salmon were running eagles congregated *en masse* high in the conifers overlooking stretches of shoreline that were popular for trolling. Looking up, "snowballs"—white heads—were everywhere, looking for a free lunch. Trollers catching all-too-common nuisance fish, small members of the cod or pollock families, tossed them over the stern after roughly unhooking them; almost instantaneously one or more eagles would leave their perches and swoop down upon the still-floating prey. The lucky winner of the competition seized the hapless fish in its talons on the fly and made off with it—often harassed all the way back to its perch by fellow eagles not so quick on the draw. An oft-repeated show, and always fun to watch.

Their scavenging was on display when we brought our boat into an anchorage at the end of a commercial halibut opening, where halibut boats had been dressing their catch and offloading onto a fish-buying tender. Quantities of entrails were floating about on the water, and much had washed up on the beaches. Eagles that we estimated as well over a hundred in number occupied one gravel bar, bloated and waddling about after having gorged on the smorgasbord. We did not see one even attempt to fly, and doubted they could. The FAA would have grounded them.

Scavengers though they might be, Southeast residents were well advised to keep pets—kittens, puppies, and small dogs—under close watch when out of doors, as they were known to occasionally disappear. An article appearing in Juneau's daily newspaper related the following story: An RV from the lower 48 had stopped at a gas station in Haines (on Lynn Canal north of Juneau, the only town in Southeast connected with the continent's road system). The elderly couple were taking stretch breaks while fueling, he on one side and she on the other with their canine companion, one of those annoying, yippy little dogs that Linda and I call "appetizers." An eagle perched atop a nearby tree obviously concurred with our definition, as it swooped down, snatched the hapless critter from beneath the nose of the woman, and soared off with its prize. The woman proceeded to wax hysterical, while her husband, hidden from her view on the other side of the camper, pumped his fist with a silent "Yes!"

The bald eagle, despite the fact that much of its diet is water-sourced, is not an aquatic bird. It does not alight on the water and doesn't swim—at least it's not supposed to do either. Imagine my surprise when, while steelhead fishing on Petersburg Creek, an eagle came floating by me in midstream, riding the current, looking not in the least distressed and making no effort to either take off or reach dry land. I've no idea how it got there, or why, and it disappeared around a bend in the river looking every bit as elegant and stately as a Mississippi River steamboat.

On our way home from an outing in our boat, we encountered one eagle in the water almost a mile from the nearest shore. At first it appeared to be swimming, doing a reasonable imitation of a giant seagull, but venturing closer, we could see that its talons were hooked into the back of a salmon of perhaps six or seven pounds, and it was trying mightily to lift off with its oversized trophy. We watched an evenly matched struggle for perhaps half an hour, during which time we began to wonder whether what appeared to be a struggle for a meal was actually a struggle for survival—the eagle being unable to release its grip on the fish. All the while a second eagle had been circling low overhead. Eagles mate for life; this may have been the concerned mate. We could not intervene, and could not stay around long enough to know the verdict, but it wasn't looking good for either party.

We were privileged to have once witnessed a brood of eaglets earn their wings. It happened while we were anchored up not far off the beach on Homeshore, fly-fishing for coho, but fishing was forgotten as we watched: On a large fallen log lying parallel to the beach at the junction of beach and fringe timber were perched a mature bald eagle, which we figured to be Mama, and three eaglets. We didn't see where they had come from, but there must have been an "eagle tree" with a huge nest in the immediate vicinity from which the eaglets had tumbled—or perhaps been nudged. Mama, first in line, walked to the end of the log and simply hopped down to the ground; she turned to watch as each eaglet in turn imitated her performance. Mama walked back to the midpoint of the log and easily hopped back aboard. The eaglets followed and also hopped back aboard, although not near as easily. Mama again strolled to the end, and this time flapped her wings and launched in a gentle arc to the ground. All three eaglets did so in turn, exercising at least passable form. The getting-up-on-the log process was repeated. This time Mama launched more purposefully, flapping her wings more vigorously to propel her into a slightly higher arc, one that carried her into the lower branches of a nearby spruce. Two of the eaglets followed, their flaps and arcs more faltering and haphazard, but make it they did. The third, unnoticed by Mama, had failed to mount the log, its attention gathered by a yellow plastic pail that had washed up on the beach nearby. Mama returned alone to the beach, no doubt irked at the short attention span of this offspring but unwilling to wash it out of flight school. The recalcitrant eaglet was coaxed back onto the log, and this time proceeded to follow Mama into the low branches, where we lost sight of all. It appeared to us that this was all the teaching they were going to get, flying 101 and the top gun course rolled into one.

———

It would be a slight not to mention the raven, every bit as common as the eagle in Southeast Alaska. Ravens are the largest members of the corvid family of birds that includes crows and jays, and are known for their rare intelligence. Their antics are great fun to watch, their range of vocalizations fascinating, and their aerobatic displays, apparently done for the sheer fun of it, mesmerizing. Both the eagle and the raven, portrayed as the sly trickster that he is, occupy revered places in Tlingit culture and lore.

Guns

As this is written I am following in the news the latest in a dreary litany of tragic and senseless school shootings, wishing we were back in a more innocent time and place. Once, we were.

Guns are an emotionally and politically charged issue today, and most people have come down firmly on one side or the other. Try to put your sentiments aside as you read on, realize that yesterday was not today, and also realize that, as in many other ways, with respect to guns Alaska was simply different from everywhere else.

It is impossible to discuss living in Alaska without discussing guns. Guns have been a part of the fabric of Alaskan life since earliest territorial days, a means of subsistence and survival. It is easy to forget that while most of the lower 48 was suburbanized, urbanized, and otherwise civilized, Alaska was, and still largely is, the Last Frontier.

The percentage of households in which guns were present over the time we lived in Southeast Alaska was extremely high, probably even more than that of the rural south. It might have been a bit lower in Juneau than anywhere else in Southeast, owing to the number of state and federal government employees who were there despite, rather than because of, the Alaskan lifestyle.

A major difference between Alaska and the rural south was that in Alaska, gun ownership and use cut across educational, occupational, cultural, and political lines. Another difference between Alaska and virtually everywhere else was that, particularly in the smaller outlying villages, guns were—and still are—essential tools for putting food on the table. While they might not have been so absolutely necessary in the larger population centers like Sitka or Juneau, they were still perceived to be by many of the residents (like ourselves, and many we knew). Guns and their legitimate uses were an immutable part of Alaskan life and culture, and anyone who didn't like it didn't have to stay.

While guns were deeply imbedded in Alaskan culture, there was no such thing as a "gun culture" in the Alaska that I knew. Many residents owned and used guns but some didn't, and there was no line in the sand drawn between them. In many cases we didn't know, and certainly didn't care, whether our friends and neighbors were the former or the latter. Neither did they. We had no militia types, special forces wannabes, vigilantes, or other assorted wackos running around with AR-15 assault rifles. Open carry was legal everywhere in the state—bars, banks, public buildings, you name it—but guns were rarely seen outside of homes or the places where they were used, for the simple reason that carrying them to make a statement—just to tell everyone which tribe you belonged to, and to piss off or scare the snot out of the wussies in the other tribe—would have been considered ludicrous in the Alaska of that time.

Southeast Alaskan gun owners were a far from homogeneous group. They were not bound together by the common element of gun ownership, and they came in many flavors. At one end of a spectrum were those for whom guns were but tools of necessity—essential for bringing home waterfowl, moose, or venison in the same way that chainsaws were essential for stockpiling the winter's firewood. They were hunters, with little or no interest in recreational shooting. Some hunted only seldom, some a lot. They owned only those guns they needed, and used them only when necessary. They maintained their arms because they had to work when called upon, and by and large were competent marksmen, again because they had to be. Their interest in firearms was limited to what they needed to know, and they relied on factory ammunition for the small amount they used. Rural subsistence hunters fell into this category, but so also did several of the friends I regularly hunted with.

At the other end of the spectrum were serious firearms enthusiasts, the hobbyists. We had plenty of those. Many, but not all, were hunters. Some were into various aspects of competitive shooting, everything from biathlon to military-type events to precision benchrest shooting to trap. Others enjoyed informal recreational target shooting for its own sake. The hobbyists tended to be highly knowledgeable about firearms, ballistics, and related subjects. They knew and appreciated quality, form, and function, owned more guns than they actually needed (sometimes many more), and since they shot them a lot, tended to be highly skilled in their use. Some had guns customized to meet their needs or desires, or even had them custom-built. They handloaded their ammunition. For the enthusiast, Southeast was a good place to be: There were plenty of kindred souls about, plenty of space and opportunity to exercise their passion, and no stigma attached to what they did. It was looked upon as a pastime, not much different from bowling or golf. None that I knew suffered from any compulsion to shoot up things or people.

Most were somewhere in between; I myself was nearer the serious hobbyist end. I did a lot of shooting—to upgrade and maintain my skills, and because I enjoyed it. I handloaded all of my own ammunition. I had several of my guns modestly customized to improve form and function—sight alterations, custom grips for handguns, custom stocks for my two centerfire hunting / bear protection rifles—ones I styled, inletted, checkered, and finished myself (more learning curves ascended). All of the guns I owned were "shooters"; I was not a collector. I wound up owning more guns than actually needed, but my guns were still tools and I balked at purchasing some I greatly admired but had no practical use for.

In the years 1969-late 1990s gun-associated crime was uncommon in Southeast Alaska and the rest of the huge state as well, with the notable exception of Anchorage, a big city with all the urban baggage that went with it. In Southeast there were no gang wars (no gangs). No drug-related violence (drugs there were, but it was mostly pot use by teenage stoners and cocaine snorted by a white-collar clientele, neither particularly conducive to violence). Despite plenty of alcohol use and abuse, guns were not part of the equation. The use of firearms in robberies, home invasions, and for the settling of domestic and other disputes was not quite, but almost, unheard of. No school or other mass shootings. We certainly had our share of nutcases and malcontents— maybe more than our share—but packing heat and shooting up people to air grievances real or imagined wasn't something they did. Why, or why not? This armchair sociologist-psychologist doesn't know. Perhaps the small size of even our largest communities had something to do with it, maybe it was our isolation from the gun-violence epidemics of the lower 48, or maybe it was our very lack of a gun culture.

The rarity of gun violence made each incident memorable. Juneau did have one shooting that occupied the newspaper headlines for a week, and it was a doozy—possibly one of the most inept gun homicides in the history of crime. The perpetrator had borrowed the handgun he used in the murder earlier on the day of the shooting, and returned it to the owner the morning after. He had a motive known to several acquaintances (a falling-out with the victim over money), left copious evidence of his presence at the crime scene, and during the course of the police investigation borrowed the handgun a second time for the purpose of mutilating the barrel rifling with a cold chisel so that it could not be confirmed as the murder weapon. Needless to say he was bagged in record time, and so far as we know is still serving out his time in Juneau's Lemon Creek Jail, the State's only maximum security prison. The crime affected us personally in that we had to look for a new dog groomer. Some friends of ours were not so lucky: They had just paid this individual in advance on a long-term contract for the grooming of their dog.

We in Alaska couldn't help but be aware of the escalating pattern of gun-related violence the lower 48, including the assassination attempt on President Reagan, that was producing the nation's first calls for gun control. But it was like it was all taking place on some other planet. We, in our bubble, didn't have the disease, and neither needed nor wanted the cure. This attitude cut across the political spectrum. We considered ourselves environmentalists, as did most in our circle, and like them held liberal views on some other issues—but we were also recreational firearms users and hunters. Almost anywhere in the lower 48 we'd have been tarred as "tree-huggers" by the cretins on the far right, and feathered as "gun-lovers" by the gooneybirds on the far left—but in Alaska we were the simply the norm. Alaskan politicians of both stripes knew enough to keep silent on the subject of gun control.

Just as there was little gun-related crime, there were few accidental shootings—particularly considering the ubiquity of guns, ease of access, and popularity of hunting and recreational shooting. Only two hunting accidents were known to me; one was fatal. It was our observation that Southeast Alaskans were, in general, far more skilled in the use of their firearms, and knowledgeable and observant of the essentials of gun safety, including safe storage, than was (and is) the average gun owner in the lower 48.

There are exceptions to every generalization. The most bizarre that came my way (it did so in that I was Juneau's *de facto* urologist that day)—or that I ever heard of—was the result of sheer stupidity on the part of the teenager who was both assailant and victim. Perhaps he was competing for a Darwin award; I never asked. The dimwit had been practicing quick-draws from his belt with a loaded .44 magnum revolver, and I will leave to your imagination the location of the wound and appearance of the unintended target. If you've ever seen a sea cucumber, one of the ickier denizens of the Southeast Alaskan sea floor, you will not need much imagination (for the uninformed, I suggest googling). Our Dirty Harry wannabe had nailed it, dead center (for those of you who require happy endings, this story had one. I saw him for follow-up months after he'd undergone reconstructive surgery in Seattle, and he proudly volunteered how pleased his teen female acquaintances were with the result. Perhaps his urologist had done his work too well.).

The incidence of firearms mishaps involving children was almost nil, despite the prevalence of firearms in homes. Alaskan children, including our own, learned from an early age that the firearms in their home, while strictly off limits, were neither exotic novelties nor instruments of the devil but simply tools—common, useful, even essential tools, that had the potential to do grievous harm if misused. Kids, ours included, weren't tempted to impress their friends with them, first because they themselves were not impressed, and second, because their friends all had exactly the same "tools" in their homes.

Our children were thoroughly schooled in the fundamentals of gun safety, handling, operation, and use as soon as they were old enough, and attended evening gun-safety classes held at a local school. Their reward was the enjoyment of plinking clam shells and pop cans with a .22 rifle or pistol at deserted beaches on family outings. The destructive power of firearms was on display there, and more so every time I brought back deer from a hunt. This approach, while it worked well enough for us and most fellow Alaskans, might not in locales where gun ownership was less prevalent and less informed.

———

As a latecomer to the game, thirty years of age and newly arrived from suburbia, I had a lot of catching up to do in the firearms proficiency department. I didn't have the luxury of starting at the logical beginning, learning the basics of marksmanship with .22 rimfires, guns of mild muzzle blast and almost negligible recoil, and working slowly up from there. One of my "starter guns" was the quite powerful 30/06 rifle, as this was the minimal U.S. forest service-recommended caliber for carry in the brown bear country of the Tongass National Forest as well as a versatile all-around big game hunting caliber. I would find this venerable workhorse to be a popular choice among Alaskans who hunted deer or other game in bear country. The other "starter" was a .357 magnum revolver; we'll get to it.

Some folks who start near the top, as I did, never become decent shots, and may even drop off the wheel completely; powerful weapons have intimidating muzzle blast, even with good ear protection, and definitely unpleasant recoil (it's simple Newtonian physics: What hits on one end hits back just as hard on the other.). The instinct to flinch—to close one's eyes and jerk the trigger, often fostered by starting too near the top, can be difficult to overcome and impossible for some.

I was doggedly persistent in learning to shoot my newly acquired weapons well. In addition to starting at the wrong end of the power curve, I was not "natural" marksman (as a fortunate few are)—I had to study, learn, and concentrate on, the mechanics of shooting, and practice, practice, practice. In the process, I found that I enjoyed shooting for its own sake, and the satisfaction that came with the gradual mastery of something that, for me, was difficult and challenging—including the largely Zen process of learning to tune out the muzzle blast and recoil of powerful weapons.

Lots of practice requires lots of ammunition, which can get expensive. The cost can be greatly reduced by handloading—home-brewing your own ammunition, reusing your fired cartridge cases with purchased bullets, powder, and primers (cost is far from the only reason for handloading, but going there is outside the scope of this narrative). A lot of Alaskans loaded their own ammunition, and components were easy to come by.

Handloading would eventually cost me a new kitchen floor, in Juneau. I cast my own lead alloy bullets for my most powerful handguns, in an effort to give them a performance edge should they ever have to be used against a bear. This involved heat-treating them in Linda's oven to increase hardness. Just before one Christmas, a batch fresh out of the oven wound up on our kitchen floor before making it to the pan of quenching water; the large, deep scorch-mark on the floor put me deep in the dog house. A Christmas gift of a new hardwood floor, with all-new kitchen cabinetry thrown in, got me out.

———

Getting back to handguns, and the .357 magnum revolver I'd brought with me. I became aware that handguns occupied a significant but peculiar niche among Southeast Alaskans: Many owned them, a fair number carried them afield, but, like handgun owners everywhere, few were capable of hitting anything with them. Although shooting fundamentals and mechanics are the same for both handguns and long guns, handguns are far more difficult to master—and not many were willing to put in the time, effort, and ammunition to do so. Consequently almost no one considered them suitable for hunting, and for those who carried them for protection against bears it was suggested by cynics that, in the event of an attack, the best use of the handgun would be to end the fracas quickly by shooting oneself.

This wasn't something I wanted to hear. My sole reason for bringing a handgun to Alaska had been to have a light, handy weapon I could carry on my person when stream-fishing, as security against the big bears I'd heard about. For better or worse, I wasn't about to give up on this. When I learned that my .357 magnum, as ferocious as it was considered in the lower 48 where I'd bought it, had only enough bite to get a large bear properly pissed off, I wasted no time in moving up to a .44 magnum—at that time the world's most powerful handgun—and was willing to do the work required to shoot it well (for me, a prerequisite for carrying in the field). As protection against the big bears even the .44 magnum, no matter what you might have heard about its awesome power (or seen the wonders wrought with it by Clint Eastwood on the silver screen), left something to be desired—but I felt, and still do, that it was far better to have a handgun on your person than a far more powerful rifle leaning against a tree 20 feet away, closer to the bear than to you. Moving to the .44 added considerably to the degree of difficulty of the handgun learning curve, but I found that I enjoyed the challenge and the process. More on handguns for both deer and the big bears in later chapters.

I never owned a shotgun. In Sitka I don't recall hearing much about waterfowling, but maybe I just wasn't listening. Juneau was another story. Located as it was along a major flyway, a great many residents took to the wetlands every fall in hip boots and/or camo-painted skiffs to go after mallards, pintails, and Canada geese. One devotee was Gary Hedges, a lifelong Juneauite, friend, and one of my fellow surgeons. From his duck-hunting tales related in the surgical lounge, I gathered I wasn't missing much: putting out decoys before first light, then hunkering down on one's ass in sodden marshland in the cold and drizzle, waiting for the legal shooting hour to arrive, and maybe, just maybe, getting a shot or two at the quarry (Gary actually did okay. We had goose for dinner at his house once and it was excellent, except for the occasional piece of shot.). The shotgun crowd also had an active trap-shooting club, and Gary was pretty good. I know I missed a lot of fun there, but looking back, I already had more than my share of expensive and time-consuming outdoor vices.

———

Finding a store that sold guns in Juneau was about as easy as finding a bar in Hoboken, New Jersey. When we arrived the largest of these was Skinner's Gun Shop downtown, which dated to territorial days, but over the years there were many: Chandler's and Rayco sales out near the airport, Western Auto, Fred Meyer, and others whose names I can't recall. In the early days when federal firearms licenses (FFLs) could be had by virtually anybody for $25 a year, some people dealt out of their homes or garages. I purchased my S&W .44 magnum revolver, at that time in short supply in gun shops everywhere, new at the Alaska Bar in Ketchikan.

Most gunshops in the lower 48 didn't stock rifles in calibers such as the 338, .375 H&H, and .458 magnums—there was no call for them—but they fulfilled a role uniquely Alaskan: There were large bears in the woods not found anywhere else in North America, and they could on rare occasion be hazardous to one's health. Those who spent much time in the Alaskan bush, and those who hunted the bears, required guns appropriate to the task. I'll save most of that discussion for the chapter to come on big fuzzies. Suffice it to say here that Juneau gunshops, and those throughout Alaska, regularly carried these exceedingly powerful rifles in all makes, as well as ammunition and reloading components for them.

Sitka had been similar, but on a much smaller scale. In both Sitka and Juneau I did a lot of window shopping—the gunshops were the Montgomery Ward annual hunting catalogs of my teen years come to life. And of course it wasn't always just window shopping.

Finding places to shoot in Sitka and Juneau wasn't hard. Sitka had no designated range, but a couple of suitable and safe places out the road were regularly used by locals. Juneau had a shooting range, out Montana Creek Road on the far side of the Mendenhall Valley and miles from the nearest home. It had covered shooting benches, was able to accommodate many shooters at a time, and was maintained by volunteers from a local sportsman's organization. It was free and open to the public all the time, and totally informal—i.e., no rangemaster. From what I saw there was no need for one. Those who used the range were savvy and meticulous about gun safety and etiquette, and invariably courteous. As far as accidents go, I believe the range to have had a perfect safety record. Most who used the facility policed their own trash, and were helpful to those new to the game without being intrusive.

I used this range often, getting away for an hour or two on week-days when my schedule permitted, when it was least likely to be busy. On one occasion the only two guys I encountered were giving their ri-fles a final check before an upcoming black bear hunt in Yakutat. They were just finishing up when a large black bear strolled across the range, about 150 yards out. One of the guys decked it. They drove their pickup out to the downed trophy, and I helped them load it into the bed.

On another occasion I was there alone when a vehicle drove up and discharged four young yahoos, who promptly plopped down an AR-15 assault rifle, several boxes of ammo, and a six-pack of beer on the nea-rest shooting bench. I packed up my stuff as rapidly as possible, and left. This was the only time I ever encountered alcohol at the range, and one of the few times I encountered an AR-15. The latter is now the single most popular firearm in America, for reasons I can't begin to fathom, but at the time very few were to be seen in Southeast Alaska.

Big Fuzzies

Whenever the subject of Alaska comes up, people want to know about the bears. I can't blame them. When we first arrived we wanted to know about them too. I got an unexpected introduction within days of my arrival at Mt. Edgecumbe from one of the O.R. techs, a young Alaska Native that I would be working with on a daily basis. Two years before he had been deer-hunting with his brother when he was knocked flat from behind by a bear neither man heard approach. As the bear clawed him he got of a single, unaimed shot, driving the animal off (it was never found). He got off lightly; his most severe injuries were on display when he wore his scrubs: several long scars down one forearm. When he flexed that forearm, more than a half-dozen golf-ball-sized lumps popped up beneath the scars, muscle hernias through tears in the enveloping layer of fascia (connective tissue) produced by the animal's long, powerful claws. I think it was that same tech that told me of a logger who had succumbed in the hospital at about the same time after sustaining a penetrating bite to the skull.

For most of our two years at Mt. Edgecumbe, the bears remained more a myth, unseen bogeymen, than a reality. We heard many more stories before we saw our first bears. With only two months remaining in my tour Linda and I finally saw two, foraging out on the grassy flats at the head of Idaho Inlet, while in the company of guide Ben Forbes. All of our other sightings and encounters occurred later, while living in Juneau.

The bear of which we speak is the coastal brown bear, a massive creature whose range encompasses the Alaska peninsula and Kodiak Island in the west, around the coastal arc of the Gulf of Alaska to the narrow band of mainland and certain islands of the southeastern panhandle. The brown bear shares the coastal mainland with the far more common and much smaller black bear, the same bear so readily found in every state of the lower 48. What is odd is the distribution of the two bears on the islands of the Alexander Archipelago: Brown bears are the exclusive inhabitants of the three large "ABC" islands of northern and central Southeast—Admiralty, Baranof, and Chichagof—and their smaller satellite islands. The remaining islands of central and southern Southeast, including Prince of Wales, the archipelago's largest island, harbor only black bear. Wherever one species has encroached on the other's island, it always ends badly for the black bear. They are killed and eaten by brown bears (an interesting aside: The distribution of wolves in Southeast Alaska precisely parallels that of the black bear—present on the mainland, and all islands of the Alexander Archipelago *except* for the ABC islands and their satellites. I'll say here that during our time in Alaska we never saw a wolf. Few do.). Sitka and Juneau residents, ourselves included, recreated extensively in the ABC islands, so all the bears we encountered there were coastal brown bears.

Despite the color designations, color is not at all reliable in distinguishing a small brown bear from a large black bear. The brown bears of Southeast Alaska can range from blonde to black, and everything in between. Much more reliable are some physical characteristics: The brown bear has a pronounced hump between the shoulders, and in profile its face is dished in contrast to the Roman nose of the black bear.

Coastal brown bear are oft referred to as "Kodiak bear" by outsiders, even though only a modest percentage of the overall population resides on Kodiak Island in the western gulf. Others, again mostly from outside, call them grizzlies—and in a moment we will see that they are not entirely wrong. To locals they are brownies, or to some, affectionately or not, big fuzzies. Once DNA studies became available they revealed *the coastal brown bear to be genetically identical with the grizzly*, which inhabits all of interior Alaska and some remote places in the northern Rockies of the lower 48 and Canada. The difference is one in which nurture has trumped nature; coastal bears have access to an almost inexhaustible source of high-grade protein from midsummer through fall in the form of copious salmon runs. Interior bears have to work harder for lower-quality food. The result is a considerable difference in average size. A mature coastal brown bear boar in prime condition can easily top 1000 lbs. and measure well over 9 feet, while its grizzly counterpart may be 500 lbs. and 7 feet. Bear biologists have opted to define the difference between the two by geography; bears living on the interior side of an arbitrary and imaginary line 100 (or is it 200?) miles from the coast are grizzlies, while those living on the coastal side of that line are coastal brown bears.

The gristly introductory tales notwithstanding, coastal brown bear are as a rule solitary and reclusive, preferring to avoid contact with humans when it is an option (they also prefer their own company to that of other bears. When they do interact, if it's not for sex one is likely to kill and eat the other.). Most visitors to Southeast Alaska never see one. Even among residents they're not frequently seen even when looked for, or when fishing, deer hunting, or hiking in their domain. That said, anyone who spends enough time in the bear country of Southeast Alaska will eventually have a few encounters. A few will have a confrontation. The majority end well enough with the bear retreating from the field with a "woof," and no harm done to either party. There are, however, exceptions, and for that reason those encroaching on the bears' turf are well advised to carry some form of deterrent. Not everybody does, and most who don't get away with it. I liken carrying a deterrent to wearing a seatbelt in an automobile. The law aside, the one time you decide not to buckle up might be the one time you wish you had.

When we arrived in Alaska, and until quite recently, the only deterrent options were firearms. At that time the U.S. Forest Service recommended as a minimum for carry in bear country the quite powerful 30/06 rifle, the gold standard amongst Southeast Alaskan outdoorsmen for generations (the word was that anyone unwilling or unable to master the 30/06 had best stay clear of bear country, or go only in the company of someone adequately armed). The 30/06 is where I started.

I read a lot—and the best advice for carrying in bear country, distilled from a variety of knowledgeable sources, seemed to be: *Carry the most powerful rifle you can shoot well and get off repeat shots with quickly.* For many that will be the 30/06; for most mere mortals, the upper limit is the .375 H & H magnum.

The .375 H & H magnum began as a proprietary cartridge, introduced by the London gunmaking firm of Holland and Holland in 1912 for the hunting of medium and large African game. It has stood the test of time, and with the improved propellants and projectiles of today, is better than ever. There are yet more powerful rifles out there, but they're heavy, highly unpleasant to shoot, and fail to measure up to the "shoot well and get off repeat shots quickly" criteria for all but a handful of supermen.

While more gun than needed for North American game short of the big bears, the .375 is a superb all-around rifle for those willing to take the trouble to master it, as it can handle everything from mice to mastodons. It has a large following in both Africa and Alaska, where it is the choice of many professionals. Over 50% more powerful than the 30/06, it is a caliber favored by Alaskan bear guides as a "stopper" to keep their clients from being chewed on, and was also the rifle issued to U.S. Forest Service timber cruisers who ventured into the Tongass alone to explore tracts for potential timber sales.

The great bears long ago acquired a near-mythical reputation for being able to absorb firepower and keep on coming, and I had heard a number of antidotal claims about the .375's near-mythical ability to put those same bears down and keep them down. Although there was probably a little more truth to the former than the latter, the mystique surrounding the .375 produced a hankering to have one.

Long story short, about three years after moving to Juneau I bought one, when a shipment of Sako .375 rifles that had come in to a local gun shop went on sale at an irresistible price. Mastery did indeed require practice, but by then I had learned a few tricks—there are some—for dealing with intimidating recoil, and within a short time I shot as well with it as I did with the '06 (or a .22 rimfire, for that matter). I had it fitted with "express" open sights for rapid target acquisition at close range, and it became our beachcombing rifle, carried on family outings in bear country.

I was anxious that Linda, and David when he was old enough, become familiar and competent enough with this rifle to use it if a situation arose where it had to be used, and they happened to be closer to the rifle than I. This they both did, passing a test involving a stopwatch and a nine-inch bullseye at 20 yards (women actually adapt to shooting powerful weapons more readily than many men, as they are not encumbered with the psychological baggage that the fearsome reputation of a particular caliber can bring on). Our girls weren't really interested, and I saw no reason to push it as long as they weren't going to venture into bear country by themselves.

There are those who argue that a short-barreled 12 ga. pump shotgun loaded with rifled slugs or 00 buckshot is the equal of any rifle against a bear at very close range. I wouldn't argue back. This weapon has been used effectively in the killing of some problem bears by wildlife control officers or their designatees. A large bear that had become habituated to the town garbage pit in Tenakee Springs was so dispatched by Big Bob Smith, a gentle giant of a man that I had known personally before his untimely passing. The bear had expired at the bottom of the deep, steep-sided pit. As Big Bob told it, he left to get help in skinning the animal, and when he returned some twenty minutes later the carcass was gone. All that could be seen were a few telltale drag marks; in that short time the massive carcass, weighing well over 500 lbs., had been picked up and carried off by another bear.

We've already heard one cynic's take on handguns vs. bears, but it wasn't the only one. There's the tale of the grizzled old-timer who, after listening to saloon-talk from a greenhorn blathering on about how his .44 magnum revolver would blow away the biggest, baddest, bear, gave him some considered advice: "Son, before you take that revolver out in the bush be sure to grease the outside of the barrel thoroughly. It will smart less when the bear takes that gun away from you and rams the barrel right up your ass." Definitely food for thought.

Despite such ominous warnings I opted to carry a .44 magnum revolver, ungreased, in a shoulder holster whenever I was fishing or otherwise trespassing in bear country with only myself to worry about. Its marginal power was a justifiable criticism, but largely unsaid was that most people who carried them simply didn't know how to shoot them. I had become capable with the .44, hunted deer with one, and knew of a few instances in which a .44 magnum had been successfully used against the big bears in self-defense situations. I wouldn't go courting trouble with it, and would use it only in the court of last resort, at point-blank range.

The .44 magnum was knocked off the throne in 1983 with the advent of the considerably more powerful 454 Casull revolver, essentially the .45 long colt peacemaker of Old West fame on megadoses of steroids. This brought the handgun at last and at least into the ballpark as a reasonable bear deterrent, but was a handful to shoot well. I bought one. Actually, I bought two (with different barrel lengths), learned to control them, and hunted deer with them as well.

Those of you who hunt, or read hunting publications, may be aware that Alaska's great bears have indeed been taken by trophy hunters using

.44 magnum, 454 Casull, and similar ultrapowerful handguns. *Do not equate this to a confrontation with an aroused bear that you didn't ask for.* In a hunting situation the hunter holds all the cards—rock-solid shooting position, a stationary, unaroused target at a favorable shooting angle, a comfortable range, the luxury of time, possibly optical sights—and a backup with a powerful rifle if things go south. In a defense-against-attack scenario it's the bear who gets to shuffle and deal, from its own deck. And bears cheat.

——

When bear encounters escalate into confrontations, it is the result of one of the following: (1) A sow instinctively protecting her cubs when they've inadvertently been approached too closely, or separated from her, by an intruder. (2) A bear wanting something you have (a salmon, a deer or moose carcass). (3) A bear thinking you want something he has (a deer or moose carcass). (4) A bear just having a really bad day. Bears have personalities, and included here are those constitutionally cranky bears for whom *every* day is a bad day. (5) Rarest of all but most potentially lethal is the predatory attack. The bear wants to eat you. The culprits are sometimes, but not always, old, sick bears on the brink of starvation, looking for the easiest possible meal. Veteran Sitka bear guide Ben Forbes estimated that one out of twenty-five incidental bear encounters at close quarters result in a confrontation; of those, a few will end in a charge, and a disagreeable result for one party or the other.

When it did, sometimes the verdict went to the humans. During our time in Alaska I was aware of eight self-defense killings of bears in Southeast, six of which involved friends or acquaintances. I'm sure there were more I didn't know about—maybe many more. Those that I knew of all involved veteran outdoorsmen, highly competent with firearms. None took pleasure in doing what they had to do, and all were relieved that the decision had gone their way.

Sometimes the verdict went to the bears. Nine maulings that I know of occurred either while we lived in Southeast, or before that to people I eventually came to know. Actually I was acquainted with, or had at least met, all but two of the victims. Injuries were severe in all but two. Two were fatal, both predatory attacks, and part or all of both victims was consumed (one mauling was technically a draw, the hunting partner of the victim killing the bear before further damage could be inflicted). The number of bear victories within my recollection is probably closer to the number that actually occurred than is the number of people victories.

More than half the mauling victims were deer hunters, armed, skilled with firearms, and experienced in the woods. The element of surprise was common to most maulings, owing to the nature of the habitat and also to the stealth and great speed of which these huge creatures are capable. Being familiar with the circumstances of many of these unfortunate incidents, I found it perplexing that those victims who were armed would probably have fared no better had they been carrying bazookas rather than hunting rifles—while the unarmed victims might all have fared better had they been armed.

A brown bear is capable of killing even the largest, most powerful human with one swipe of a paw, or one bite down on a skull. The wonder of it is that more maulings didn't end in fatalities. The only answer that makes sense, and the one to which bear experts subscribe, is that most brown bear attacks are not made with the intent to kill (the rare exception being the predatory attack). They attack to either neutralize a perceived threat, to get what they want, to keep what they have, or to work off their mad—and when they've accomplished their objective they will leave it at that. If they really wanted you dead, you'd be dead.

Most of the incidents alluded to in which the bears won have been recounted in detail in at least one of the many books written about Alaskan bears and bear attacks. Those sources also include the many incidents occurring outside the temporal and geographic limitations of this book, and I'd recommend them to any who are interested.

While I never chanced to be on call when seriously mauled victims were brought to our emergency room, I was once summoned to check out an off-duty Coast Guardsman who had been deer hunting Admiralty Island's Point Barlow with several of his buddies. They had started a drive at the base of the peninsula, hoping to flush out any deer trapped between them and the tip. At the beginning of the drive, the men spotted a bear out ahead of them, which shortly disappeared from view. This would have been an ideal time to abort the drive—but they didn't (and then there would be no story.)... As they approached the peninsula's end the bear reappeared out of the brush, running full-tilt at the drivers. It ran right over and flattened the man I was examining— and just kept going. It was no doubt just as petrified as my patient. The man complained of a really sore chest where he had been stomped on, and did have a nasty bruise, but otherwise didn't have a scratch on him.

Sitka guide Ben Forbes tells of a client who, when presented with a perfect shot at a trophy bear, took aim and proceeded to rapidly cycle the action of his rifle until all of the cartridges had been ejected. As the bear meandered off, the hunter expressed disbelief that that the animal was not lying on the ground with its toes in the air. He was convinced he had emptied his rifle into it, rather than onto the ground.

Ben also related the experience of a friend who had left his float-plane at the mouth of a stream while he walked a few hundred yards upstream to fish a good run of silver salmon. He had reached his limit of six when a bear came from upstream, probably to fish too, but became sidetracked by the fish market standing in front of him. The angler backtracked toward his plane, throwing fish at the bear's feet as he retreated and the bear advanced. Each fish distracted the bear just long enough for another few steps backward. The last fish was tossed just as the angler reached his plane, pushed off, and hopped in.

———

All of our Alaskan friends who shared our love of the out-of-doors have their own set of bear stories. Some had more, and more exciting ones, than we did. None of ours were hair-raising, for which we were and remain thankful.

Several of our encounters took place in one of our favorite weekend getaway spots, Neka Bay on Chichagof Island, about 50 miles from our home in Auke Bay. The saltchuck there—a tidewater estuary—was a great place to flyfish for sea-run trout, and was also considered a great place by bears. On one occasion we took a picnic in to the beach, where we also beachcombed and the kids shot up a lot of clam shells with a .22. After the few-minute row back to our boat, anchored only 50 yards off that beach, we turned around to see two big fuzzies—most likely a sow with a close to full-grown second-year cub—nosing around our picnic site, looking for goodies we may have left behind (we were always careful to leave none). They had probably been lurking in the fringe timber mere yards away during the entire time we were on the beach, just waiting for us to take our leave. I think it a safe assumption that, during our time spent in the outdoors of Southeast, we had been far closer to more bears that we didn't see than to bears that we did see.

On a later trip to Neka Bay, just Linda and myself, we took our skiff to the very end of the estuary on a high tide, hoping to see bears foraging in the grassy meadows at the estuary's head. We weren't disappointed. A sow with three small cubs (a bit unusual—two is more the norm) was out in plain view. We watched for quite some time, as the sow was unaware of our presence. At some point there must have been a subtle wind shift, because she abruptly stood up, turned toward us, woofed once, and lumbered off toward the woods with two of the little fuzzies right on her heels (we had earlier learned something borne out by subsequent experiences, that bears that stand up on their hind legs are not exhibiting aggression, but are just trying to get a better take on whatever has gotten their attention). The third cub, oblivious, continued nosing around in the meadow. Seconds later the sow came bounding out of the woods and whomped the youngster a blow that would have felled most people, whereupon the cub hightailed it into the woods with mom close behind. Then commenced a piteous bawling that went on for some time, and we could only imagine the thrashing being administered the wayward little fuzzy. When the show was over, Linda remarked that it was a good thing we had been observing from our skiff at a safe distance from the water's edge. I asked her to look over the side; the water we were floating in was little more than a foot deep.

Our last visit to Neka Bay was made with friends Barb and Roy Greening, in their boat. Their small inflatable had no outboard, so we rowed it in to the beach (at the same spot we'd seen the fuzzies years before) and walked, with our fly rods, a mile or so up the beach to our favorite fishing stretch, well out of sight of the inflatable. After having fished about an hour, my attention was caught by the sight of a bear swimming across the estuary from the other side, toward ours. It made landfall about 200 yards upstream of us, shook like a dog, and literally scratched its head as though deciding where to go next. It decided to walk down the beach in our direction.

This is the part where it's wise to pull up stakes and make tracks for the inflatable. The hard part was trying to impart a sense of urgency to Barb, a talented watercolorist but also something of a free spirit and space cadet, who was engrossed in painting. She was not about to be interrupted by something so trivial as an approaching bear. The rest of us almost had to rip the brush out of her hand to get our foursome started down the beach. The bear had gained ground, perhaps halving the distance before it picked up on our presence. When it did, it reared on its hind legs, stared at us a moment, then took a sharp left and high-tailed it into the timber. We watched with relief, only to see, when we turned back around, yet another fuzzy out on a point 100 yards ahead, studying us. On being noticed, this bear wheeled about and lumbered off away from us. It was quickly lost from view, but we thought it likely it was walking the beach in the same direction we were headed.

After giving it time to put more distance between itself and us, we resumed our trek and were finally within about 50 yards of our inflatable—which despite being close was obscured from view by a hump in the beach. Upon summitting the hump, we were confronted with the sight of a large bear butt disappearing into the fringe timber, leaving behind a totally trashed inflatable, flat as a pancake. Each air chamber of the hapless gasbag had been gashed with multiple foot-long rips produced by long, powerful claws. For good measure, the bear had also decimated the four orange life vests left in the skiff. Almost certainly, the perp was the second bear we had seen.

We'd have been in unfortunate straits, facing the possibility of a night or two out in the elements, had it not been for a commercial crabber tending pots in the immediate vicinity of our anchored boat. The crabber had watched the entire show unfold, and on seeing us motored in with his skiff to take us and our sad-looking inflatable back to our boat. For this act of mercy he was rewarded with a bag of chocolate-chip cookies baked by the women earlier that day. Our rescuer related that from where he was he could have easily shot the bear and saved our gasbag, but he didn't believe the act to be justified. He was right, and we were in agreement. Barb and Roy's gasbag lived to float another day, as they sent it back to the factory where it was successfully repaired.

Another of our favorite haunts was Pavlov Harbor, also on Chichagof and about the same distance from home. We sometimes spent as long as two weeks there in late July or early August, when runs of pink, chum, and coho salmon were coming in. We often saw evidence of bears in the form of fresh tracks, partially eaten salmon, and monstrous mounds of bear poop up near the falls at the head of the bay where bears had been fishing, and were occasionally treated to the sight of bears in the act of fishing (these we watched from a safe vantage point on the other side and over 100 yards away).

During one stay at Pavlov we observed a particular bear that made a daily ritual of circumnavigating the harbor along the beach in leisurely fashion, taking about two hours to complete the circuit. I didn't believe it to be a particularly huge specimen as fuzzies went, but it would walk up or down the face of the falls—steep, and perhaps fifteen feet high at low tide—more easily than a tank or half-track.

This bear was different, displaying an unsettling indifference to the presence of humans. I was able to approach it in the skiff to within 15 or 20 feet (the water depth dropped off sharply) as it munched blueberries near the bank—drawing entire branches through its jaws and stripping them clean. It was quite aware of, and unperturbed by, my presence as it periodically looked up and stared at me for seconds at a time. Unfortunately, I had no camera with me.

On another day our entire family was on shore at the foot of the falls when the bear came strolling up the far bank and began crossing over directly opposite us. Again, it was obviously aware of our presence. It was in no hurry, and the fact that we were in its path seemed to be of no consequence. There were no signs of either fear or aggression. We didn't wait to find out what would happen when it reached our side—and us—and beat a measured retreat to the safety of our skiff, waiting a ways down the beach.

A high-school friend of David's, there at Pavlov for a few days with his family in their own boat, had rowed their small skiff in to the beach. We were aboard our boat and happened to be looking in the right direction when the skiff took off from the beach at warp speed, Christopher rowing like a madman, the skiff throwing up a wake like a speedboat. There, at the water's edge where the skiff had been moments before, was the bear.

This indifference to the presence of humans may have been the bear's undoing. One year later, we were beachcombing just outside Pavlov when we came upon the almost-complete skeleton of a bear, absent the skull. From the location, the condition of the bones, and absence of the skull, I gathered that the bear had been shot by a hunter during the previous fall season, only a few months after we'd last been there. I had little doubt that it was the same animal we had watched daily in essentially the same area. We took home a few vertebrae and one humerus, the large bone of the upper foreleg. The humerus makes that of a human bodybuilder look absolutely puny in comparison.

Of my time spent in bear country, by far the most was in the course of deer hunting—the subject of a future chapter. Much of this was in mid-November when, according to Alaska F & G research data, on average 50% of the bears were already denned up in the high country. That left, of course, 50%. Over the many years I hunted, my companions and I would have encounters, a few close, but nothing approaching a confrontation. One of our number, curious as to the source of a sound resembling heavy twigs snapping, discovered it to be a bear in the process of chomping through the ribcage of a deer carcass. Needless to say, he quietly reversed course. Our lack of issues with bears while hunting was as much a tribute to luck, and to the forbearance of the fuzzies, as to anything we did or didn't do.

———

Admiralty Island, with a brown bear population density estimated at one per square mile, is the big fuzzy equivalent of Tokyo, Hong Kong, or Singapore; the Tlingit name for Admiralty is Kooznoowoo—Fortress of the Bears. Pack Creek lies near the upper end of Admiralty's Seymour Canal, a 40-minute hop by float plane from Juneau. Its large and reliable annual salmon runs attract large and reliable numbers of fuzzies, who stay on to fish throughout the summer. The grassy flats at the Creek's outlet were homesteaded many, many years ago by Stan Price and his wife Edna, and when she passed, he stayed on. Over the years, Stan became a legend. The Pack Creek bears became *his* bears; he knew each of the regulars on sight, knew their peculiarities and behavior, and gave them names. And the bears knew him. Stan never crowded the bears, but sometimes they crowded *him*. The only deterrent he carried was a stout walking stick or shovel, and when they got too close, uppity, or threatened his garden, he'd give them a whack on the snout. They always got the message (author's disclaimer: This is for professional bear-whisperers only. Do not try it yourself.). The only bears Stan was wary of were aggressive strangers that sometimes showed up, apparently driven over from Hawk Inlet on the west side of Admiralty when the Kensington Mine opened there and brought increasing human activity.

All this I learned from friend and hunting companion Kim Smith, who had been Stan's physician. Kim made regular house calls at Pack Creek, as Stan was in his eighties then and had some health issues. Kim was the beneficiary of all manner of stories, as well as bear-watching without parallel.

With Stan Price's passing, Pack Creek became a bear sanctuary, jointly administered by the U.S. Forest Service and the Alaska Department of Fish & Game. It featured an observation tower, and quickly became such a popular attraction that visitation was—and still is—by reservation only, made far in advance.

———

In territorial Alaska, when and wherever civilization encroached on bear habitat in the form of canneries, homesteads, logging, or mining, the bears paid a price; bears that didn't retire from the field gracefully were eliminated. Times, and values, were different then. A bear breaking into a homesteader's shed where harvested deer were hanging was a threat to a family's food supply, a matter of life and death. Bears hanging out around canneries were seen as a threat to the workers, and to the operation of the cannery. Such scenarios rarely existed in the Alaska of our time. When it came to the killing of bears, "justification," and the definition of "self-defense," were now stringently defined, as they had not been in territorial days. Since attaining statehood Alaska has become concerned about the status of its coastal brown bears, maintaining ongoing research and enforcement programs as well as establishing protected areas, to insure stable populations.

The killing of a brown bear alleged to be in self-defense was a big deal. Every reported killing was thoroughly investigated by the Alaska Division of Wildlife Troopers, a part of the Department of Public Safety charged with the enforcement of wildlife protection laws. This was to insure that a claim of self-defense was not used as a pretense for wanton killing or to procure an illicit trophy. The hide and skull were required to be taken and turned over to the Department of Fish & Game, and no other part of the animal—the impressive claws, for example—could be kept. The investigation would do credit to a CSI team on TV, and if the killing was ultimately ruled not to have been justified, penalties were severe. All of us who spent time in bear country knew the law: *The killing of a bear in defense of property, including game one had taken, was not considered justifiable, nor was it justifiable to instigate a confrontation that resulted in a dead bear.*

The killing of a bear in what you perceived to have been a self-defense situation may have saved you a mauling, possibly your life. But... if the letter of the law were followed, your actions would be judged by others who had not been in your shoes. Tom Parke, the sourdough guide and charter skipper that took a group of us on annual deer hunts for several years, and who had himself years before dropped a charging bear at his feet with the last round in his 30/06, advised that should any of us have to do it, leave the bear where it lay, walk away, and never disclose it to a soul.

Trophy hunting of brown bear was carefully controlled and monitored. Non-residents were charged a hefty fee for the privilege, as well as having to engage the services of a registered guide. Many clients were wealthy Europeans, particularly from Germany. Klaus, the builder of our home who you'll meet in a later chapter, used to hire on for these hunts with bear guide Karl Lane (another sourdough, who I met only once) as cook and translator. Alaska residents did not require a guide, but were permitted to take no more than one brown or grizzly bear every four years. Some friends and hunting companions did take brown bear, and have handsome rugs to show for it. Others, like myself, never had the desire.

Poaching, or surreptitiously taking the skull and hide of a bear killed in self-defense? Virtually impossible to get away with. And no guide would risk his license and livelihood by allowing a client to shoot a bear illegally.

Bears were the only Alaskan game animal from which the hunter was not required to harvest the meat. Guides Ben Forbes and Tom Parke both told of hunter clients, basking in the macho glow of success after taking a trophy, insisting that a steak being cut from their bear and cooked for their dinner. One bite of leathery meat with the rank flavor of rotting fish was always enough.

———

A relatively recent entry into the arsenal of bear deterrents is bear spray, utilizing capsicum as the primary ingredient. It is basically the same as the pepper spray carried by people closer to civilization for protection against aggressive dogs or potential muggers or rapists, but a much more potent concoction in a supersized cannister with a more powerful aerosol. I don't know precisely when bear spray was first introduced— it may have been as long as 20-25 years ago—but its acceptance was slow among veteran Alaskan outdoorsman, largely because it was new, unproven, and because of a traditional reliance on firearms.

We have taken two recent cruises through our old haunts in Southeast Alaska with National Geographic/Lindblad (our do-it-yourself years now far behind in the rearview mirror), and our interest was piqued to find that the leaders of the shore expeditions all carried bear spray as the sole deterrent, and had been trained in its use (*also mandated was a minimum number of five people for those shore ventures, a number confirmed by experience as a tipping point in determining the behavior of a confronted bear*).

I did a post-cruise internet search on bear spray, and found a lot out there—all positive, and not just advertising. Over time the product has been improved, and an impressive body of data on its use has been accumulated—demonstrating that bear spray, when used according to direction, is indeed extremely effective in deterring attacks from aggressive bears. And, it is non-lethal. Both parties can walk away from a confrontation. Not a pleasant experience for the bear but, like a hangover, it is temporary.

Were I able to do over today everything we did in the Alaskan outdoors, I think bear spray might now be our deterrent of choice for at least some activities.

———

Some professional photographers approach the big fuzzies quite closely in the company of an experienced, armed guide. But... *it is a sound maxim not to take the carrying of a deterrent as license to approach a bear any more closely than one would without a deterrent.* You owe it to yourself, and to the bear, not to allow an encounter to escalate into a confrontation if it's within your power to prevent it. And there is no room for foolishness, such as following bear trails through brush and alder thickets along streams when the salmon are in. Remember that when you enter bear habitat, you are a guest in their house.

During our time in Alaska were we afraid of the big bears? At some level the answer has to be yes. But it was more a matter of respect that engendered awareness, caution, and appropriate behavior on our part. We invariably carried a firearm in bear country, but at least as important we learned, and abided by, the rules for minimizing undesired encounters and confrontations, knowing that in doing so the dice were loaded heavily in our favor when we went out to enjoy the Alaskan outback.

Juneau: We Come to Stay

One evening in the spring of 1973 I got a call from out of the blue, from my old Mt. Edgecumbe friend, Tom Stengl. Tom was calling from Juneau, Alaska. When his stint at Mt. Edgecumbe was over, he had returned to group ENT practice in Minnesota, but the call of the wild had been too strong. He left after a year to establish a solo ENT practice in Juneau. He was calling to tell me that one of Juneau's two general surgeons was in the process closing his practice and moving back to the East Coast, and an opportunity for me was there for the taking, if I chose.

For our family, this had to be a joint decision. We had been gone from Mt. Edgecumbe almost two years, and I'd never considered the possibility of a practice opportunity in Southeast Alaska more than a distant pipe dream—although I have to admit to having had that dream. Pulling up stakes would mean leaving the security of salaried group practice, rolling the dice on an uncertain future, and the daunting prospect of becoming involved in the business side of medicine. Linda loved her life in New England, and the marvelous house we were renting in the country outside of Concord, N.H., built in 1796, held together with pegs, and without a square corner in it. Both of our families lived an easy day's drive from us—and close to 4000 miles from anywhere in Southeast Alaska. But, wise and perceptive woman that she was, Linda knew even before I did that we were going. She knew that I, like Tom, had tasted the Kool-Aid.

———

Last time we were pushed. This time we jumped. Our furniture and belongings preceded us, but this time Uncle Sam was not picking up the tab. Our Conestoga wagon on this westward trek was a VW Square-back, and now carried five rather than four-and-a-fraction pioneers—real ones this time. And this time we were beset by hostiles almost from the beginning—*microbes*! By the evening we reached Des Moines, Iowa, three-year-old David was running a temperature of 104. Linda stayed at our motel with the girls while I took David in search of a hospital emergency room, finally finding a medical center with a crowded E.R. at about midnight. I knew the hospital game, and It was impossible to miss the funny look from the E.R. receptionist when I signed us in: no permanent address, no employer, no medical insurance, out-of-state I.D. Had I been behind the desk, I'd have been thinking the same thing: deadbeat.

The harassed E.R. doc who examined David couldn't find any-thing amiss other than the extremely high fever, but going with the percentages thought he probably had a middle-ear infection, and pre-scribed an antibiotic. The receptionist's eyebrows went up right over her hairline when I actually paid the fee for the E.R. consultation and medication.

Two days and another doctor visit later he was no better, and we seriously considered diverting our wagon train to Denver so that Linda and the children could fly back to the East Coast and the safety and re-sources of our parents. We ultimately continued on and spent the next night in Yellowstone at a cabin we'd reserved near Old Faithful. The weather was unseasonably cold, well below freezing, and our cabin was uninsulated and unheated. It had two double beds—our two girls had one, and Linda took poor miserable David into the other with her. I bedded down on the freezing board flooring in David's Winnie the Pooh sleeping bag, which came up to my waist.

Whether it was the wearing of sackcloth in the guise of a Winnie the Pooh sleeping bag, the medication kicking in, or both, David improved and was fine by the time we reached Seattle. This time we put ourselves and our vehicle on an Alaska state ferry, arriving at Juneau's Auke Bay terminal near the end of September 1973, well after midnight and in a driving rain. As we'll see in the next chapter, by later on the following day we weren't so sure we should be happy to be there.

———

Juneau is located on the mainland coast northeast of Sitka, about 120 miles away by water but far closer as the crow flies—a 30-minute slingshot hop by jet. It began life as a boom town circa. 1880 after gold had been discovered in Gold Creek, the stream coming out of the basin separating Mt. Juneau from Mt. Roberts and running through what is now the center of town. Hard-rock mining evolved with the Alaska-Juneau Mine, and the Treadwell Mine on Douglas Island on the other side of the Gastineau Channel that actually tunneled beneath the channel. Millions of dollars in gold were extracted before the high-grade ore petered out, as it always does. The last survivor, the A-J mine, closed up shop in 1944; its remains still cling to the mountainside overlooking town.

In 1906 the seat of territorial government was moved to Juneau from the old capitol at Sitka. At the time we came, and for most of the time we were there, state and federal government were the largest employers and sustainers of the economy.

At the time of our arrival Juneau's population was around 20,000—far greater than Sitka's—and grew to about 25,000 during our time there. The downtown residential area was built up on the steep slopes behind the business district. A large segment of the populace lived in the subdivisions of the Mendenhall Valley nine miles north, built on the glacial moraine left by the receding Mendenhall Glacier. There were other, smaller residential subdivisions at Lemon Creek and Switzer Creek, and in the satellite town of Douglas across the channel. We would eventually have a home at Auke Bay, twelve miles north of city center. The road system was more extensive than that of Sitka, extending forty miles north to Echo Cove at the foot of Berners Bay, and six miles south to Thane, home to a handful of residents. The road to the north was paved for only the first 24 miles, and civilization petered out even before pavement's end. Douglas Island, containing the town of Douglas and connected with Juneau via a bridge over the Gastineau Channel, had a road system of its own along its eastern shore to the north.

All in all, Juneau had a more cosmopolitan flavor than Sitka. Sitka was a small town, but in addition to the population difference the strong state and federal government presence gave Juneau a slightly white-collar aura that helped make it a city. But a look at its large and crowded small boat harbors, and the number of business establishments catering to boaters, hunters, and fishermen, revealed where its priorities lay— and the short drive in any direction, or foray by boat, confirmed that the wilderness was everywhere at its doorstep, no less that it had been at Sitka.

Unseen up behind the city was the Juneau Icefield, 1500 square miles of snow and ice that was, in places, thousands of feet deep. Seen from the air, as we saw it a number of times, it appeared as a vast white blanket pierced at irregular but frequent intervals by inverted ice-cream cones—nunataks, the peaks of high mountains barely poking their heads above the ice. Spilling out of the icefield were 36—or was it 38?— major glaciers, rivers of ice obeying the pull of gravity and sculpting the landscape as they did. Most were "hanging" glaciers, no longer reaching saltwater, and the only one visible from the road system was Lemon Glacier. The Mendenhall, accessible by road at the head of the

Mendenhall valley, was one of two remaining tidewater glaciers. The icefield was part of the incorporated borough of Juneau, which bordered on Canada to the east, and made it, geographically, one of the largest in the nation.

Despite the fact that Juneau was on the continental mainland, the Juneau Icefield to the east, and impenetrable terrain to both the north and south that extended vast distances, rendered Juneau isolated and inaccessible by road or rail—no different than Sitka and the other island communities of Southeast Alaska.

Juneau, although over 70 miles removed from the Gulf of Alaska as the crow flies, connected with it by a network of major waterways and was a major port along the so-called "inside passage" that extended from Seattle to Skagway, a distance of over a thousand miles. Like the rest of Southeast its climate was maritime—but with a twist. Its climate was also shaped by the vast unseen icefield above it, and by its vulnerability to sometimes violent weather systems coming down from the north via Lynn Canal and through a number of topographic slots such as Taku Inlet. Downtown Juneau was wet; moisture-laden air from the Pacific would meet the abrupt walls of Mt. Roberts and Mt. Juneau behind the city, and just dump. Downtown averaged around 90" of rain annually; we in the sunbelt at Auke Bay, twelve miles north, averaged around 60". In winter, high-pressure systems coming down from the Yukon brought with them clear skies, frigid temperatures, and winds spilling off the icefield that could clock over 100 mph as they funneled through the slots of Taku Inlet, Sheep Creek, and Gold Creek Basin. One target zone was the parking lot at the downtown Foodland supermarket, where shoppers would go down like tenpins. Winds roaring out of Taku Inlet, eight miles south—"Taku winds"—would whip the waters of Stephens Passage into a raging frenzy, the froth and mist visible from downtown.

Much of downtown, including Juneau-Douglas high school where our kids would go, was located in an avalanche zone; there had been a

129

near-miss during the severe winter just before our arrival. Some spectacular images had been caught on film from across the channel on Douglas Island, which produced the illusion that the entire town was being annihilated. Avalanches and slides were a regular occurrence just south of town, frequently blocking off the road to the residential area of Thane, and responsible over the years for some fatalities among those tasked with clearing the roads.

Juneau's airport was built on the moraine at the mouth of the Mendenhall River, the only land flat and spacious enough to accommodate it. The north-south approaches were through a narrow slot separating the mountains of the mainland and those of Douglas Island. Juneau weather, like that of Southeast in general, had a propensity for overcast, and the airport was prone to being fogged in at any time of year. Inversions that frequently accompanied high-pressure systems could cause the airport to be selectively blanketed with a low-lying layer of fog thick enough to cut with a knife, while everywhere else for miles around was blue-sky clear. This combination of factors made for frequent fly-overs, and might close down the airport for days at a time. Nonetheless, we locals had great respect for the Alaska Airlines pilots who were veterans of this run, and time and again made it in when it seemed they wouldn't.

Just about all Juneauites, ourselves included, used the airlines for occasional weekend getaways to Seattle. Seahawks football was a big attraction even though the team was mostly awful in those years, but other sporting events, shopping, sightseeing, and just plain curing cabin fever were also part of the agenda. We all got cabin fever occasionally.

Flying, even with a major carrier like Alaska Airlines, was more casual in our early years there. On a few occasions when we were blessed with clear weather, pilots approaching Juneau from the South would alter their approach to come in low over the Juneau Icefield and down the path of the Mendenhall Glacier. Those were flights to remember.

The airport was also home to a number of flying services—mini-airlines—that served outlying communities in northern Southeast with

CHEECHAKOES IN WONDERLAND

regularly scheduled flights, carrying mail, freight, and passengers. Many of the villages had no airport and were accessible only by float plane; the Juneau airport, located as it was at the edge of northern Gastineau channel, could accommodate the fleet of workhorse Cessna 185s and larger DeHavilland Beavers on floats. We had missed by a scant few years the era when almost all air travel within Southeast was by WWII-vintage amphibious aircraft, the Catalina PBY and the Grumman Goose; Linda and I had actually flown from Ketchikan to Sitka aboard a Grumman Goose, operated by Alaska Airlines, during our Mt. Edgecumbe years.

The same air services were available for charter flights to wherever one wanted to go, within range. Most Juneauites availed themselves of these services from time to time, as we did. These flights, conducted as they were in typical Juneau weather, were frequently bumpy and always interesting. Low overcasts could force planes down on the deck, where the pilots navigated from marine charts.

Juneau had a significant cadre of private pilots, many of whom we knew. Just about everyone new to the country at least thinks about becoming one—I did, briefly—as at first glance it appears able to open up tempting vistas in the way of outdoor opportunities. But most of us soon realized, as I did, that piloting in Southeast is a daunting enterprise best left to those who love flying for its own sake.

Many of Juneau's private pilots owned super cubs fitted with balloon tires, aircraft that could land and take off in extremely short distances, and weren't choosy about runway surfaces. Sandbars and gravel beaches were all the same to them. Two of my good friends—superb, experienced pilots—had them, and I flew with them on occasion. Most of the "airplane people" didn't own boats; their planes, and their interest in them, consumed all of their free time. They were a close-knit group, meeting for breakfast every Sunday at the local Taco Bell.

Given its terrain and weather, Southeast Alaska was an unforgiving place to fly. In 1973, during the interval between our Sitka and Juneau years, an Alaska Airlines jet on approach to Juneau had gone down in the mountains of the Chilkat Peninsula with the loss of all aboard, including Alaska's sole congressman. Despite a prolonged and intensive search, the crash site and the wreckage were found only years later. During our time in Juneau a few small aircraft, private and commercial, also crashed or simply disappeared.

Among the private pilots that I knew other than those mentioned above, there were a number of near-misses: One made an emergency landing on Egan Drive, the city's major highway. Another set his disabled plane down on the North Douglas Highway. Yet another wound up high in a giant spruce near our Eaglecrest ski area, his super cub suspended vertically, nose-downward. No significant injuries resulted from any of these incidents.

——

Prior to our arrival Tom Stengl had arranged for us a first-floor downtown rental not far from his own home, and within walking distance of a grammar school. We bought a second car, an ancient red VW Bug that ran well but had a see-through floor. Our apartment was nice, but Linda and I, approaching our mid-thirties, were looking forward to, at sometime soon and assuming that my practice would succeed—owning the first home of our own.

Housing in Juneau was perennially tight, prices were high, and the best places sold even before being listed. Our banker knew we were looking, and suggested we take a gander at a spec house going up in a small subdivision overlooking Auke Bay, 12 miles north of downtown. We did, and loved both the location and the potential of the house. It would have over 3000 square feet, enough for our young family to grow into, and to accommodate Linda's and my hobbies. It also promised to be good-looking in a traditional way (neither Linda nor I, with our New England background and biases, could understand how so many Juneau homes had been built with no apparent regard for aesthetics. Particularly incomprehensible was the penchant for flat roofs in a place with so much rainfall and accumulations of wet, heavy snow.). It was at an early-enough stage of construction to allow us to modify the interior plan to fit our needs and desires. The price seemed right, things were starting to look up for my practice, and we signed the papers.

Klaus, the contractor/designer/builder, was an Austrian with a heavy accent and a mastery of old-world craftsmanship to match, and the traditional Austrian love for beer. His craftsmanship was rivaled only by a total lack of business acumen, and the building process morphed into a soap opera—actually, more of a suds opera. Klaus was both perfectionist and procrastinator, doing, and doing over, things until he was satisfied—or not doing them at all. All the while the clock was running, and the cost of building materials steadily going up. As the escalating costs and passing time gnawed away at the profits he would receive from our agreed-upon price, he spent more and more time at Squire's Rest, the pub a short ways down the road, drowning his concerns. When we needed to discuss something and couldn't find him, we knew where he'd be and roust him out.

He was always seeking advances over and above what our agreement called for. A few of these he got, most he didn't. He once sent his wife Christina, equally Austrian and who looked the part of a heroine in a Wagnerian opera, over to do the dirty work. When her alternate demanding and pleading fell on deaf ears, she suddenly clutched at her chest, let out a piteous groan, and collapsed to the ground in the driveway. Wagner would have been delighted.

Klaus had built other homes in the area, and we'd been briefed to anticipate the performance we were seeing. Linda and I just stood there and took it in. Christina's son, about age six, was along, possibly to evoke sympathy for his mother's cause. He also just stood there. He'd seen this show before.

At length the woman picked herself up, dusted herself off, and bid us a curt adieu without having squeezed another advance out of us.

Eventually our house was "completed," and we moved in on New Year's Day 1975. There were a lot of loose ends hanging when Klaus, lured by the prospect of outlandish paychecks and a chance to leave the money pit that our house had become for him behind, lit out for the North Slope to work on the Trans Alaskan pipeline. Despite the loose ends, we were not sorry to see him go. His assistant finished up the house, paid from Klaus's forfeited contractor's bond. Among other things, Klaus had left our front deck supports resting on stacks of shingles originally intended for the roof ridgeline, rather than on proper concrete footings. He left without insulating the hot-water heating pipes that ran under a cantilevered main floor, and which froze in the sub-zero weather during our first night of occupancy. The cinderblocks below ground level in the back had not been properly sealed and backfilled, which we discovered when the snow melted in the spring. We never bothered with the beer cans we knew to have been trapped between the studs, beneath the sheetrock and paneling. We sometimes thought we could hear them rattling together during the not-infrequent earth tremors that our area experienced, but it was probably our imaginations.

Klaus left us with a well that produced a scant 8 gallons per minute, but only on a good day, and was always losing its prime. The line from well to pressure tank in the garage ran above ground, and was haphazardly insulated. Our chronic water shortage and crises fostered a close relationship with George the Plumber, and precipitated our enrollment in the Juneau Racquet Club so that we could enjoy the luxury of regular showers.

Some years later we brought in a local driller in to deepen the well. He left the process in charge of an assistant over 4th of July weekend, who in turn left the bitt turning while he quenched his holiday thirst at Squire's Rest. The unattended drill froze solid in his absence, prisoner in a sludge of rock dust and water the consistency of cement far beneath the earth's surface. The rig's owner spent days extricating his incarcerated equipment, at one point offering to sell it to us for a song. We ultimately ended up with a well that produced good water in good quantities, drilled to a depth of over 370 feet. It remained a source of wonder to us that a country that provided so much water from above could be so stingy with water from below.

After all these trials and tribulations, we wound with a soundly built, spacious, finely crafted and well-designed home, with a southwest-facing view out over Auke Bay to North Douglas Island and the mountains of the Chilkat Peninsula in the distance. There was nothing behind us but forest that continued right into the wilds of northern British Columbia. It was twelve miles from downtown but only nine miles from both the hospital and my office, a quick trip on the newly opened Egan Expressway, and only blocks from the marina where we kept our boat. Eagles, ravens, and great blue heron made a good living along the margins of Auke Bay at the foot of our street; blue heron roosted in favorite trees near our home, one close enough to the front deck to touch. On clear nights we could take in nature's amazing light show, the aurora borealis, from our driveway.

———

As we habituated to life in Juneau we would learn that civilization had pushed the people-intolerant big fuzzies to the margins, and there were plenty of places within the Juneau road system where it was considered safe to live, hike, berry pick or otherwise recreate without the encumbrance of a firearm. Although the probability of encountering a fuzzy in these "fuzzy-free zones" never fell to zero, it was only slightly greater than that of encountering a sasquatch.

Some favorites were the moraine and East Glacier Trail at the Mendenhall Glacier, and frozen Mendenhall lake in winter, where Linda and the children often took our dog for a run. Eagle beach to the north out the road was also a great place, although perhaps not quite as fuzzy-proof. Another was the all-day trek on the trail up Mt. Roberts, directly behind downtown. The view from "the cross" at the 2000-foot level was worth the effort: Looking straight down, Juneau's two boat harbors and the Juneau-Douglas bridge. To the north was Gastineau Channel, the Mendenhall moraine at the airport, Auke Bay, and beyond. Mt. Roberts was also a favored destination for the few local paragliding enthusiasts. One achieved his fifteen minutes of fame when he landed in the settling pond of Juneau's sewage disposal facility.

In the 1990s the Goldbelt Native Corporation received permission to install an aerial tram to the 1700-foot level on Mt. Roberts, where they also put in a restaurant and gift shop. It has proven a big attraction, and we've enjoyed it on recent visits. Should you visit Juneau, by all means take it.

In those areas vacated by the big fuzzies, black bear thrived—but because they weren't big fuzzies, they got little respect. They were the Rodney Dangerfields of the Alaskan bear world, but take note: While attacks by black bears are extremely rare, when they do occur they are always predatory. The only one to have taken place in Southeast Alaska during our lengthy tenure was in Glacier Bay National Park, not far from the Bartlett Cove Lodge. All that was found of the unfortunate camper were his boots, complete with feet.

Black bear all too regularly made their presence known in the downtown and residential areas, and Juneau imposed hefty fines for the unsecured garbage containers that attracted them. On one weekend a bear had to be removed from the roof of the Triangle Club bar in the middle of downtown, and another was apprehended after wandering into the Bartlett Hospital emergency room. The live-trap operated by the wildlife division of the state troopers got a lot of work; although its home was outside the trooper detachment building near my office, it was seldom there. Nuisance bears were relocated far out the road, but not all stayed there. Rarely, multiple-time losers had to be euthanized. The youngster bagged in the emergency room, deemed too young to survive on its own, wound up in a zoo.

This story was related in the surgical lounge by one of our orthopedists: A gent who lived in a less-than-savory downtown neighborhood returned home in the wee hours, drunk, one time too many. His irate wife proceeded to pitch him down the outside stairs of their second-floor flat. Arriving at the bottom, our inebriated friend took out his mortification on the nearest object—a large black dog nosing in a garbage can. He gave it a mighty kick in the rump, and when the animal turned to face him it proved not to be a dog. That realization sobered up our friend in a hurry, and as the critter ambled off our friend was soon feeling every step of the many his body had just bumped down, including the one that had dislocated his shoulder.

———

Juneau had its quirks. We would learn that in Juneau there was no such crime as grand theft auto. It was called "joyriding," a misdemeanor, and punished as such. The tenuous rationale for this was that it was impossible to get off the rock in a purloined vehicle. Small comfort to the vehicles' owners: Misappropriated vehicles were always found quickly and within a few miles of their abduction site, generally trashed and half-immersed in some creek.

Juneauites harvested their own Christmas trees, and there were a lot to choose from. Most popular were bull pines from the muskegs; small Sitka spruce and hemlock had a more classic look, but would begin shedding needles copiously within days of being cut. Linda and the children usually performed this rite on their own (my sensible tree choices were regularly overruled until I finally gave up trying), coming back every year with specimens far too large for our living room, even given its 16-foot ceiling. Our vehicle, dwarfed and camouflaged by its trophy burden, resembled the forest advancing on MacBeth's castle as it wended its way home from a successful tree hunt. I always had to cut several feet off the bottom, and even then the trees were so wide and heavy as to require buckets filled with cement for stands.

A physician friend, out on a December deer hunt, encountered the perfect Christmas tree. Not having a saw with him, he felled the tree with multiple shots from his .338 rifle. There are many places where people cut down their own trees, but where else but Alaska do you shoot them down?

That physician happened to be a Seventh-Day Adventist, many of whom eschew meat in their diet. When asked what he was doing hunting deer, his reply was "Everyone knows deer are vegetables."

It is fortunate that golf—such an important source of recreation for so many down south—was never on my recreational radar. Nowhere in the greater Juneau area was there enough suitable land for even a par-three course. We had heard that some diehards played on the Gastineau Channel mud flats just south of downtown at low tide, but I believe that to have been a short-lived venture.

Juneau opened a community ski area, Eaglecrest, near the north end of Douglas Island in 1977. During the development stage some of the boosters beat the drum for it as a potential godsend to the local economy, claiming it would attract jumbo jets packed with skiers from Japan. Of course they were full of applesauce. With a base elevation of only 1000 feet, it was at the mercy of the weather gods; a midwinter warm spell could cause the area to close for weeks at a time. Those same gods provided it with fog, flat light, and heavy, wet snow—"Sierra cement." Despite this it was a popular attraction for hordes of locals, including us. Linda took our children every weekend it was open during the winter of 1977, and since it looked like she was missing out on some fun she started taking lessons the following year. A year later it was my turn. Although the area had only slightly more than a 1600-foot vertical, much of the terrain was as challenging as any found in North America, and those who could ski the whole mountain would be at home on any slope. Over the years Juneau produced some elite skiers, including an Olympic medalist, and a lot of extraordinarily good ones, including all of our children. Linda and I were sufficiently hooked to retire in ski country.

Juneau, and in fact all of Alaska, was entering a tumultuous decade as we arrived in late 1973. The Trans Alaskan pipeline, being built to transport crude oil from the newly developed fields of Prudhoe Bay on the North Slope to the port city of Valdez on the Southcentral Gulf, was at the root of much of it. A statewide boom was already in progress as roughnecks drilled on the North Slope, pipeline construction crews labored the length of the vast state, port facilities were established on the Gulf, and the major oil companies established infrastructure in Anchorage. Rumors of high pay for workers on the pipeline—true—produced a stampede from the lower 48, much like a gold rush; this in spite of the State admonishing people not to come unless they had a guaranteed job awaiting. The glut of people wanting in on the bonanza was overwhelming the resources of virtually all points of entry to Alaska. Even in Juneau, far from the action, the energy radiated by the boom was almost palpable.

The prospect of riches rolling in by the barrelful when the oil started to flow awakened a sleeping ogre that had been stirring fitfully since statehood: the idea of relocating the capitol from Juneau to the State's major population center of Anchorage, or somewhere close to it. Juneau had long been looked upon as a dreary, rainy, backwater, isolated and geographically removed from the rest of the state, by legislators from in and around the metropolis of Anchorage, some 1000 miles away to the northwest—and they detested it. Egged on by a powerful Anchorage newspaper publisher, who for some reason harbored an visceral hatred for Juneau, the latest incarnation of this plot would move the capitol to a new city to be built in the Matanuska Valley, just north of Anchorage. Land purchases had already been made on the speculation that it would happen, and Anchorage developers were falling all over each other to be first in line at the gravy trough. Millions, maybe billions, in spoils for the greater Anchorage area was at stake, and their politicians, lobbyists, and media were working and spending overtime to convince the rest of the state to go along. The capitol-move faction had a powerful lever in the promise of endless oil revenues which, the public was assured, would cover the obscene cost of this extravaganza.

Juneau lived under a cloud of uncertainty for the years it took this drama to play out. Every resident, ourselves included, was justifiably concerned, and the town fathers and politicians petrified at the prospect of their city going into an economic death spiral if its reason for being were snatched away. Their concern was well-founded but some of their responses, governed by panic rather than reason, were not. The sitting mayor and council had clandestinely petitioned the Federal Department of Transportation to move Juneau and all of Southeast Alaska from the Pacific (Seattle's) to the Yukon (Anchorage's) time zone; the ostensible but flimsy rationale was to make it easier to transact government business between the center of population and the capitol city. They had consulted neither their constituents nor any of the communities of Southeast Alaska that would be affected, and we the public only learned of it when the petition appeared as a *fait d'acompli* in the newspaper headlines. We'd been blindsided by our elected officials.

The brouhaha that ensued went on for months, and for that time was a complete distraction from the issue that had precipitated it. It pitted Juneau's politicians and wealthiest business owners against virtually everybody else; most of us enjoyed the benefits of Pacific Time—more afternoon and evening daylight—and the economic and travel axis of Southeast was tilted toward Seattle rather than Anchorage. Most folks had the common sense to realize that this self-flagellating act of appeasement would score no points with the capitol-move proponents; we, and they, knew that it was always about the money. And, we were pissed that this was being pulled off behind our backs. I became a member of a committee devoted to keeping Southeast on Pacific time—my first and only foray into public life—and even debated Juneau's mayor on prime-time local TV. As a semi-articulate non-politician with stage fright I couldn't match his polished, oily unctuousness, but given the malarkey he was peddling, I didn't have to.

In the end it came down to a plebiscite in a special election, and the Pacific Time faction won in a landslide. The petition to the Federal Government was withdrawn by popular mandate. It also led to a recall election directed at the mayor and the entire council, all of whom narrowly survived (I took no part in the recall movement).

The capitol-move proposal was ultimately torpedoed in a statewide referendum; Anchorage alone could not withstand the weight of votes from everywhere else in the state. Some years later, and well after the issue had been laid to rest, a new mayor quietly petitioned the U.S. DOT to have all of Alaska, which encompassed four different time zones, incorporated into a single zone, to be called Alaska-Yukon time (moving Juneau and Southeast one hour to the west, as per the original proposal). This time it went through without so much as a whimper, as I and everybody else was tired of fighting city hall. Alaska-Puke-on time it would be, and still is.

The second cockamamie idea spawned by the capitol-move threat was that of a road connecting Juneau with the rest of the continent's road system, i.e. with Anchorage and the lower 48. It also was not entirely new. It was (re)proposed with the intent of making Juneau more "accessible," thus negating one argument for relocating the capitol. Great in theory, but for anyone with a map who was in the least familiar with the territory, it was off-the-wall goofy—but that wasn't deterring Juneau's movers and shakers from pushing it. They proposed a road connecting Juneau with Haines, seventy miles north and on the opposite side of Lynn Canal. Haines was the only community in Southeast to be connected by a road spur—the Haines Highway—with the Alcan Highway, and thus with both Anchorage and the lower 48. The logistics were impossible, and even if a feasible plan were to be developed the cost would be in the billions. And after all that both the Haines Highway, and the Alcan Highway to which it connected, were literally 1000 miles of bad road in each direction, and impassable because of weather for well over half the year.

Most locals actually felt Juneau's isolation to be a good thing. Connecting us by road to the rest of the country would only make us more susceptible to the evils ranging freely through the lower 48, out of proportion to whatever benefits it might bring.

The idea smoldered on for several years but never gained much traction with the public, ultimately dying of common sense. I've only recently learned of a movement to resurrect it; the looniest ideas just don't want to stay dead. Maybe this one needs a silver bullet.

————

Just prior to our arrival in Juneau the Alaska Native Land Claims Settlement Act of 1973 had been passed; the details were still being worked out, and the impact still reverberating. The Act created village and regional Native corporations throughout the state, and ceded to these corporations vast tracts of land of their choosing as well as vast amounts of money. Every Alaska Native was automatically a member of one or more, had a say in the election of officers, and received dividends if there were any. The Act had no direct effect on us, but did have some major ramifications for the State and the communities within it, including Juneau. Native Alaskans were now a collective political and economic force to be reckoned with; it made non-native Alaskans aware that there was indeed a line drawn between themselves and the Native populace that many had not been seeing, but that Native Alaskans had known was there all along.

The doings, and the fortunes, of the various corporations were often in the news, and we knew that the political infighting within some was brutal. Also that some had chosen their leaders wisely and prospered, while others hadn't. They were handicapped in that an Alaska Native leadership class had to be built from the ground up, but in time some talented and farsighted leaders emerged within the Native community. We were sorry to see some land allotments in Southeast logged off by their corporations, but some are using their allotments in more sustainable ways.

———

Even as Juneau labored under the threat of the capitol move, another industry was growing rapidly: tourism. It would eventually equal, and seasonally surpass, government as the mainspring of the economy, and for Southeast as a whole would more than fill the void left by the demise of the timber industry.

In the early 70s Juneau was visited by perhaps one cruise ship every two or three days during the summer. The ships came in at South Franklin Street, a thoroughfare at the south end of downtown that ran along the waterfront. In those days South Franklin was Juneau's skid row; the inert drunks lying on the sidewalks made them an obstacle course, a place best avoided by respectable locals like ourselves, and doubtless repellant to tourists.

The numbers of cruise ships rose every year; more per week, and they came earlier and stayed later. By the mid-80s, four per day was not unusual, May through October. The town fathers and the laws of economics partnered in cleaning up South Franklin. The drunks disappeared, to be replaced by small shop after small shop, hawking everything from cheap trinkets and T-shirts to high-end local arts and crafts, furs, Gucci, and Rolex. Fortunate indeed was the tourist who could run the gauntlet of South Franklin Street without maxing out a credit card. Locals still generally avoided the place: four ships at 3000 tourists each, milling around in the middle of the narrow thoroughfare, produced downtown gridlock all day long.

The tourism boom spawned all manner of concessions and offshoot businesses. Bus tours to the Mendenhall Glacier and other points of interest. Many small boat owners got "six-pack" licenses and began running half-day sportfishing charters and whale-watching trips out of

Auke Bay. Nightly salmon bakes in Gold Creek Basin. Flying services offered sightseeing tours over the icefield. Several helicopter services sprang up, offering trips up onto the higher reaches of the Mendenhall and other nearby glaciers. A friend of our daughter's worked for one during the summers, and would call us whenever they had a partially open flight. Thus we all got to go on a few of these spectacular trips.

Juneau had an auspicious tourist in the mid-'80s—President Ronald Reagan, there for a well-hyped, one-day pit stop. It happened to be a late-summer Saturday, and our family had trekked over to the University of Alaska Southeast campus where thickets of ripe blueberries lined the road. We were industriously filling our buckets when a white stretch limo with smoked windows happened along and slowed to a crawl as it passed. We, the hearty local hunter-gatherers living off the land, the stalwart exemplars of the American pioneer spirit, waved and smiled. We never knew for sure whether the president was in that limo.

———

When oil did start flowing through the Trans Alaskan pipeline, it was indeed matched by a flood of royalty money flowing into the state coffers. Alaska's state senators and representatives were quick to pick up on a thing that would virtually guarantee them reelection, and wasted no time in abolishing Alaska's state income tax. That had been fine with us.

At the same time Gov. Jay Hammond, a former bush pilot from the boonies of Southwest Alaska and arguably the best governor the state has ever had, established the "permanent fund"—putting a percentage of the royalty money into an investment fund, the returns from which would be used to pay an annual dividend to every Alaskan man, woman, and child. Within a decade each divided check would rise to over $1000; for us as a family we realized over $5000 per year, a great boost to our children's college funds.

Our daughter Susan celebrated the passing of her driver's exam by taking a girlfriend along in our car for a spin through town. While traversing a residential area up in back of downtown the engine stalled, and she coasted to a halt in front of an imposing house with white columns and a large front lawn. The engine wouldn't restart. A kindly looking middle-aged man with a short salt-and-pepper beard emerged from the house, ascertained their problem, and asked if he could take a look. After just a minute or so of hocus-pocus under the hood he asked Susan to turn the engine over and, lo and behold, it caught. The man waved and turned to head back toward his house, never having introduced himself. The house was the governor's mansion, and the anonymous good Samaritan-mechanic none other than Gov. Jay Hammond.

(L) Mt. Edgecumbe volcano, from John Brown's beach near our home

(R) A Sitka evening winterscape from our window. Mt. Arrowhead at right

(L) Summer 1969, outside our Mt. Edgecumbe residence: Linda, the Lieutenant Commander, Susan, Betsy, Taffy in foreground. David's here too. Can you find him?

(below) Mt. Edgecumbe Alaska Native Hospital: no mistaking government construction

Looking out over Peril Strait: A Southeast Alaskan autumn land-marinescape

Ginger, high and dry at the mouth of Eva Creek, 1970

(below) Elfin Cove in 1971, looking little different than it did forty years later

A piece of Southeast
Alaskana: an aging salmon
troller on the grid at Elfin
Cove, 1971

Shore boats: the
Sitka-Mt.
Edgecumbe ferry,
1970

A day at the beach behind our house,
Mt. Edgecumbe, 1971

Tlingit dugout canoe in front
of Sitka's Centennial Hall

(L) An annual rite of summer: the Sitka Salmon Derby, 1971

(R) GMO Ross Brudenell, Sitka guide Ben Forbes, 1971

(L) Rebuilding St. Michael's cathedral, downtown Sitka, 1971

(Below) About to board a piece of aviation history: an Alaska Airlines Grumman Goose in Ketchikan, 1971

Downtown Juneau, nestled at the foot of Mt. Juneau and Mt. Roberts, from Douglas Island. Remains of the Alaska-Juneau Mine cling to the flank of Mt. Roberts (R)

(L) The Mendenhall Towers (in the Juneau icefield), Glacier, Lake, and Valley from the air, 2019 (Kim Smith photo). The falls seen at center was behind the face of the glacier until some time in the 1980s.

(R) View from The Cross on Mt.Roberts, 2000 feet above Gastineau Channel. Below, the Juneau-Douglas bridge and Juneau's two small boat harbors. To the north the airport, Mendenhall Peninsula, and Auke Bay beyond

Our home in
Auke Bay, 1975

The nearby
Mendenhall
Glacier and
Lake, early
1970s

Mendenhall
Glacier as it
looked in 2020,
seen through a
veil of smoke
from wildfires in
the Yukon.
When we first
saw it fifty years
before, the
waterfall at right
was well behind
the face of the
retreating glacier

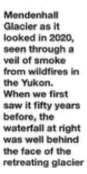

(above) The falls at Baranof Warm Springs, 1977

(L) Fishing at the base of the falls, 1977

(R) "Main St.", Baranof Warm Springs, 1977

(R) Lone orca, Icy Strait

(L) Linda on bear watch with the .375 H & H magnum while we fish Eva Creek, 1981 (she knew how to usit it, too)

(below) Humpback whales bubble-net feeding at Point Couverden

153

(R) South Sawyer
Glacier,
terminus of
Tracy Arm Fjord

(below) David
and Linda with
her giant halibut
from Holkham
Bay, 1983

(R) Sumdum
Glacier behind
Holkham Bay,
with bergs from
Tracy and
Endicott Arms
stranded on its
moraine. Tom
Parke's
second-best
halibut spot is
just out of the
picture to the
right

Raccoon III, anchored at the head of Neka Bay. The saltchuck - the river's estuary - lies ahead around the point

(L) Big fuzzies on the beach, above far right, at Neka Bay, sniffing around where we had been minutes before

(below) The saltchuck, Neka Bay

(L, below) Linda plays, lands a Neka Bay cutthroat

(below) The remains of a fallen giant on the beach at Neka Bay

(below) Dr. Watson on one of his early boat trips

(below) Berg near the head of Tracy Arm Fjord

(L) Author on moraine of Muir Glacier, Glacier Bay, 1971, dwarfed by his surroundings

(R) Barb Greening smooches Pavlov Harbor's Halibut-Lips Rock

(L) Betsy, Linda, David, Susan pose in our apartment with our first Juneau king salmon, 1974

(R)Family marshmellow roast on Flea Point, Pavlov Harbor, circa. 1978

The Deep End of the Pool: Private Practice in Juneau

Scan back to our arrival in Juneau: The first surprise awaiting us was finding that with the exception of Tom Stengl, who apparently kept the knowledge to himself, we had not been expected. The hospital administrator gave me a "What the hell are you doing here?" look when I appeared in his office the next day, despite my having met with that selfsame individual during a trip up in late spring to discuss matters like credentials, state licensure, and hospital privileges, and having made my intentions crystal clear both to him and to Gary Hedges, Juneau's remaining surgeon.

The second shock, and far more disturbing, was finding that I'd been preempted. A young general surgeon, Bill Palmer, had done a locum tenens for Gary during the early summer, filling in to cover his practice for a month while otherwise passing through on his way to setting up a practice in the Matanuska Valley just north of Anchorage. He'd found Juneau to his liking, decided to stop right there, and had set up his own private practice a few months prior to our arrival. We had not been forewarned, although there had been plenty of time to do so. Had we been, we would have pressed the abort button. Juneau had never had more than two general surgeons. Could it support three, and could Tail-end Charlie catch up?

Some economic help from the hospital and community had been hinted at by the administrator on my earlier visit, when enlisting a second surgeon had been an urgent priority—but now that a second surgeon was already on board, there was nary a mention of it. The welcome wagon's cupboard was bare, and we were on our own.

What had happened? I don't know, and made no effort to find out either then or later. It wouldn't have done any good, and some anthills are best left unkicked. Our most immediate concern was survival; the wagon train's resources were about spent. At that moment I felt like the wagonmaster of the Donner party, arriving with his charges—my family!—at the summit of the pass with winter coming on.

———

I'd known there was no way to enter the Juneau medical scene as a surgeon other than by opening a solo private practice—and there was nothing about either medical school or residency that had prepared me for doing so. It had once been easy: Virtually all of my clinical mentors in both medical school and residency had been, despite attending status at teaching hospitals, in private practice and for the most part solo. They were, however, the last of American medicine's Innocent Age. Forces were already in play that were changing the face of medical practice: the intrusion of government in the form of Medicare and Medicaid; the rising power of the insurance industry as it drafted in the wake of the government programs; the advent of managed care and corporate medicine; an increasingly litigious public; the age of consumerism. These had already caused most in my generation of physicians to opt for situations that would shield them from the distracting battle for survival that private solo practice was becoming. I had been among them, choosing to take a salaried position with a multispecialty group upon leaving the U.S.P.H.S.

And now here I was, jumping out of the lifeboat into the deep end of the pool, and not knowing how to swim. It was a plunge I wouldn't have contemplated anywhere but Southeast Alaska, but now I was actually in midair, looking down at a pool that was not only crowded but also full of piranhas. Anyone opting to set up a solo private practice at this time—anywhere—was voluntarily boarding the *Titanic*, joining the ranks of the dinosaurs even as the giant meteor was making things uncomfortably warm on the Yucatan Peninsula.

There was no alternative but to plow ahead. Suffice it to say that, on the back of a $24,000 loan from the federal small business administration—and being steered toward a capable accountant and attorney—I found office space to rent near the hospital, outfitted it with mostly second-hand furniture and equipment (largely thanks to a sympathetic and generous Juneau pediatrician named Ken Moss), found a capable R.N. willing to double as receptionist and bookkeeper, hung out a shingle, and had at it. The first several months would pass uneasily.

It was fortunate that four part-time state and federal government contract positions for physicians were going begging as I opened for business, and I signed on for all of them. None required more than two hours per week, they paid well, two could be done in my office, and all had extremely flexible hours that would not interfere with a surgical schedule. They were invaluable in paying the bills and putting food on the table during the first years when my surgical practice was getting off the ground.

It was also fortunate that both of the growing family practice groups were almost as new to Juneau as I, and therefore had no preestablished referral allegiances. There evolved an unspoken referral protocol whereby almost every Juneau physician delivering primary care, whether pediatrician, internist, or family practitioner, sent their elective as well as emergency surgical referrals to the surgeon on call for that day, unless the patient expressed a specific preference. It helped that all three surgeons were accessible, affable, and good at what they did, and I think the referring medical community recognized the wisdom of this democratic system as a means of keeping all three of us *in* the community.

All but one. The unfortunate exception was an established internist with a huge practice. His referral policy was also democratic: He did not refer to *any* local surgeon. He referred all elective surgery outside, to Seattle; the only patients of his to be seen by any of us were sent for minor office procedures (lumps and bumps, warts and moles), for suture removal or wound complication treatment after having undergone major surgery in Seattle, those rare patients who dug in their heels and resisted being sent outside for elective surgery, or for emergencies where he had no choice in the matter. Over the years I well recall performing difficult emergency surgery on a few of his critically ill patients, all of whom had excellent outcomes—but it changed nothing. My two surgical colleagues endured similar experiences in their dealings with this internist. It wasn't something we talked about, but they liked it no better than I did. I thought then and even decades after that his behavior in this regard was not only an affront to us, but also a disservice to his patients and to his community.

There were no full-time physicians staffing the emergency room when we arrived in Juneau. Every physician with hospital privileges had to rotate on an E.R. coverage call schedule, a duty universally detested, and by myself as much as anyone. Some on the staff were unable or unwilling to venture beyond their very narrow comfort zones, and sought consultations for just about everything. For the surgeons, this meant being called in to treat the most minor of lacerations and boo-boos, and seeing virtually everyone presenting with abdominal pain—things most E.R. physicians would handle in stride or selectively seek consultation for. The good parts for me were the badly needed fees for E.R. work I otherwise would not have gotten.

My days on E.R. call, as much of an annoyance as I found them, did produce the occasional priceless antidote; this one had a truly Southeast Alaskan flavor.

Late one sunny spring afternoon I was summoned to the E.R. to see two men who had been brought in, unconscious and unresponsive, by our EMTs; for the sake of clarity and brevity they will henceforth be designated Alphonse and Gaston. The sparse information initially available was that the Coast Guard had evacuated the two from a small boat in Auke Bay, Alphonse having been found in a stuporous state at the helm, Gaston passed out on the floor of the cabin. Evidence at the scene consisted of several six-packs of beer, mostly empty.

It had been a long time since I had anything to do with working up comatose patients, but I proceeded with the usual checking of airways and vital signs, physical exams, and lab work—nothing alarming or revealing of anything found save the unmistakable odor of used beer. As I pondered just what was going on with these two, a piece of the puzzle filtered in from the Coast Guard rescuers: The boat in which the men were found contained a propane stove in the cabin, the propane cylinder for which was empty with the valve in the "open" position.

At length both Alphonse and Gaston began to stir, through no effort of my own. As G came around, every movement elicited an agonized groan. A came around more quickly, and a story finally emerged: The two friends had been salmon trolling off Funter Bay, each in his own boat, and had been quaffing brewskis at a steady pace since early morning. At some point G had gone below to his cabin to heat a bowl of soup, and when he didn't return topside and his boat began behaving erratically, A became concerned and pulled alongside. A found his friend out cold on the floor of the cabin and, resourceful fellow that he was, lifted him onto a bunk, closed the cabin door behind him, lashed the two boats together, and took the helm of G's boat for the trip home.

The wind kicked up on the slow trip back to Auke Bay, and as the boats pounded into a stiff chop the ever-solicitous A checked on G every few minutes. Each time he found G unresponsive on the floor, bounced off the bunk by the rough ride—and each time he put him back and closed the cabin door behind him. A continued to self-lubricate over the several-hour run back, and the last thing he remembered was passing Coghlan Island at the entrance to Auke Bay.

Alphonse's final diagnosis was nothing more than alcoholic stupor, from which he was recovering nicely on his own. Gaston's was a bit of the above, plus close-to-lethal propane inhalation—and painful total-body contusions caused by the repetitive trauma of falls from bunk to floor. A few x-rays confirmed that nothing was broken. His well-meaning friend had undoubtedly saved him from asphyxia each time he opened the cabin door, contributed to his bodily miseries by setting him up for repeated falls, and came close to snuffing him each time he closed the door again. Alphonse had never noticed the open propane valve.

When I returned home at the conclusion of this episode, friend and next-door neighbor Jerry Quigg was outside and we stopped to chat. "I saw the funniest thing from my living room window this afternoon," Jerry said. "Two boats lashed together, going around in circles in the middle of Auke Bay. I finally called it in to the Coast Guard...."

We all breathed a collective sigh of relief when, a few years down the road, physician Jim Thompson—whom we would dub "Dr. Vacation" for his frequent, exotic, and extreme outdoor escapades—put together an E.R. group that provided coverage 24/7.

It turned out there was work enough for three general surgeons, despite the drain of all too many elective procedures to Seattle—and with only two, the call schedule would have been oppressive. The relationship with my two colleagues was good from the beginning: We worked together in coordinating a surgical on-call schedule that kept the hospital and community covered 24/7, covered one another's patients, and assisted one another at surgery. The prospect of consolidating into a group was never broached by any of us over the many years we practiced alongside one another; looking back, it might have made economic sense to do so, but I think each of us was individualistic and ornery enough—as surgeons tend to be—to realize that we were better off being our own bosses.

Small hospitals in small cities are commonplace across America, but Juneau's Bartlett Memorial, because of the happenstance of geography, was unique—or close to it. Juneau was a mini-hub, situated a thousand miles from anywhere. Anywhere larger, that is. While 1000 miles can be covered in two hours by plane, in practical terms that time might be two days or even more; for over a decade after my arrival, the only way to triage critical patients to a major medical center (usually Seattle, occasionally Anchorage) was via scheduled commercial flights, of which there were only a few per day, and which required bumping passengers and removing seats. And, capricious weather could shut down our airport for days at a time. The bottom line: For the critically ill or injured, resident and visitor alike, the buck stopped at our doorstep.

The hospital and its medical staff were called upon to provide definitive care to patients that would have been quickly waved on to major referral centers or upper-level trauma units by virtually all hospitals of similar or even larger size in the lower 48. Our hospital had to be geared for it, and was. For the surgeons, it meant that we were periodically confronted with the kind of challenges residency had prepared us for, but were seldom experienced by our smaller-hospital surgical brethren in the lower 48. Such cases could be exhilarating but were also exhausting, as we had no resident staff, intensivists, or hospitalists to share the load of the ongoing complex care such patients often required.

Alaska Airlines had been unfailingly cooperative in making the triage of critical patients as expeditious as possible, but the establishment of a medivac service by Seattle's Harborview Hospital in the mid-1980s was a major step forward. A Learjet based at Seattle's Boeing Field could make the round trip in four hours of flying time, but the weather at the Juneau end was still problematic. It was not until the late '90s that a medivac jet was based in Juneau. I was no longer in practice then, but it must have made a huge difference. It would have been no longer necessary to err so strongly on the side of conservatism in triaging patients south—for instance, patients with head trauma. Also, timely, reliable triage made available to critical patients the most recent advances in medical care then coming online at major centers—for example, routine early cardiac catheterization for heart attack victims.

Juneau's general surgeons did wear extra hats, but not as many as I'd worn at Mt. Edgecumbe—and those hats were actually vital in helping the community to support all three of us. We did the gynecologic surgery, and two of us the C-sections; after the arrival of a second orthopedist we were rarely involved in fracture work. At that point in time vascular surgery was still a young discipline that had not attained subspecialty status; while not all general surgeons partook, I had sound training and experience in it during my residency, and enjoyed doing it. My two surgical colleagues did the fiberoptic endoscopies. We all did emergent things that might have been handled by plastic, pediatric, or thoracic surgeons, urologists, or trauma specialists, in larger centers. Laparoscopic cholecystectomy—gallbladder removal—was the first of the minimally invasive abdominal procedures to go mainstream, but it did not do so until circa 1990. It was so totally alien to my generation of surgeons, requiring vastly different skillsets—more like playing video games than doing surgery—that only one of the three of us chose to climb the pitfall-filled learning curve so relatively late in our careers, and it wasn't me.

The practice of general surgery in Juneau involved a great deal of unscheduled, after-hours, and weekend work—emergency C-sections, appendectomies, bowel obstructions and other acute abdominal conditions, acute vascular issues, trauma of all kinds, assisting on emergency orthopedic procedures, E.R. or hospital consultations. Thus a significant portion of my work was conducted between dusk and dawn. Linda and I had an unspoken deal of sorts: I never heard the children when they awoke at night, and she never heard the phone when it rang or me getting out of bed. Were I to be called in for, say, an emergency C-section, it might be as little as two hours from the time the phone rang to the time I was back in bed. Linda always knew the next morning when I had been gone, however. It was the socks. If I got out of bed in the morning and my socks were on, I'd been out the night before. There was an occasional bonus encountered on the late-night drives home from the hospital. On clear nights I would stop at a highway pull-out to marvel at the Northern lights as they played over and animated the whiteness of Lemon Glacier. Worth losing a little sleep over.

With just three surgeons oftentimes there were two, and sometimes only one, available for days, a week, or rarely even two weeks at a time. Given the frequency of emergency work in Juneau, it was during those times that I was thankful for training in an era when there were no restrictions on the hours a resident could work. Those of my era learned how to continue functioning at a high level in the face of fatigue and lack of sleep. We had to, and we did. It wasn't ideal, or anyone's idea of fun, but in a practice setting such as Juneau's there were times when there were no options—and I think we took a sort of perverse pride in being able to do it. And it wasn't my scheduled Monday 8 A.M. cholecystectomy patient's concern whether I had enjoyed a good night's sleep the night before, or been operating nonstop all weekend; that patient expected, and was entitled to, my best either way, and he or she got it.

———

As tourism blossomed during our Juneau years, our emergency room saw ever-increasing numbers of visitors who had arrived on cruise ships or in motorhomes via the Alaska Marine Highway. The cruise ships, which we dubbed "Red Cross ships," brought elderly people who had postponed retirement to save for the trip of a lifetime, all the while accumulating snowballing medical issues. A number would get only as far as Juneau before the snowball rolled downhill and deposited them, critically ill, on our doorstep. Sick as they were, they often arrived at our hospital with a greater fear of those who might be treating them than of whatever was wrong with them. From their perspective, they might as well have been in some third-world country: Any doctor driven to practice in such a quaint, remote, and backward place, with such miserable weather, had to be a bumbler at best, perhaps a quack, last in his class if he or she had even been in a class, and unable to cut it in the Big City where the *real* doctors were (never mind that all three general surgeons were graduates of elite schools, had been university-trained in our specialty, and were here because we wanted to be here). The casual dress code of the medical staff probably didn't help—every day was casual Friday—but hey, this was Alaska! And for reasons that we've seen, it was sometimes not possible to beam these patients back to their comfort zone in the lower 48 for definitive care.

The attitude wasn't entirely limited to visitors. It spilled over into a segment of the local population—some state and federal employees and their families who had migrated north from urban centers, and particularly those who were patients of the aforementioned internist. Those same folks who wouldn't think of having elective surgery in Juneau were all too happy to have us here when their child's appendix burst at two in the morning.

The reality was that Juneau's medical community was, and remained, remarkably free of bad apples. The community was proud of its collective competence and guarded it jealously; its modest size made black sheep easy to spot, and most with less-than-stellar references, reps, or credentials were culled even while trying to get a foot in the door. Not that some didn't try. The few that made it didn't last long.

———

So how did I fare over a career as a medical entrepreneur? The verdict is mixed, but the *Titanic* didn't sink. I made mistakes along the way, mostly errors of misplaced trust and naivete in the zero-sum world of business. I never bought into advertising and promoting my practice after it became legal and ethical to do so. On the plus side I did get some sound advice that I listened to, made some decisions that turned out to be good. I was able to keep my practice in the black, send our kids to college, prepare us for retirement, and keep us out of trouble. I'd give myself a B-.

Would I have preferred my practice to have tilted more toward elective surgery and less toward emergency work, and with less call? Yes. This often happens in surgical practices in more populous areas as they evolve over time, as young and hungry surgeons move into a community and eagerly take on the after-hours and weekend work the established surgeons no longer need. But I knew going in that this would never be possible in Juneau; it was pedal-to-the-floor or full stop. It was a price worth paying to be able to live, work, and raise a family on the Last Frontier.

> *An Ironic Postscript: I practiced for most of a career in a place where a number of folks thought that no local physician was educated or smart enough to be trusted. We then retired to a state—Idaho—where a significant portion of the populace thought that all physicians were too educated and smart to be trusted. Go figure.*

Messing About in Boats II: Juneau

"Twenty years from now you will be more disappointed by the things you didn't do than by the ones you did do. So throw off the bowlines. Sail away from the safe harbor. Catch the trade winds in your sails. Explore. Dream. Discover."

- Mark Twain

"Boats, like whiskey, are all good."

- R. D. Culler

By the spring of 1974 it had become clear that my surgical practice, launched the fall before, was not going to crash. We plunked down the down payment on what would become our home in Auke Bay. We also attended the annual boat show at Channel Marina, Juneau's largest dealership, and walked away the owners of a brand-new 23' Bayliner cabin cruiser. It also marked the beginning of a friendship with the dealership's owner, Hank Bryson, that endures to this day. If you think this purchase frivolous, remember that in Southeast Alaska a boat is a necessity, not a luxury. Makes one wonder if the government should have been giving out boat stamps.

We named our new craft *Raccoon* (raccoons were son David's favorite animal, although, oddly, one not found anywhere in Alaska). In terms of size and everything else it was a prototypical Southeast boat, powered by a single big gas engine with an outdrive. It was fast, able to get us out for an evening's fishing and back without spending most of the time in transit. A modest fuel capacity limited our range to about 100 miles round trip. It provided adequate-but-not-great protection from the elements, and was a good fishing platform. At its best for day trips, it worked for overnighting and even weekending, but was cramped, chilly, and a bit like camping out five to a pup tent. I installed a second-hand VHF radio, which was just starting to be considered essential equipment for boats of this size. We began learning the local waters, and discovered that our *Raccoon* had a nose for fish. For newbies still finding out where the best spots were, we had extraordinary early success trolling for king salmon.

Ship-to-shore transportation was by means of a sport-yak, just as it had been for both of our Mt. Edgecumbe boats. Sport-yaks were light, inexpensive dinghies molded of bright-orange plastic, a bit smaller than a bathtub, double-hulled to provide flotation. They were to be found atop most boats of this size throughout Southeast Alaska. Two people was a crowd, and set the craft so low in the water as to swamp or capsize in the slightest chop, or if either occupant so much as sneezed. During our second season with *Raccoon* we moved up to an inflatable which was safer but not much bigger, and an 8-foot aluminum pram that we could power with our auxiliary outboard kicker, and even fish from.

A year after we moved from downtown to Auke Bay we gave up our boat stall in town. Auke Bay was not only more convenient but also a lot closer to most of our preferred destinations—but alas, no stall space was available there. So, we went to plan B and bought a 4 WD International Scout SUV and trailer. We kept the boat at our house, and put in at a launching ramp only a quarter-mile away. I became an accomplished trailer jockey, able to get our boat in or out in under two minutes.

Our new Scout was the most miserable vehicle we ever owned. It handled like an 18-wheeler, and had the suspension of a horse-cart. Linda hated to drive it. Its 4-cylinder engine had no get-up-and-go but absolutely devoured gasoline (I couldn't believe it when I ran out of gas on Egan Drive only days after the tank's first filling). It got about 9 mpg, and only 6 mpg in 4WD, which we had to use almost constantly in winter; in 2WD the Scout either bogged down or skated with even the slightest trace of snow or ice on the road. As a bonus, watching the body rust out was like watching, or listening, to corn grow. No wonder you can't buy International Scouts anymore.

The Scout's front drive shaft once fell out while Linda was homebound on Eagan Drive. By a stroke of good fortune Horst, an auto mechanic we knew, was in the car behind her. He got under the Scout in the middle of the highway and put the shaft back in.

We moved on to *Raccoon II* in 1977, also a Bayliner but 27 feet in length. The kids were getting bigger, our family had outgrown the smaller *Raccoon* for weekending, and three engine failures over three years had convinced us that with a single-engined boat we were putting ourselves at risk every time we went off the beaten path (over the years we ourselves would tow in a number of disabled single-engine craft). *Raccoon II* had twin gas engines, and the insurance did pay off a couple of times. Our range was still limited to around 100 miles before a pit-stop for fuel. *Raccoon II* had a few more creature comforts, but our trips were still limited in distance and duration; our countertop propane stove was a cut above the alcohol stove of the *Raccoon*, but we still ate a lot of spam and Dinty Moore stew. We trailered this boat as well.

Three years later we were ready to move on to boat number three—boat owners among you are probably smiling at the familiar pattern. Our Scout's body was almost completely rusted out by the end of the 1979 season, as was our patience with it, so when we put the *Raccoon II* up for sale, we put the Scout up for sale as well. It didn't sell until we changed our add in the classifieds to read: "Buy our ski rack for $50 and we'll throw in a '76 International Scout for free" (I actually don't recall our asking price, but if it was over $50 it was an unconscionable rip-off).

———

We did a lot of research before purchasing our next boat, scanning through ads in yachting magazines, sending for and studying brochures, nosing around at the annual Seattle boat show, and stopping at some dealerships on Seattle's Lake Union. We eventually chose a 34' Californian, powered by twin 200-hp turbodiesels. We'd been impressed with the design, a melding of the deep-vee hull and broad stern of an offshore sportfisherman with the best features of a pure displacement trawler, and with its heavy fiberglass construction. It promised diesel reliability and economy, twice the range we'd been accustomed to, considerably greater speed than a pure trawler but with the same comforts, and good rough-water capability. After much soul-searching we cashed in our whole life policy to help with the down payment, and with interest rates going to record highs, financed it through my corporate retirement plan (paying usurious interest is less painful when you're paying the interest to yourself).

It had a spacious salon that was a combined pilot house, lounge, galley, and dining room, easily convertible to an extra bedroom, with large windows all around. The flying bridge had lots of comfortable seating and a second helm station. Storage space was seemingly endless, and it could sleep up to seven adults without undue crowding. The cockpit was a perfect fishing platform, whether for trolling, bottom fishing, or fly casting for coho in the salt (a later chapter). The galley featured a small AC/DC fridge and a Dickinson stove that ran on the same diesel that our engines did, and served for both cooking and keeping the cabin warm and dry. Within a short time I would install radar, an autopilot, an elaborate fish finder fathometer, and a 3 kw generator for brewing the morning coffee, running the girls' hairdryer and a microwave oven, and, most importantly, keeping our three big D-8 batteries at full charge when we stayed in one place for any length of time. If we were careful with water, we could stay out for two weeks at a time and be comfortable doing it.

A 10-ft. fiberglass skiff, for which we carried a 6 hp outboard in the lazarette beneath the cockpit, mounted on the swimstep for ship-to-shore use and for chasing coho salmon around Pavlov Harbor with a fly rod. Depending on our destination, we might in addition bring along an 8-ft. inflatable. We carried spares for most things, and a tool kit that could manage repairs to anything short of major engine issues. Our new "pocket battleship" would be, of course, the *Raccoon III*.

By this time I had ascended the learning curves for troubleshooting and fixing most of the things that could go wrong on boats. I performed all of the routine maintenance and servicing of the engines, transmissions, generator, batteries, etc., and did a number of system upgrades and all the after-installations—generator, autopilot, and more—myself. A saltwater environment is hard on everything, and in a boat with so many systems there was always something to repair or replace. Everyone in the family pitched in on the seasonal maintenance inside and out, and the spring haul-out ritual of power-washing and applying a fresh coat of copper antifouling paint to the bottom. I was not a natural do-it-yourselfer, but the fact that this was a boat was a powerful incentive for learning and doing. Again, boaters will understand. In Southeast Alaska, 95% of boat-owning families did it the same way. It would be otherwise unaffordable, no one else could do it quite the way you'd like it done, or when it needed to be done.

———

Our boat was trucked from Tustin, California, where it had been made, to the dealership on Seattle's Lake Union, where it would be outfitted to our specifications. We would then make the almost-1000-mile run up the inside passage to Juneau. We timed the trip for late May-early

June, to coincide with a usually favorable weather window. I arrived in Seattle with friend Tony Rivera two weeks prior to D-day, to oversee the operation and work alongside the riggers. We went back and forth to ship chandleries, checking things off the list as we went, and trying to stay within a preestablished budget. We installed custom name boards on the transom and front of the flybridge, fashioned by a colorful chap with a small shop on the Seattle waterfront, Omar the Woodcarver. Made sure we had all the appropriate marine charts and cruising atlases for the entire route. Linda, and Tony's wife Judy, came down a few days before D-day to outfit the galley, buy the food, and take care of all those things that only a woman would think of.

Late on the afternoon before departure I noticed an ad in the paper for a huge sale on Imperial survival suits at Doc Freeman's, Seattle's premier ship chandlery at the time. These red neoprene suits had already gained a well-deserved reputation for saving lives: Surface water temperatures in Southeast Alaska seldom got out of the 50s even in summer, and these suits could extend survival time in the water from hours to days. They had not been within our original budget, but now they might just be. At precisely 5:00 P.M. on the Friday heading into Memorial Day weekend, I called Doc Freeman's hoping they'd still be open, as it would be our last chance. A male voice answered: "This is Doc Freeman's, we're closed." Before he could hang up, I blurted that we wished to buy four of the on-sale survival suits. A pause, and then the same voice: "This is Doc Freeman's, we're open."

Thus we came into possession of four Imperial suits. We, and later the entire family, practiced the one-minute drill in getting them on; in them, we looked like grotesque red teddy bears. It was our good fortune never to *have* to use them, but they were great fun to bob around in. The kids would play water-frisbee in them.

Our route took us out of Lake Union through the Ballard locks and into Puget Sound, thence past the Strait of Juan de Fuca and through the San Juan Islands into Canadian waters. As we approached the white-water rapids of Dodd Narrows, the gateway to the Strait of Georgia that separates Vancouver Island from the Canadian mainland, it looked like we were headed over Niagara Falls in a barrel. We went through Canadian customs at Nanaimo, B.C., on Vancouver Island, then traversed the long, wide Strait of Georgia staying on the Vancouver Island side, as it offered the most direct route. We'd heard from friends who had done the trip that the mainland side offered more interesting opportunities for gunkholing, but we had been a few days behind schedule getting off and had to take a reluctant pass. Just beyond Campbell River we entered Johnstone Strait, which would take us into Queen Charlotte Sound.

Queen Charlotte Sound was one of the three open-water gauntlets that boats taking the otherwise "inside passage" had to run, the other two being Milbank Sound and the Dixon Entrance. All were wide open to the Gulf of Alaska. Of the three, Queen Charlotte was by far the longest stretch, and had the most fearsome reputation.

As we approached, the marine weather channel on VHF radio had been posting gale warnings for Queen Charlotte for the past few days. We elected to hole up in Alert Bay, a small native village on the mainland opposite the northern tip of Vancouver Island, and wait out the weather. The forecast for the following morning informed us that the gale-force winds would be abating, and were expected to continue to do so. Off we went.

A mile or two beyond Alert Bay we cruised past God's Pocket, a hole-in-the-wall where we had heard that northbound boats would duck into to await a weather window. Numerous boats, most larger than ours, were rafted up in the tiny anchorage. What wimps, we thought aloud. We should have taken the hint.

Within minutes we had left the lee of Vancouver Island, and were headed into building seas. Another few and we had passed the point of safe return, where turning about would have put us at the mercy of a frightening beam sea. The wind had indeed abated, but as so often happens after prolonged gales, the sea wasn't quick to get the message.

For the next four hours we took huge, breaking combers bow on, taking green water on the windshield with every one and then pounding down in the troughs. The sea-keeping qualities of our new *Raccoon III* were being proof-tested, and she was living up to expectations. Tony and I had our hands full, busy steering, jockeying the throttles, and just staying upright. Linda sat on the floor at the rear of the salon, her complexion a sickly green, hugging a trash bucket into which she heaved every few minutes. She later related that rather than being afraid she was going to die, she was afraid she wouldn't. It was the first and only time on any of our boats that she would be seasick. All the while Tony's wife Judy, a confirmed landlubber born and raised in Iowa, sat propped on a bunk in the bow, contentedly munching on snacks and reading a paperback novel.

For the next few days we traveled within the protection of the Queen Charlotte Islands, the southern extension of the Alexander Archipelago known since 2010 as Haida Guaii, or home of the Haida people. We limped into Prince Rupert, B.C., on one engine, having lost oil pressure in the other due to a cracked fitting. We were forced to lay over a day while repairs were made, and took the opportunity to walk the town. We all craved a long-overdue shower, and found a YMCA where, for a quarter apiece we could use the showers and get towels to boot. The guys went one way, the gals another, and Tony and I were soon soaping up in a locker-room-type shower with multiple heads on the wall. We could hear voices and splashing, so knew we were close to the pool. Suddenly an alarm clanged, and a voice from the pool yelled, "Everybody out, fire drill!" Moments later a girl in a bathing suit, looking to be in her late teens, came around the corner exclaiming, "Bob, fire drill." Then, as she took in the lathered specimens before her, "Oh, you're not Bob." I was lost for words. Far too late they came to me: "No, I'm Will, but will I do?"

The following day we crossed the Dixon Entrance into Alaskan waters, and the morning after were in Ketchikan, going through American customs. Departing Ketchikan, we were mooned by the entire crew of a passing barge.

A few days later we were home, fortunate to have a slip awaiting us at newly enlarged DeHart's Marina in Auke Bay. We'd come a thousand miles in fourteen days, including layover days for weather, repairs, and fishing. Other than for Queen Charlotte the weather had smiled on us, with fair skies much of the time, light winds, and calm seas. It was curious that in both the native villages in British Columbia that we stopped at, we detected the same faint whiff of hostility we'd encountered in their Alaskan counterparts. On arrival in Auke Bay we were all glad to be home, and at the same time wished the trip might have gone on for far longer. Our kids were glad to have us back; the wonderful couple that stayed at our house and took care of them in our absence were tougher disciplinarians than their mother.

———

Raccoon III would live up to our every expectation, allowing us to stay longer and in greater comfort at all our favorite haunts, and, with its greater range, to explore new ones. Like all craft with broad, flat sterns she could be a handful in a short, steep following sea, but safe and sea-kindly in the sloppiest weather if well-handled. Our home waters out of Juneau—Lynn Canal, Stephens Passage, Chatham Strait, Icy Strait—were wide, long, and not well-protected, but we were able to run in conditions we wouldn't have thought of bracing in our previous boats. We would learn from experience, when approaching places like the turn at Point Couverden in snotty weather, to place the heavy microwave oven, which lived atop the fridge, on the floor. It we didn't, it would find the floor by itself.

I took *Raccoon III* to Petersburg, 120 sea miles from Auke Bay, on a few spring steelhead-fishing trips. We could now make Baranof Warm Springs and back without a thought about stopping for fuel, and also Bartlett Cove, inside the entrance to Glacier Bay.

Glacier Bay National Park encompasses a considerable expanse of mainland northern Southeast Alaska. The entrance to the Bay, on the north side of Icy Strait, is a bit closer to Cape Spencer in the west than to Point Couverden in the east. The Bay itself is presently a vast body of water with two long, converging arms, Muir and Tarr Inlets; into each spills multiple tidewater glaciers. It challenges the imagination to realize that, a little over 200 years ago, when Captains Cook and Vancouver first surveyed the area, there *was* no Glacier Bay—only a single megaglacier whose face extended out to what is now the entrance on Icy Strait—appropriately named, as it was then choked with ice calved from the face. We never traveled farther west in Icy Strait than Glacier Bay, although we'd visited outer Icy Strait, Cross Sound, and the outer coast with Ben Forbes in 1971, and I would later become intimately familiar with that territory on hunts out of Elfin Cove. On our boat trips to Glacier Bay we always elected to anchor near the lodge at Bartlett Cove, and take the day-excursion offered out of Bartlett Cove up the Bay to the face one of its tidewater glaciers.

Our favorite among newly accessible getaway spots became Tracy Arm fjord. Tracy Arm is a deep gouge in the earth's crust carved by glaciers over eons; its mouth lies inside the entrance of Holkham Bay, some 50 miles south of Auke Bay. From there it winds inland 24 miles between sheer rock walls rising 2000 feet or more on either side, to terminate at the face of the North and South Sawyer Glaciers. Its jade-green waters, opaque with glacial silt, were studded with icebergs of all sizes calved from the glaciers. Some dwarfed our boat; many were a glistening, iridescent blue, and some had carved themselves into bizarre and grotesque shapes. Some massive ones had been deposited by the tide on the moraine at the entrance to the Arm; we also caught some, overbalanced by the melting of their submerged portions, in the act of majestically toppling over.

Innumerable waterfalls cascaded hundreds of feet down the rock faces. Narrow gullies, so deep that they never saw the sun, creased the rock and held patches of snow at sea level even into July. The pack ice near the glacier faces was, in June and early July, a nursery for recently born harbor seal pups; they and their parents seemed to be all over the place, and had little fear of us. Curious, if anything. Daughter Susan's dog Tara seemed to have a mysterious rapport with them. Mountain goats could sometimes be made out on high ledges.

The air temperature always dropped as we made our way deeper into the Arm; the temperature at the mouth of the Arm and at the face of the glacier could differ by as much as much as 20 degrees F.

The narrow fjord is reputed to be extraordinarily deep, but we were never able to confirm the depth, as the glacial silt-filled waters confounded our fathometer. It is said to also confound the echolocation sonar of orcas on the prowl for seals near the glacier face.

About midway along the fjord's length the rock walls of the south side have been cleaved to form a long, wide, and deep green valley— Linda and I both felt this to be one of the most beautiful places within Tracy Arm. I thought of it as "Happy Valley." Linda envisioned having a cabin near its mouth. One of my unfulfilled wishes was to someday explore this valley on foot; in my mind's eye I could imagine encountering colonies of Hobbits there.

Floating ice, we learned, was to be characterized by size: Smallest were "bergy bits," always a bit larger than they appeared and best steered around. Our kids scooped up the smallest of these in our salmon net for the cooler, and for our glasses at happy hour. We, and the kids, had to learn from experience that bergy bits looking to be the right size could be several times that, and threaten to pull the salmon net, perhaps with kid attached, overboard.

Glacier ice is dense, highly compacted, and lasts far longer than anything your freezer can produce. If we were planning an extended boat trip to an area where such ice would not be there for the plucking, we'd sometimes send the kids out to Mendenhall Lake, only a few miles from our home, armed with hip boots, a boat hook, a hatchet, and a few empty coolers, to gather a supply from ice calved off the Mendenhall Glacier. They were doing so once when a busload of tourists from a cruise ship stopped to watch, and several offered the kids hard cash for chunks of genuine glacier ice.

Next up in size were "growlers," the smallest of which might be fended off from a drifting boat with a boat hook. The biggies, bona fide icebergs, were to be given a wide berth and not to be messed with, as they owned the road. Depending on tides, weather conditions, and glacier activity, there were times when some ice would make it all the way out to into Stephens Passage, over 25 miles from where it had been calved.

The face of South Sawyer Glacier—the larger and more accessible of the two—rose straight out of the water to a height of around 200 feet, enclosed within rock walls, with peaks up to 7000 feet as a backdrop. We've heard the water depth at the face to be around 600 feet. When we were lucky—and often we were—we would catch the calving of massive slabs of glacier face, announced by a crack like a rifle shot and followed by a thunderous roar as the gigantic chunk hit the water below. The waves radiated outward to rock our boat, standing off hundreds of yards to avoid being caught in the shifting pack ice (given the incredible scale of things, it always seemed much closer). Most spectacular were the "shooters"—massive calvings that plunged deep beneath the surface, remained there for suspenseful seconds, and then shot upward through the surface like corks from a champagne bottle.

There are no adjectives, at least in my vocabulary, up to the task of describing Tracy Arm. It was magical, *surreal*, something out of Tolkien's *Lord of the Rings*. We made this place our annual 4th of July weekend pilgrimage, and when there we never hurried; it was always as though we were seeing it for the first time. We have, over the years, accumulated hundreds of photos of Tracy Arm in all its moods. Some, quite by accident, approach professional quality. But best of all are those etched in our memories.

Throughout all of our adventures in *Raccoons I, II, and III* Linda was our quartermaster, in charge of seeing that the troops were well fed, appropriately clothed, and otherwise well supplied. She was a logistics magician. She planned the menus, bought the food, and supervised the packing, getting everything stowed away to make it seemingly disappear until needed. She was so good at her job that over time I think the rest of the family took it for granted, but we shouldn't have.

She was also a master chef who could play *Raccoon III*'s Dickenson oil range like a fine instrument. And when I and/or the children came in cold and wet from the cockpit or an outing in the skiff, we could count on hot chocolate and freshly baked chocolate-chip cookies being there to greet us.

Linda hated to run the boat (all of our boats, from first to last). But even the skipper had to visit the head occasionally, so at times there wasn't an option. When king salmon trolling I liked to follow the bottom contours along a given depth, say 20 fathoms, which sometimes put us within mere yards of the shore. When returning to the helm from a short break, it was not unusual to find our boat out in the middle of nowhere, closer to the international date line than the shoreline we were supposed to be hugging. Nonetheless, both she and I knew that in an emergency she would be fully capable of getting us home on her own.

Our children did more and more on the boat as they got older and grew into their responsibilities. As he advanced through his teens David became a more-than-capable navigator and ship handler, and actually enjoyed the chore of cleaning salmon and filleting halibut on the back deck at the end of the day as we made our way in to our anchorage for the night.

Taffy, our trusty bloodle, never boated with us. It wouldn't have worked on our earlier, smaller boats, and by the time we got *Raccoon III* she was 14 years old and simply not able. She lived to the ripe old doggie age of 17.

Dr. Watson, the old English sheepdog we got as a puppy a few years after we got *Raccoon III*, was a constant companion on family boat trips and provided entertaining company. On one of his first trips as a puppy, the weather kicked up and we were unable to take him ashore for doing what doggies do for a full 24 hours. He lasted an incredibly long time, but it was finally obvious that the tide was coming in over whatever dogs have for tonsils. At length he stood up on his hind legs with his front paws on the rail cap, looking like a furry little old man as he piddled into the scuppers for what seemed an eternity.

He got to know all the shipboard routines, and where to be when. His nominal sleeping place was beneath the double berth that the salon settee made into, but he usually ended up on top of it, and on top of our kids sleeping in it. When salmon or halibut were brought aboard he'd harass them mercilessly as they flopped about the deck, but once they'd been subdued with the conker he immediately lost interest. When we anchored up to fish in a bit of a chop that repeatedly slapped at our transom, he went on "troll patrol," barking incessantly at the trolls he was certain lurked beneath our stern. Definitely effective; the trolls never got us.

He learned the ritual of getting into and out of the skiff or inflatable, not easy but essential for making potty trips and excursions to shore. Watson loved walks on the beach, and never required a leash. He was never at risk for running off into the woods and getting lost, or perhaps becoming a bear snack; with his herding genetics, he felt it his job to keep *us* from getting lost. His shore outings often included sitting patiently on barnacle-encrusted rocks while we fished or picnicked, and invariably resulted in a painful inflammation of his underpinnings (his privates, but because they're not private in dogs we referred to them as his "publics"). We termed that affliction "barnacle bottom." Watson couldn't resist slurping saltwater on those beach forays, which, unfortunately for him and for us, gave him the "saltwater droozles." If he tired of shore activities before we did, he'd go perch in the front of our beached skiff as a reminder to us that it was time to go.

Sheepdogs as a breed are not water dogs, but Watson did charge in to help us land and release our trout. He also got few inadvertent dunkings. As a puppy, out on the water with David in our inflatable, he once stepped off the bow like he was stepping off a sidewalk; the water was mirror-smooth, and we think he took it for a solid surface. Nonplussed, he paddled to the swimstep of the mother ship only yards away, to be plucked aboard. It was a relief to know he could swim if he had to.

Years later, while we were anchored up fishing at Homeshore, I happened to be looking forward just as our now large and klutzy animal launched an impromptu half-gainer off the bow, where the freeboard— the distance to the water—was about six feet. I gave him a 9.6 for both form and degree of difficulty. It looked intentional, but I think not. A brisk current swept him toward the stern, and he wasn't helping his cause by panicking and trying to climb back aboard himself, keeping him upright in the water and making it difficult to keep his nose above the surface. I tried to scoop him in the big salmon net, but the net was overmatched by the flailing 100 lb. animal. After some tense moments we finally wrestled him onto the swimstep by the collar. Once aboard, the relieved crew belatedly fitted their sodden, bedraggled pet with a life jacket for a photo shoot. I hope he felt as foolish as he looked.

A semi-regular crew member was Susan's dog Tara, a 57-varieties little animal she adopted as a puppy while in high school. Tara (aka Madam Grumpus) looked just like an Alaskan sled dog, and was extraordinarily good at running off and getting lost, finding porcupines, and rolling in filleted halibut carcasses left rotting on the beach by fishermen. We loved her anyway.

———

Given our range, which we could extend to almost 400 miles by cutting our cruising speed to 7 knots, there were many places we could have gone but didn't. Many we wish we had: the bays of lower Chatham Strait beyond Baranof Warm Springs—Red Bluff, Tebenkof, Bay of Pillars—and the bays of south Admiralty. Endicott Arm, Tracy Arm's southern counterpart, terminating in Dawes Glacier and including spectacular Ford's Terror. Outer Icy Strait and the Inian Islands. It was all a matter of time, and how we chose to use what we had. When we found places we liked, we tended to return to them time and again rather than try something new. Some of those mentioned we eventually got to experience, but only much later in time.

Raccoon III would be our last boat. We had no use for a bigger one, and couldn't conceive of a better one. It was, for us, the ideal Southeast Alaskan boat, and for fifteen years it was our magic carpet, taking us on adventures most can only dream about.

————

Our last adventure in the *Raccoon III* took place in late summer of 2000. A few years earlier we had sold our beloved boat to Greg and Jan Trigg, who had three children the ages that ours had been when we first got the boat in 1980. They kept it at the same stall in DeHart's marina, and had maintained it well. They used it much as we had, and Greg had also taken on some charter work with it. They bare-boat chartered it to us twice, the last time in 2000 so we could enjoy a week on it with son David and his wife Miho, who had come all the way from Japan, and daughter Betsy, who had invited along her old college roommate, Zorana. Greg had installed a state-of-the-art GPS, which during our years with the boat had been both too inaccurate and technologically unevolved to justify the cost. David and I had a great time using it; I wished we'd had one like it years before. It would be considered indispensable today.

Zorana—"Z"—lived in Washington, D.C., and was a city girl through and through. We'd suggested she bring along a bare minimum of clothing and personal items, packed in a few small duffels—that's the way you do things on a boat, where space and weight are always at a premium. Z arrived at the dock with a single huge suitcase that must have weighed 90 lbs. A harbinger of things to come.

To streamline our day-before-departure food shopping Linda, our quartermaster, made up separate shopping lists for everyone. The lists were specific, what to get and how much of it, and were not to be deviated from. Z was delegated the produce list, fruits and veggies. She, however, was accustomed to instant gratification when it came to satisfying her gastronomic whims, and it had always been easy with a supermarket steps away from her apartment door and a phone even closer. Resourceful young lady that she was, she decided that under the present circumstances she would bring the supermarket along with her. She arrived back at the boat with enough produce, in great variety, to last our crew a month. It required several filled-to-the brim coolers to hold it all. So it was also with liquor. We hadn't customarily made out a list for this, and hadn't bothered this time either, as our usual requirements for alcoholic beverages were sparse in quantity and basic in variety. Z took it upon herself to supply us with all manner of exotic microbrews, stout, malt liquor, wines of every persuasion, and an assortment of hard liquor that would have done credit to the poshest D.C. bar (Z had bartended in the past, and knew the recipes for scores of exotic drinks we had never heard of). *The Raccoon III*'s inexhaustible storage capacity was taxed to, and beyond, its limit. We left Auke Bay more heavily laden, and sitting lower in the water, than ever I could remember.

We had an easy run to Swanson Harbor the first afternoon, enjoying a good humpback whale show on the way. Tied up at the public float there, as we often did when there was space. Had happy hour, which didn't put a perceptible dent in the booze supply, followed by one of Linda's trademark dinners. Everyone was in fine spirits, looking forward to the week. And that was when the shit hit the fan. More precisely, it was when the shit didn't go anywhere.

One of our number emerged from the head bringing news that it wouldn't flush. I went below and confirmed the unpleasant fact—the switch that worked the macerater and flush wouldn't produce a peep. Going topside, I gathered our crew around and presented the facts and alternatives: I didn't know what the problem was, but would go back down and try to fix it. If I succeeded, great, we could proceed as planned. If I didn't, we as a group had a choice: We could return to Auke Bay on the morrow, shortening or even aborting our barely begun adventure, or...we had a flybridge that offered privacy, several empty buckets, and an inexhaustible supply of saltwater. I asked for a show of hands: If I couldn't fix the head with what we had on hand, who was willing to rough it for the rest of the week? There were six of us, and five hands shot up. Z had the look of one just propositioned to perform some unnatural act.

Realizing she'd been outvoted in a landslide, she graciously suggested we go on tomorrow without her. She would walk her way back to Auke Bay. It had been an easy three-hour run into Swanson, so how hard could it be?

Earth to Z: The journey on foot from where we were to where she proposed to get to would require trekking the length of the Chilkat Peninsula north to Skagway at the head of Lynn Canal, a distance of 80 miles, thence down Lynn Canal on the other side for an equal distance. And these were distances as the crow flies. Taking into account the obstacles that would have to be gotten around or over—mountains, rivers, bays, snowfields and glaciers—and the total lack of habitation or amenities—no Holiday Inns or Burger Kings—the time, distance, and degree of difficulty would increase by some unknown exponential factor. Had such a trek been proposed to the great naturalist John Muir, who had explored the wilderness of northern Southeast Alaska a century before and had spent more time, and trod more miles in it, than anyone before or since, he'd have laughed his dour Scottish ass off.

Nonetheless, logic was proving no match for delusion. Realizing our trip hinged on my ability to get the toilet functioning, I went below with a few tools and had at it. It took five minutes. The switch had corroded; all it took was removing it and stripping a bit of insulation from each of the leads to expose fresh, uncorroded wire. Just cross the wires, and voila! A flush every time. Even Z could cross those wires. We proceeded on schedule the next morning.

Zorana proved a fine shipmate, hilariously funny, interested in and appreciative of all the new things she was seeing and might never see again. She certainly pulled her oar in making our trip an enjoyable success for all aboard. One night she went out on deck while everyone else was sleeping soundly, and was treated to a magnificent aurora borealis display, the first she'd ever seen.

Our itinerary included Tenakee Springs, Pavlov, Homeshore—where everyone caught a coho or two—and Excursion Inlet, part of which lies within the boundaries of Glacier Bay National Park. On our next-to-last day we made a stop at the Excursion Inlet cannery, the last operating salmon cannery in Southeast. The cannery featured a small general store that served both employees and transients like ourselves.

In addition to her already mentioned excesses, Z had brought along a stock of exotic cheeses, most of which had been hardly touched—but the one she had a hankering for at the moment had already been consumed. Her eyes lit up when she saw a package of that very cheese on a shelf in the cannery store. This time, though, the quartermaster was looking over her shoulder and said "no." And "no" it was.

———

One of the many cornball sayings of surgical colleague Gary Hedges was: "It's better to be lucky than smart." On the water, it's best to be both. We stayed out of major trouble on the water during our time in Alaska; the worst to befall us was damage to two of *Raccoon III*'s propellers in separate incidents. We were smart (mostly), but when you consider some of the stories within this narrative (and some others not in the narrative) you'd have to conclude we'd been lucky, too.

Not all were so lucky, or smart. We've heard about "Million-Dollar Rock" in outer Icy Strait, but Point Couverden, closer to home, claimed its share of the unlucky or unwise. Couverden, at the confluence of Lynn Canal, Icy Strait, and Chatham Strait, was a 22-mile run from Auke Bay, and we either passed or rounded it going and coming on the majority of our longer outings. We often fished there. A long reef projected from its tip, to be given a wide berth especially at high water when most of it was submerged. It had almost bagged us the very first time we rounded it in the original *Raccoon*; that it didn't had been luck.

Once, heading home northbound in lower Lynn Canal having turned Point Couverden about ten minutes before, we passed a southbound luxury megayacht of over 70 feet making good speed as it hugged the shoreline to port of us—a little close, Linda and I observed to each other at the time. We anticipated it would round the Point, and in a matter of minutes. Sure enough, it disappeared from view behind us as it began the turn, and we had to assume the skipper would respect the Point and give it wide clearance, as it was well-marked on the charts. Unsolicited advice is seldom taken with good grace on the water, especially by the professionals who skipper luxury yachts of this size—even when they may be unfamiliar with local waters. We stayed off the radio and trusted that this one knew what he was doing.

He didn't. Minutes later we picked up his call to Coast Guard Juneau on the VHF. He'd struck the submerged reef doing 18 knots, momentum driving the vessel far up onto it. I would not have wanted to be in that skipper's shoes. We later learned that it required several days and two tugs to pull the vessel off the reef on a flood tide, and it had to be towed to a dry dock in Ketchikan for extensive repairs.

Point Couverden was nothing if not democratic in distributing its dubious favors to the mighty and the humble alike. While anchored up and fishing off the Point, we watched as a small craft that appeared to have been put together in someone's backyard out of scraps of discarded plywood cut the corner, inside not only us but the kelp bed as well. Watching the drama unfold was akin to watching Alfred Hitchcock's movie *Psycho*. You knew what was about to happen to Janet

Leigh in that shower, but were powerless to stop it. We heard the "thunk" and saw the lurch as the odd craft struck and rode up and over the submerged bar. As it settled lower in the water, its skipper gunned the engine and ran it up on the exposed reef to keep it from going down. Friend and frequent fishing companion Mike Franklin, fishing from his own boat near ours, already had his inflatable in the water and rowed in to see what was going on, and if we could be of assistance.

As we had surmised, they'd holed the hull. To Mike it looked beyond salvage and we offered to transport the occupants to Juneau, but the two guys on board—from Haines, 70 miles up Lynn Canal—weren't having it. They had a few tools but no fastenings, so both Mike and I rummaged through our inventories and brought them an assortment of nails and screws, nuts and bolts. Working through the night, they used floorboards and seats to patch the bottom. We couldn't imagine how they'd done it. They floated off the reef on the tide in the morning, and headed for Haines. We'd offered to keep in touch on the marine radio in the event they encountered difficulties and required assistance—we fully expected they would—but their VHF had a short antenna and limited range, so we soon lost contact with them. Since nothing about them appeared in the newspaper in the days following, we assume they made it.

We were again anchored up off Point Couverden when a small cruise ship struck a submerged rock in Glacier Bay and ran itself aground to avoid sinking. We were 40 miles from the scene but heard the vessel's distress call, and once again eavesdropped on channel 22, the VHF Coast Guard frequency. Point Couverden lies in a fairly direct line between the Juneau airport and lower Glacier Bay, and we watched as Coast Guard helicopters out of Juneau shuttled back and forth overhead, ferrying heavy-duty pumps and other equipment to the scene. We heard the first helicopter call the ship, wondering where in hell it was. He'd followed the coordinates given him by given by an apparently

191

flustered radio operator aboard the vessel, and found himself hovering over the town of Gustavus, just outside the entrance to Glacier Bay. Days later they had a provisional patch over the hole, were pulled off on a flood tide, and were able to limp back to port.

Fishing Southeast II: Trout, Coho, Steelhead, and Sockeye on the Fly Rod

Flyfishing had captured my imagination years before I would ever try it, in the outdoor magazines of my teen years and even a seasonal weekly column in *The New York Sunday Times*. *This* was the way the elite, the fishermen's fishermen, fished—not a mere monied elite, but a *skilled* elite. It seemed an art, impossibly difficult—so I knew then that at some point I would have to get into it. I would eventually teach myself fly casting (practicing on dry land when no water was available), fly tying, and the rudiments of fishing with flies, from books and articles, getting better at all of the above over time. *Remember that this, and all you read in this chapter, transpired decades before the Robert Redford film A RIVER RUNS THROUGH IT transformed fly-fishing from elitist outlier into the affluent-populist phenomenon it would become in the 1990s, and is today.*

A common conception about Alaska is that the State is a mecca for fly-fishermen. Overlooked is the fact that Alaska is a huge state, and only the Alaska Peninsula in the far southwest corner, a small part overall, has ever become that. When we first arrived in Southeast Alaska, and indeed throughout our tenure, fly-fishing was far out on the margins. There were few practitioners and no mentors; I would have to establish the learning curves even as I negotiated them. In the process I would eventually become a mentor of sorts.

While a seeming disadvantage, it worked out well enough. I'd always have rather been the guide than the client, and enjoyed the challenge and satisfaction of finding out what worked for myself—even while having no choice in the matter.

We'll take up fly-fishing for trout first, as something most fly-fishers from the northern tier of the lower 48 can relate to. There are many lakes throughout Southeast, but most are accessible only by air and some are sterile. We did fish a few of the exceptions with success, but Southeast trout fishing proved for us, by and large, to be stream fishing.

The streams of Southeast are uniformly short and connect with saltwater. Often the interface is a brackish tidal estuary, or "saltchuck." The trout that inhabit these ecosystems are dolly varden—actually a char, a close relative of the brook and lake trout—and a particular strain of cutthroat, the native trout of the American West. They are anadromous, as are Atlantic and Pacific salmon, but with a difference: While salmon spend the beginning and end phases of their lifecycle in fresh water and the balance in saltwater far at sea, these trout, although they spawn and winter over in fresh water, are otherwise at home in the brackish saltchuck and the fresh and saltwater at either end, able to move easily from one to the other in going where the food is. They never stray far from the shoreline. They are known as "sea run" trout, and are native to the Pacific Northwest, coastal British Columbia, and Southeast Alaska.

Dolly Varden had over the years been maligned in Alaska, and not thought highly of as game fish; although native, they were regarded as an undesirable species for their predation on salmon eggs, and thus detrimental to the State's lucrative salmon fisheries. Fisheries research eventually proved this a bad rap, but for years the Territorial Department of Fish and Game placed a bounty on them—25 cents for each dolly varden tail turned in. Unfortunately, the tails of dollies were indistinguishable from those of cutthroat, rainbow, steelhead, or small salmon, and much bounty money went out in payment for the tails of the very species the bounty was designed to protect. In more enlightened times the dolly has been recognized as the superb game fish it is.

Both dollies and cutts are handsome fish. Dollies are silver-grey on the back and sides with pale yellow or pinkish spots, and their bellies and the tips of their fins turn scarlet at spawning time. Cutthroat have iridescent olive-green backs and sides peppered with black spots, and defining crimson slashes beneath their gill plates. The intensity of color of both varies with the amount of time they have been spending in fresh vs. saltwater: Saltwater fades the colors and renders the fish more silvery. In some systems dolly varden can grow to several pounds, but are more likely to be in the twelve to twenty-inch range. Cutts are in that same range, but larger specimens are unusual.

It is said that dolly varden and cutthroat seldom jump when hooked, but the Southeast Alaskan sea run variants certainly did. The fight of the cutthroat of the lower 48 has been commonly maligned, but that did not hold for the sea runs of Alaska.

There were some stream-fishing and saltwater opportunities "out the road" heading north from Juneau, particularly Echo Cove at the end of the road system where our children caught their first trout—dolly varden—on spinning gear, but our favorite trout spots were on Admiralty, Baranof, and Chichagof Islands, accessed only by boat. We learned of these by word-of-mouth. Because of their remoteness, we almost never had company when we fished.

The trout we were targeting were predators of smaller fish—needlefish, sculpin, or stickleback. We used bucktail and streamer flies—baitfish imitations or attractor patterns—and both seemed to work equally well. It was fun conjuring up and tying new patterns, but it probably didn't matter that much. We fished them using the standard streamer tactics well known to fly-fishermen everywhere, casting across stream and strip-retrieving as the fly swung downstream with the current to mimic a baitfish in distress.

Success was more about location and timing than being a whizbang fly-fisherman—although proficiency helped. We would learn by trial and error where the most productive stretches were, and what time of season to fish them. The best stretches of two of our favorites were below tidewater, in the saltchuck, and what tide to fish them on was critical: Both had fishing windows on an outgoing tide, announced by "popcorning" trout breaking the surface as baitfish were brought down to them on the ebb current. These windows, when the trout fed ravenously, could be compared with insect hatches on trout streams of the lower 48, where dry-fly-fishermen waited for the hatch to begin, and trout to dimple the surface, before wetting a line. When we arrived on a high tide, we waited for the popcorning as the tide ebbed before wading in and starting to cast. While the "bite" lasted, fishing could be fast and furious. Fished at the wrong phase of the tide, these same waters could seem barren, devoid of fish.

Tackle needed not be expensive or elegant, but since much fishing was in brackish tidewater it did need to be up to the rigors of saltwater use, particularly reels. Some high-end trout reels intended for freshwater use will wizzle in the salt like the Wicked Witch of the West. The venerable and ubiquitous Pflueger medalist, favorite of old timers but spurned by nouveau tackle snobs, was all you needed. Add a five- or six-weight rod, sink-tip line to match, and any leader you happen to have along with you. As a preventative against the effects of the salt, my gear always went into the shower with me at the end of a trip.

Overall, trout fishing in Southeast Alaska was not rocket science—very much unlike fishing the spring creeks of Pennsylvania or Idaho's Silver Creek, cerebral games where intense concentration, tiny flies, matching the hatch, long, light leaders, and stealthy, precise fly presentation were crucial to success. All the same, it was great fun—and more relaxing. It never gave you a headache. It was a great way for Linda and the children to break into flyfishing, as the neophyte could enjoy some success amidst the irritation of untangling snarls and wind knots, unhooking flies from vegetation (or one's own clothing) snagged on the backcast, and recouping from abortive casts that deposited the fly at one's feet. Son David began flyfishing at age 8, catching small dollies in the stream below the falls at Pavlov Harbor using flies he had proudly tied himself. As I watched him pull in fish after fish, I noticed that his fly had become undone to the point where it was just a short strip of orange chenille clinging to the hook shank by a thread. But it was still catching fish. Within a few years he would become a master with a fly rod. Linda and daughter Betsy had to work harder at it, but eventually became quite capable. Oldest daughter Susan was too busy thinking about boys to be bothered.

Frequent fishing partner Mike Franklin once took a total newbie along. Newcomers to fly casting have to be coached out of "cracking the whip," which is not only ineffective and grossly inefficient but also snaps off flies. Mike watched as his pupil cracked and flailed away, and finally, when he was getting the hang of it, told him it was time to tie on a fly. The first one had been long gone.

We sometimes kept a few cutts or dollies for the frying pan, but for the most part released the trout we caught—in keeping with an increasingly pervasive flyfishing ethic in the lower 48. Fishing barbless—mashing down the barbs on our hooks—made this easier and far less traumatic for the fish. We didn't do this just to be trendy. Not only did we have plenty of salmon and halibut in the freezer, but we suspected the ecological balance in these systems to be more fragile than the plentiful numbers of trout we caught suggested. Trout matured slowly and reproduced late in these high latitudes, and we wanted no part of depleting stocks, even though it seemed as though we couldn't.

It came as a surprise to learn the Alaska Native take on catch-and-release. One would think they'd embrace it in the name of conserving a precious resource. But they detested it. To them a fish, in allowing itself to be caught, was offering up the most valuable thing it had, its life, in order to sustain that of the fisherman. To release a fish was to refuse its gift, an unconscionable act and an insult. When viewed from the native perspective it made sense, sort of. Recently some native village corporations have gotten into the sportfishing business, including flyfishing. Some of their number are now guiding flyfishers from the land of catch-and-release. Wonder how that's going.

Some of the streams we explored in mid- and late summer were literally choked with spawning pink (humpy) and chum (dog) salmon. The nickname "humpback" derives from the grotesque hump males develop, and "dog" from the outsize canine teeth that species develops, as they near the end of their lifecycle in preparation for spawning. It was almost impossible to cast for trout without inadvertently snagging one; we enjoyed these streams as much or more for the spectacle of the salmon glut as for the fishing. We walked the banks along deeply worn bear trails, punctuated at intervals with partially eaten salmon carcasses and mounds of steaming poop. Although we avoided streams whose banks were lined with brush and alder thickets, I always had the unsettling feeling of being in the presence of unseen company. Maybe we shouldn't have been there.

All Pacific salmon species undergo profound, degenerative physical changes as they enter fresh water in preparation for spawning. Death isn't far away, and they have neither much fight nor much table appeal. Salmon this advanced in their lifecycle aren't sought by either sport or commercial fishermen, even though they may occasionally strike a fly or lure. On one occasion David hooked a sockeye at the inlet to Pavlov Lake while trout fishing that was spawned out and awaiting the Grim Reaper. It was a dead weight coming in, in an advanced stage of decomposition, and yet was hooked fairly in the jaw. When beached it exhibited absolutely no sign of life.

Our favorite place to fish trout would have to be Neka Bay, of which we've already heard in the chapter on big fuzzies. It held both dollies and cutthroat. We'd get two days—two tides, occasionally three—of fishing in on a weekend trip. Neka Bay had at least as many bugs as trout. On still, cloudy days the no-see-'ums would descend in great clouds, and even bug dope was ineffective against them, leaving Linda and the kids sitting out these invasions under head nets. I, though, had a strategy: I found that if I simply ignored them and let them have their way with my exposed hands and face, they would eventually have no alternative but to bite on top of their own bites. The first bites would have ceased burning and itching, and the second set couldn't reach me through the first. It kept me fishing. Small wonder I caught more fish than they did.

When the clouds parted and the sun came out, the no-see='ums vanished as if by magic—to be replaced by hordes of huge, carnivorous green-headed flies emerging from the tall marsh grass. Those same flies would invade the cabin of our boat on sunny days—but we had a secret weapon. Dr. Watson, our sheepdog, was our fly swatter, and, as a bonus, our vacuum cleaner. He'd park himself on the settee and bonk them with his nose as they buzzed about the inside of the window. When they dropped to the settee, he scarfed them down.

Our other favorite spot for trout was at the head of Mitchell Bay, behind the native village of Angoon on the east side of Admiralty Island, which I had first "discovered" while we were at Mt. Edgecumbe. Given its distance from Auke Bay we went there less often, but the lure was irresistible. Mitchell Bay was accessed via a narrow but deep winding passage several miles in length through which big tides ripped through at great velocity, creating eddies and whirlpools that could wreak havoc with underpowered craft. The passage eventually opened out into the bay itself and a rich ecosystem that provided a haven for fish and wildlife of all sorts; the people of Angoon frequented it for hunting deer and waterfowl, and subsistence harvesting of salmon. The head of Mitchell Bay featured a reversing falls—actually, more of a long, reversing rapids—and could be fished effectively either above or below on an outgoing tide when the trout were "popcorning." Mitchell Bay was exclusively a cutthroat fishery.

In our earlier and smaller boats we would anchor in a small basin at the foot of the reversing falls, which provided just enough room for a boat of that size to swing about its anchor in the constant, swirling movement of the water. When Mike Franklin made his first trip there in his own boat but in our company, he rafted up to the *Raccoon*; when we returned to the boats after a morning's fishing, we found that the receding tide had left Mike's boat high and dry on a reef and tilted at a crazy angle, while the *Raccoon* to which it was tethered floated freely. His boat floated off on the next tide, and miraculously had sustained no damage. We've not heard the last of Mike's sometimes not-so-excellent adventures.

We seldom had company here either, but on a later trip Mike and I were fishing at the upper end of the reversing falls when a chartered floatplane came over and landed on Salt Lake above, taxiing in to make shore and deposit fishermen just above where we were fishing. The current grabbed the plane as it approached the bank, and as it accelerated toward the rock-strewn rapids Mike and I both waded out and pulled it to safety. This was obviously the young pilot's first venture into the back of Mitchell Bay, and no one had prepped him for it; it was fortunate we were there to bail him out, saving the plane and possibly the pilot's job. Trite but true: Alaska has old pilots and bold pilots, but no old, bold pilots.

The places where we fished for trout had a common denominator: They offered safe and secure anchorages where we could leave our boat without worry. There were many, many more streams that held trout and offered excellent fishing, but were as a practical matter inaccessible to us and almost everyone else—either too far away, without a protected anchorage, or both. A neighbor of friend and hunting partner Larry Depute, a biologist and avid flyfisher who worked for Alaska Fish & Game, was one of those who had the enviable task of cataloging virtually every stream in Northern Southeast as to whether it held trout, and if so what kind(s). That knowledge is in the public domain, and with the explosion of flyfishing's popularity among the affluent, has over the last two-plus decades been utilized by Juneau outfitters that offer day flyfishing excursions via floatplane to streams within a 40-minute-or-so flying radius. Guide and client(s) are dropped off and picked up later at beaches near the stream mouths. The sons of two Juneau friends worked as guides for one such outfit during their college vacations; maybe I was born too soon.

———

From my first exposure to silver, or coho, salmon the first summer at Mt. Edgecumbe, I began plotting an assault on them with a fly rod. They looked just like the Atlantic salmon and Steelhead that were the holy grail of flyfishing; they were about the same size, and fought in the same acrobatic manner, but alas! Unlike Atlantics and steelhead, there was no flyfishing tradition associated with them. In the fly-fisherman's lexicon of circa 1970, they didn't exist. I'd have to figure it out for myself, from scratch.

Their propensity to concentrate near the mouths of spawning streams in August might, I thought, make them vulnerable to a predator with a fly rod. As with Atlantics and steelhead, they ceased feeding as they approached their spawning streams; the flies and tactics that had been worked out to goad these species into striking even when fasting were different for each, and might be different yet for silvers. I knew silvers could on occasion be coaxed into striking flashy spoons or spinners—I'd caught a few myself on spinning tackle during our first August—and reasoned they just might take a large, bright fly with lots of tinsel and flash fished in the same way.

I was ready the following season with a fly outfit suitable for steelhead or Atlantic salmon (and also saltwater-resistant) and some streamer flies that would have put a New Orleans pimp to shame. The initial testing ground would be Redoubt Bay which, according to what I'd been told, had the proper ingredients: a sizeable coho run where fish marshalled at the head of the bay before going upstream to spawn. Redoubt Bay itself posed a formidable problem—getting there. It wasn't all that far from Sitka, but the route took one through a gauntlet of pinnacle rocks along a stretch of outer coast, without markers or any aids to navigation. A local, one of the hospital maintenance workers who had allegedly made the run many times, disclosed his secrets for negotiating this minefield. The experience was as hairy as I had imagined; pinnacle rocks first on the side and then the other, just below the water's surface, waiting to rip the bottom out of our boat should we deviate in the slightest from our line-of-sight-markers. We made it safely there and back. I later heard that our "guide" had wrecked two boats in the process of working out his route.

The silvers were there, evidenced by the characteristic salmon behavior of swirling, porpoising, and even jumping clear of the water when getting geared up for spawning mode. Enough to make any fishing fanatic drool.

After wiping away the drool I hooked three coho on my fly gear that day—losing all on the first, frenzied jump. I deduced that the extremely long-shanked streamer hooks I'd tied my flies on were providing these acrobats too much leverage. As far as flies went, it would be back to the drawing board.

I had only one more opportunity that season, and with redesigned flies and a more user-friendly venue than Redoubt, finally hooked—and landed—my first coho on a fly. I couldn't wait to return home so Linda could snap a photo of the Mighty Fisherman holding his fly rod in one hand and his trophy in the other. Snap she did. The photo showed me, grinning like an idiot, holding a fly rod in one hand and—Linda's blurred thumb in the other.

That might have been my fly-caught coho of a lifetime had we not moved to Juneau two years later. At Mt. Edgecumbe I had demonstrated that my formula could work—it had, once—and now I would attempt to prove that it was no fluke at Chichagof Island's Pavlov Harbor, which I'd read of in a national outdoor magazine during our first winter in Juneau. The article was about a fishing foray made there by Bing Crosby and John Wayne, guided by a colorful character named Buzz Fiorini, who we would run into several times later in our own fishing ventures.

Pavlov had much in common with Redoubt, and yes, taking that one coho on a fly had been no fluke. We would spend at least a week at Pavlov every summer when the coho were in, stalking the small schools moving about near the surface in our skiff, getting slightly ahead and staying far enough away so as not to spook the school—then, laying a bright, midsized streamer or bucktail ahead of the lead fish. Over the many seasons we fished there I, and son David when he'd become skilled enough (which he had by the age of 11), caught a *lot* of Pavlov coho on the fly, releasing most of them.

Pavlov coho were distinctive in that they seldom exceeded 8 lbs., but they were consistent and spectacular leapers. When our children were younger they had a great time catching them on Pixie spoons and light spinning gear, either casting from the mother ship or trolling from our skiff.

I would occasionally fish at Pavlov from shore, below the falls on an incoming tide, and once when I did so I had interesting company. I was confronted by an entire family of otters—I think there were five—lined up across the stream opposite me with their heads (two big ones, lots of little ones) out of water, glaring with bared teeth and hissing loudly in unison, at the interloper who was poaching their fishing hole. I felt like a standup comic who'd just bombed in front of his first club audience.

In addition to the fishing, Pavlov was the family favorite as a destination spot in which to spend time. The setting was beautiful, there were beaches to comb, deer and bear to watch, cookouts on "Flea Point" (another no-see-'um magnet), walks up to the falls at the head where we watched salmon in their attempts to leap the falls, and even portages around the falls with a small inflatable to flyfish for cutthroat at the inflow of the lake above. Both salmonberries and blueberries were plentiful. When there was a little wind we would rig one of our salmon rods with a kite, and fly it from the bridge with no fear of it hanging up in a tree. When David was younger, every year he would find a bar of Hershey's special dark in "Dave's cave," left by the mystery equivalent of Santa or the Tooth Fairy. Linda and our girls would give themselves ice-cream headaches washing their hair in the icy water at the foot of the falls.

Over time I would also successfully flyfish a number of streams for coho, concentrating on the lower reaches near tidewater where the fish were still active, bright, and in prime condition. Mitchell Bay had a run in late August that gave us the option of fishing for trout or silvers. My favorite coho-fishing memory from there had nothing to do with flyrod heroics, however: Mike Franklin's wife Beatrice, casting a Mepps spinner with spinning gear, hooked a big silver which immediately leaped high in the air and snapped the line. The fish proceeded to make another half-dozen gravity-defying leaps in succession, the spinner dangling from its jaw, literally thumbing its snout at the hapless angler. Prim, refined Beatrice had been brought up amongst the cultured, cosmopolitan elite of our nation's capital. She now let loose with a primal "SHITFUCK!" Oblivious, the coho leapt on. Mike and I cracked up.

Buzz Fiorini, mentioned in conjunction with Pavlov, knew about Mitchell Bay too. He would once in a while bring a few sports aboard his floatplane to flyfish the coho run, and it was there that both Mike Franklin and I came to know him. Once, as Mike rowed an inflatable across Salt Lake above the reversing falls on his way to the favored coho spot, he saw that Buzz was already there—up to his waist in the water, staring vacantly ahead, without a rod in evidence. Out in front of him a coho cleared the water several times, but Buzz paid no attention. As Mike drew closer, Buzz lifted his deeply bent fly rod from the water and proceeded to play his fish. "Oh, it's you, Franklin. Didn't recognize you at first." Readers who are fishermen will instantly recognize the charade; others, especially those with a devious streak, can figure it out.

Another memorable place was the lower Italio River near Yakutat, unfortunately fished but once. I'd flown up with pilot/radiologist Estol Belflower in his super cub and we camped overnight on the lower river, not far from its mouth on the sand beach of the outer coast. The flight itself was unforgettable: Estol flew us up the length of Glacier Bay's Tarr inlet and over Grand Pacific Glacier at its head, thence over miles of glacial moonscape and close by the flank of 15,000-foot Mt. Fairweather. Estol caught two coho on spinning gear near our campsite the first afternoon; the following day he went off upriver with his shotgun in search of waterfowl while I went downstream and fought one big, acrobatic coho after another, fresh in on the tide, amidst low dunes and within earshot of the surf breaking on the beach of the outer coast. Estol returned in time to see some of the fun he was missing, and on returning to Juneau ordered an 8-weight fly rod kit (Estol was known for enthusiasms never followed up on, and over years it became a standing joke between us as to whether he would ever finish assembling that rod. I think he eventually did.).

———

The silvers we fished for at Pavlov and near other spawning destinations had spent two years maturing in the far reaches of the Pacific. As nature's clock struck the hour, from mid-July through early September vast hordes made their way in from the northern Gulf of Alaska through Icy Strait, disbursing in the inside passages as they sought out their streams of origin. On the way they fed voraciously. They concentrated in areas along shorelines where tide rips, upwellings, and kelp beds concentrated feed, largely herring. There they were sought by both sport and commercial fishermen, trolling in the same places with the same techniques that they used for king salmon months earlier.

Why not take fly-fishing for silvers to the next level, anchoring up in those productive areas and casting, using even larger flies tied to imitate baitfish? Tide and current would aid in giving action to the fly, just as it did in stream fishing. My initial attempt was made one evening in 1975 at North Pass, a quick trip from Auke Bay. Again, beginner's luck! Two large—15 lb.—coho hooked and landed. It was like being handed a free sample by your friendly neighborhood dope dealer. I was hooked.

Some changes in tackle and technique had been called for. Heavier outfits—9- and 10-weight—were needed to cope with the larger flies, open water, and often windy conditions. The game was about distance casting—getting the fly out 80 feet or more—and I found that a 30-foot fast-sinking shooting head backed with small-diameter running line was better than a standard full-length fly line. Distance required refinements of technique, and mastery of the double-haul. Even during fishless stretches, I found the rhythm and grace of distance casting a reward in itself.

Much of the fishing was blind, but most exciting was casting to schools passing through near the surface, or to individual swirling, feeding fish. Coho competed to be first to the fly, and strikes were vicious. Their runs and acrobatic leaps made for great sport on fly tackle; most anglers trolled for them with the same substantial gear they used for king salmon averaging twice as large, and to my way of thinking missed out on a lot of the fun.

Saltwater flyfishing for silvers became an addiction, over the years seasonally occupying many evenings and weekends when I wasn't on call. North Pass, Handtrollers' Cove, Point Retreat, Lena Point, Point Couverden, and a stretch along the mainland coast of Icy Strait near the mouth of Excursion Inlet known to locals as Homeshore, were favored and productive destinations. On a clear day at Homeshore the towering, snow-capped peaks of the Fairweather range could be seen to the west, rising up beyond Glacier Bay. Mt. Fairweather, at over

15,000 feet, was the highest peak in Southeast. When fishing Couverden or Homeshore we usually overnighted in Swanson Harbor; we were far from the bright lights of civilization, and at that time of year—late July through mid-August—if we stayed up late enough on clear nights, we were treated to magnificent perseid meteor showers.

I gladly suffered through a few months of tendinitis in my casting elbow every season—"fly-fisherman's elbow"—as a small price to pay for the enjoyment it yielded. I wasn't the only one in the family to enjoy it: Son David became a superb distance caster, highly proficient at the game as he grew older, and Linda managed a respectable showing after paying her dues in learning to handle the heavy fly tackle well enough to get the big streamers out to fishable distances.

If taking coho on a fly was indeed doable, why hadn't others been doing it all along? The answer seemed to be good old Alaskan pragmatism. Why flail away with fancy, expensive gear that took all too much fuss and bother to master and maybe catch a fish or two every now and then, when you could troll and bring back a limit in an afternoon? It made no sense to first erecting every possible barrier to catching salmon, then investing all that time and effort in devising ways to break those barriers down. As I write this, it's hard not to be convinced by the logic. But it sure was fun.

Trollers caught far more fish per unit time invested than we did with our fly rods, but we had our moments. I occasionally limited on the good days, and some fish were in the 20-lb. range. Twice, I hooked, played, and boated one big coho after another while trollers nearby were being skunked. Sound carries well over water: "Look, that guy's catching 'em on a fly rod!" I know you aren't supposed to gloat in situations like that, but I think it a forgivable offense.

Unlike flyfishing for trout, this was not catch-and-release fishing. We caught the coho we needed for the table, freezer, and smoker by flyfishing. Every fall Linda conducted a "smokathon," devoting a week to smoking and then canning many of the coho we had in the freezer, making for several cases of smoked salmon per year. We had year-round access to this gourmet treat, and plenty left for gifts and barter (about the latter we had no qualms. Everyone in Alaska did it, and at this level it flew beneath the radar of the most constipated of IRS bureaucrats. And at this date, I'm sure the statute of limitations has long since run out.). In the years before the State's institution of "limited entry" strictly separated commercial from sport fishermen, we could have sold our fly-caught silvers to fish-buyers waiting at the dock—and perhaps become the world's first, and only, commercial fly-fishermen.

Fishing for silvers in the salt around Juneau did gradually catch on, first among a dozen or so friends and fishing companions, then, as the popularity of fly-fishing in general increased, among others who had seen us pioneers succeed at it. I wasn't the first to take coho in the salt on a fly, even in Juneau—I subsequently learned of two others that had done so some years before I did—but they hadn't pursued it and had attracted no disciples. I do like to believe I had some role in bringing it into the mainstream. I've not fished in Southeast for many years, but have heard that Juneau guides, outfitters, and charter skippers now attract flyfishing pilgrims from down south who wish to experience the thrill of taking silvers in the salt that we pioneered almost fifty years ago.

————

Why wouldn't the tackle, techniques, and flies that were successful in taking coho in the salt work for kings? Who wouldn't want to hook up with a chrome-bright 30- or 40-pound king salmon on a fly rod? Don't think I hadn't given it some thought.

At the peak of their runs, there are far, far fewer king salmon than there are coho, they're more solitary, and they're generally found deeper. The number of hours expended per fish hooked would increase by some unknown multiple, and not a small one. Improving one's odds by fishing deeper than conventional fast-sinking fly lines can do required the use of extremely dense lead-core shooting heads. These are neither easy nor fun to use, requiring a bionic casting arm and a hard hat.

A friend and I actually devoted one weekend to this quixotic pursuit. We selected Pybus Bay on South Admiralty as the place to try, given its reputation as a spring hotspot for big kings. We fished from an open Boston Whaler. The weather sucked, and between us we got no strikes in two consecutive long, cold, wet days of casting unwieldy lead-core heads, despite evidence of feed everywhere around us. At the same time we watched our spouses, trolling nearby from the mother ship, hook up with one king after another. Maybe one last cast would have done it....

A few years ago, and long after the last of my fishing years in Southeast, I read an article by a Juneau-based writer and fly-fisherman who had taken kings in the salt on a fly in the course of a chartered trip to the outer coast near the mouth of Icy Strait for just that purpose. Even before that, I had read of kings being taken on a fly offshore near Langara Island, B.C., a location offering similar conditions and high fish densities—and, high-end fishing resorts. Neither account surprised me. Taking kings on the fly in the salt is within the reach of any latter-day Ahab with enough time, enough money, and no compunctions about spending both. For those of you who check off the boxes on exotic fly-fishing ventures, put this on your bucket list.

———

Steelhead are rainbow trout that have access to the sea and take advantage of it. Born and reared in fresh water, they go to sea for a few years where they grow to sizes seldom attained by stay-at-home rainbows. Unlike pacific salmon, which invariably die after returning to their natal stream and spawning, a fair number of returning steelhead survive, return to saltwater, and repeat the process the following year. A few live to make a third spawning run. In saltwater steelhead are virtually indistinguishable from salmon in appearance; once in fresh water they rapidly acquire the classic crimson stripe along the sides that gives the rainbow its name (the process reverses on return to saltwater).

On the Pacific coast, steelhead range from Northern California on up through Southeast Alaska. Unlike coho, which they greatly resemble and whose ranges are similar, steelhead have always attracted a cult following among serious fly rodders of the Pacific Northwest. I'd known about them since my teenage fantasy years, and at last saw an opportunity to join that cult.

I found out that fishing steelhead in the short rivers and streams of Southeast would differ in key respects from fishing the large systems of British Columbia and the Pacific Northwest. These large systems had both winter and summer runs of steelhead, and the fish remained in fresh water for extended periods during which they were accessible to anglers. The streams of Southeast were limited to a single brief run beginning in early April, peaking around the end of that month or the first week of May, and lasting only until the middle of May. They were the equivalent of winter-run fish in the large systems further south. Fish were in and out quickly; bucks remained in fresh water for less than three weeks, and hens for a mere week. Timing was everything.

And, Southeast streams with steelhead runs weren't to be found under every bush; access to those that did would pose a problem. In 1970 I learned, I think from an article in *Alaska* magazine, then the *Alaska Sportsman*, that a prime one was to be found near the community of Petersburg, a short plane flight from Sitka. We had no connections there, no clue as to how we'd get to Petersburg Creek, and where we'd stay if we got there. Enter lifelong Petersburg resident Jim Hammer. A mutual acquaintance put us in touch, and without even having met me or the friend I planned to go with, he offered us the use of his family cabin—built decades before on leased forest service land right around tidewater level on Petersburg Creek. We'd get there in a borrowed outboard skiff. It was the start of an annual pilgrimage that we continued to make from Juneau. Jim and his wife Bev would become treasured friends.

Petersberg Creek is on Kupreanof Island, the mouth of its estuary diagonally across Wrangell Narrows from Petersberg. Making the run up to "Hammer's Cabin," one of only a few on the lower reaches of the Creek, involved a learning curve of its own. It required a high tide and some knowledge to keep one's skiff from getting hung up on gravel bars, in shallow riffles, and out of the numerous blind side-channels. In the early years we found them all.

Insofar as tackle, tactics, and flies went, I relied on the great stock of conventional wisdom on winter-run steelheading that was available in print from the gurus of the sport in the Pacific Northwest. In theory it was simple enough: Use a sink-tip line and short leader to dead-drift flies near the bottom, and use bright patterns that featured a lot of Day-Glo orange (they didn't have to be complicated, although we sometimes made them so). In practice, not quite so simple.

Once again, beginner's luck (It seemed I was rather good at beginner's luck.). My first afternoon of fishing yielded a bright, newly arrived buck steelhead of around eight lbs., complete with sea lice, taken, of course, on a fly. I hooked up with, and lost, a few more on that initial trip, but it would not always be that easy. I was still near the very bottom of a formidable learning curve, and it would take a few seasons of trying before I caught my next steelhead.

My companion in the early years was ENT doc Tom Stengl. He'd grown up hunting and fishing in rural Wisconsin, and by the time he arrived in Alaska had become a true predator insofar as both were concerned. A pragmatist with a knack for getting results, he fished steelhead with spinning gear and spawn bags for bait (the spawn bag, a small clump of salmon roe cured in borax and salt and wrapped in cheesecloth mesh, is far and away the most commonly used and effective means of taking steelhead in Southeast). I stuck with my flies, and think Tom felt sorry for me when, trip upon trip, he caught steelhead and I didn't—although he never said as much (I'm sure Tom would have outfished me had I been using the same gear as he). Jim Hammer had fished Petersburg Creek since boyhood and was himself a pragmatist—but he also flyfished, and once took a chrome-bright, 21-lb. hen steelhead on a fly from "Hammer's hole" out front of his cabin—a State record for that year. I still have a picture of Jim with that fish.

Over time I worked my way up the learning curve. I can't account for how it happened; seems I was still doing the same things, but now those things were working. Looking back, it was a matter of identifying productive water, detecting the subtle telltale swirls of steelhead beneath the surface in holding water, and perfecting the techniques for getting and keeping the fly down and drifting naturally through the lies and lanes where fish were most likely to be holding or traveling. Below tidewater incoming tides brought in new and eager fish, and fishing during rains as the stream level was rising but before it became turbid, could to be golden periods.

My regular companion on later trips was Mike Franklin. Mike was fine company and a fine fly-fisherman, and after paying our dues we both caught and released our share of Petersburg steelhead over the years. Our best efforts were several three-time-spawners that went about 18 lb. We were not above picking up a few tricks from the occasional fly-fisherman we encountered on the Creek that was doing better than we were. One was hooking fish in places we passed over because they were unfishable using conventional steelhead technique; we thus learned to fish deep, narrow slots using a floating line, long leader, a strike indicator (the flyfishing equivalent of a bobber!), and short, upstream casts. A technique not to be found in any steelheading literature of the day, and maybe bordering on heresy, but deadly nonetheless.

One season Mike turned up at Hammer's Cabin with brand-new stocking-foot waders. Unable to find wading shoes large enough for his sasquatch-sized feet, he had settled for the next-best thing—cheap black hi-top sneakers, size 14, with Day-Glo orange laces. He cut quite a figure. The laces were a perfect match for our preferred flies, and had he attached hooks to them they might have caught some steelhead.

At the time we arrived in Southeast, we were fortunate in that its steelhead potential had yet to be discovered far outside of the local populace. In the early years we often had the entire river to ourselves, but as the years passed sometimes did have company. We once encountered three sports from the lower 48 being guided by a savvy Petersburg local—I think their trip had been booked through the Orvis Co., the well-known Manchester, Vermont, purveyor of fine fly tackle. All had upscale gear, and were flycasting with impeccable form while their guide filmed them with a movie camera set up on a tripod on a gravel bar. Mike and I watched, unseen, from a trail above the river. Almost on cue, the camera stopped rolling and all three "fly-fishermen" parked their fly rods on the bank and picked up spinning rods bearing spawn bags.

Discouraged on one sodden day when the rain wouldn't stop and the steelhead wouldn't bite, Mike and I finally, in late afternoon, took refuge in the cabin. We had no sooner stripped off our dripping rain gear than a skiff motored up on the tide and pulled over on the bank opposite the cabin. We recognized the occupant as someone we'd occasionally run into on the stream and chatted with, a retired fish & wildlife officer from Petersburg with a reputation as a steelhead predator. As we watched out of the dark cabin window through the gloom and pouring rain, all the while thinking ourselves unseen, our raingear-clad predator rigged his spinning rod with a plastic bobber (!), baited up with a spawn bag, and on his first four casts proceeded to hook, land, and release four nice steelhead. He then parked his rod in his skiff, and before departing back down the creek, stopped to give the Peeping Toms across the way an exaggerated wave.

I also steelhead fished the better-known Situk River outside Yakutat, at Southeast Alaska's northernmost extreme, a couple of times—making a two-day float with Juneau friends over a 10-mile stretch of river in a rickety johnboat, and overnighting at a forest service A-frame cabin. The first trip featured four feet of snow on the river's banks. We caught steelhead on both trips; I took one on a fly the first cast of the first trip while my companions, fishing spawn bags, gawked (hey guys, what did you expect?).

On our second trip, some years after the first, it was apparent that the Situk had been "discovered" by fishermen from Anchorage and the lower 48. Yakutat was cashing in, having constructed a new motel and restaurant, and now offered boat liveries and a guiding service. Jet sleds were running the river, now cleared of logjams by chainsaws. It wasn't the same, and we never returned.

I came to love Petersberg Creek for far more than the fishing. There was the isolation, the silence, the tannin-stained water, the sheer beauty of the place. There was still much snow at elevation in early May, and warm days were punctuated by regular, thunderous avalanches coming off the steep mountainsides that enclosed the drainage. You heard them first, and if you looked quickly enough you'd see them. The forest service trail that paralleled the Creek all the way to the lake several miles above traversed beaver ponds, bogs with scraggly trees festooned with Spanish moss, and muskeg meadows. Fresh wolf tracks and scat were everywhere, but we never saw those that made them. We heard the mating calls of hooters—blue grouse—all around us, and if you kept your eyes open you might see one on the ground, still, attempting to blend into the landscape. At dusk, black bear regularly came out on the grass flats in front of the cabin, seeking freshly emerged skunk cabbage, and during the day occasionally meandered across the trail in front of us. Morning came early at this time of year, but no alarm clock was needed. It was supplied in the form of a woodpecker, who began his daily hammering at the sheet-metal stove stack shortly after first light.

The small community of Petersburg, on Mitkoff Island at the mouth of Wrangell Narrows, was founded by Norwegian fishermen late in the nineteenth century. It would become at one time the town with America's highest per capita income, based on its fisheries and fish processing economy. It was known as "little Norway"; even late into the twentieth century its populace was largely of Norwegian heritage (Jim Hammer's immediate forebearers had immigrated from the Old Country). Petersburg was by a long shot the neatest, cleanest, most well-kept community in Southeast. On clear days the spires of 14,000-foot Kate's Needle and Devil's Thumb, 38 miles to the east in British Columbia, stood out in stark relief. Our entire family got to know it, and the Hammers, when we attended a few of the annual 17th of May festivals, when its Norse heritage was on full display. Everything about it made me feel that, if I were able to choose anywhere in Southeast to settle, it would be Petersburg.

My last Petersburg steelhead trip was made toward the end of the 1990s, commuting from Idaho, shortly after Mike Franklin's death. I went alone. The weather was cold, it snowed, and the fishing was poor. On the last evening the weather cleared, and I hooked two big steelhead in succession in a favorite stretch well upriver from the cabin; both broke off after a first long downstream run. I looked down that run, which I had fished so many times over the years, for a long time after the second fish broke off... then headed back to the cabin, content.

Jim Hammer would pass on a few years later.

———

Finally, sockeye. This salmon, like the king and coho, is beautiful to look at and prime table fare, fresh or smoked. Smaller than coho, they seldom reach 10 lbs. As filter feeders, they were not considered a sport-fish in saltwater, but in fresh water there were exceptions: From fly-fishing magazines I'd learned that the Kenai River in Southcentral Alaska, and some river systems on the Alaska Peninsula draining into Bristol Bay, had large runs of sockeye that could provide great sport on a fly rod. They were sought with small, bright patterns; strikes were few and far between, but when hooked they put on a spectacular aerial display. Southeast had its share of sockeye runs too, including some

large ones that were targeted by the commercial gillnet fishery in saltwater, but most of those fish ran up streams or rivers opaque with glacial silt and unsuitable for fly-fishing. I put sockeye off my radar.

In late June and early July of our first year in our Auke Bay home,
the waters of the Bay in close to the outlet of Auke Creek seemed to
come alive with fish. We could see them jumping and splashing from
our front deck. I had no idea what they were.

Some asking around revealed that they were sockeye, part of an ex-
perimental run established by the research division of Alaska Fish &
Game. An estimated 20,000 fish had returned and were waiting to as-
cend Auke Creek into Auke Lake where they had been released as
smolts. The banks were lined with fishermen casting huge, weighted
treble hooks with heavy spinning gear, and retrieving with vicious
yanks. They were snagging them—and it was legal! Since it was accepted wisdom that sockeye could not be caught by hook and line in
saltwater, Alaska Fish & Game sanctioned the method for taking fish
that would otherwise go unharvested and were not needed for escape-
ment.

Enthusiasm overruled common sense. Here were huge numbers of
sockeye milling around in clear water, no matter that it was salt. Why
not try the methods I had read about? I took out our boat one evening,
stood off far enough not to be brained by the snaggers on shore, and
tied on the smallest, brightest steelhead fly in my box.

One hour later I had hooked and landed two large, bright sockeye.
Both struck hard, fought as advertised, and were hooked fairly inside
the jaw. I had invented a new sport!

Should have known better. For the remainder of that run, and all
of the run the following year, Mike Franklin and I logged untold hours
of futility (yes, I had convinced Mike I'd invented a new sport. It wasn't
a hard sell.)—never getting another strike, despite being able to feel
sockeye running over, into, and under our fly lines as we retrieved. Mer-
cifully, Fish & Game pulled the plug on their Auke Bay program, and

within a year or so the run had dwindled to nothing.

At some time in the 1980s I learned of a small sockeye run that came into Windfall Lake via the Herbert River—one of those fisherman's secrets that somehow leaked out. The Herbert was glacial, but the small tributary coming out of Windfall and joining it was clear; just above the junction of the two was a short stretch of holding water where sockeye stacked up awaiting rains that would raise the water level and allow them access to the lake. The fish that held there were silver-bright when they arrived, and had not yet taken on the bizarre coloration of sockeye in spawning mode—deep red bodies with green heads. The stretch of holding water was limited, enough to accommodate perhaps four fly anglers at the most.

The Windfall Lake trail that lead to it was 25 miles north out the road and then close to an hour's hike, and by the time I found out about it a lot of others had, too. Since the run was small, timing was critical and also hit-or-miss. The trick was to avoid weekends, arise at 4 A.M. for an early start to beat the competition, and hope you were lucky with timing. A couple of times we were.

There was an ongoing controversy among fishermen as to whether sockeye actually took a fly. In fact, the Department of Fish & Game considered a sockeye to be "fair-caught" if the hook lodged forward of the gill plate, even if outside the mouth. We were able to debunk the notion that sockeye never took a fly, as the clear, slow water of the Windfall outlet stream allowed us to often see what went on: Small schools swam around the holding water in slow ovals, and we learned to cast just far enough ahead of a school for the easily visible fly to sink to their level at the time they got there. If the fly passed by a fish by more than a few inches, there would be no response. But a fly that drifted within an inch or two might be quite obviously snapped at, and one that was dead-on would simply disappear as the fish took it. The takes were barely perceptible, and we'd have to learn to set the hook before we even felt it; otherwise the fly would be spit out. A bit like nymph fishing for trout in the lower 48. These fish were invariably hooked inside the jaw, just as the ones I'd taken in the salt at Auke Bay had been. But I must confess to also taking home a few that had been hooked *near* the mouth, and not feeling guilty about it.

More Bounty from the Sea

Most boats large enough to overnight or better carried along a crab pot, as both dungeness and snow (tanner) crab were to be found in Southeast waters in quantities great enough to support commercial fisheries. All that was required of the amateur was a sportfishing license, a small crab pot, line, buoy, and a fish head for bait.

At Mt. Edgecumbe Tom Keith and I had—once—scooped enough dungeness off the bottom with a salmon net on a big minus tide to provide a great feed for both families. But it wasn't until our Juneau years that we enjoyed this treat with any regularity. As soon as our family was old enough for overnighting in the boat, our children bought me a crab pot for a Father's Day present. The first few times I attempted to use it proved a lasting embarrassment. We caught no crab, and only then did I figure out that our pot had a collapsible frame, and I hadn't known enough to un-collapse and set it up before putting it over the side. We did better after that. One of our favorite overnight spots, Swanson Harbor, almost always produced enough dungeness for an appetizer and sometimes for a dinner, as did Wachusett Cove, a quick skiff run from Pavlov Harbor.

On one occasion we overnighted in Swanson and awakened to one of Southeast's huge minus tides. Everyone was eager to beach-comb on flats that were rarely exposed, so we hit the beach at dead low tide, 6 A.M.

In addition to sea anemones—"squooshes" to the kids—and large, multi-armed starfish were many lumps of green seaweed. Under each was a large dungeness crab, and many were legal males. It was like an Easter egg hunt.

For many years Swanson Harbor had been kept off limits to commercial crabbers, but when Fish & Game opened it to commercial exploitation, it was game over. We still put our pot down there, crowded in amongst the commercial pots, and when we pulled it, it would be brimming with crab—every one a female or sub-legal male. Those guys must have gotten tired of their regular elevator rides to the surface and then the free-fall back down, but may have learned to always expect a free lunch when they entered a pot.

King crab also inhabited Southeast waters, but in lesser numbers, and they preferred deep water. King crab pots were huge, heavy boxes with frames of welded rebar, and required a power winch to bring them from the depths to the surface. Only a few locals bothered to put out such pots; tending them was a lot of work and the returns often sparse—but one of these giant, spidery critters provided enough sweet, succulent meat for several meals.

During commercial king crab openings, a few fishermen brought their haul into the Auke Bay dock, put up a sign on the highway, and retailed them right off their boats. They'd be sold out within an hour. Fortunately for us, one of the crabbers was a friend who would call us through the marine operator on his way in, and we'd be waiting at the dock when he arrived. As I recall, his king crab went for about $10-$12 apiece. One of Southeast's great bargains.

In lieu of a crab pot we sometimes put over a crab ring when we anchored up, in hopes of hauling up a "dungie" or two or three. A crab ring is simply an iron hoop about three feet in diameter, over which is stretched mesh webbing. After wiring a chunk of bait to the center of the webbing, one lowers the ring to the bottom and ties the line off to a cleat. Every twenty minutes or so you pull it up and check it, in hopes that the quarry had discovered the bait and couldn't make its way off the webbing in time.

We were once the beneficiary of a phenomenon so rare that most locals never encounter it. We'd anchored up in Williams Cove near the mouth of Tracy Arm, in about fifty feet of water, and put down the crab ring as Linda was preparing dinner. Lo and behold, when we pulled it up the first time it contained a huge king crab! It happened again, and then again. Our son and a young friend stayed up late into the evening hauling them in. All of the females and sub-legal males went back over the side, but we still had a deck full of legal males that were alternately chasing, and being chased by, our sheepdog, Dr. Watson.

We'd stumbled onto a mass migration whereby king crab, for no apparent reason, came out of the depths to pass across shallows in a huge, rolling ball before once again descending into deep water. It had happened once before, on a hunting trip with charter skipper Tom Parke, who we'll meet in a later chapter. Tom had put over a crab ring while we hunted at Last Chance, and by the time we were back on board he had caught and cooked as much king crab as we could eat.

———

As transplants from New England who came with a taste for fried clams and steamers, we were intrigued to learn that clams were to be found on virtually every mudflat in Southeast. That's a lot of mudflats. But there was a caveat: PSP. PSP, paralytic shellfish poisoning, is caused by a marine biotoxin produced in some strains of algae, and becomes selectively concentrated in mollusks—clams, oysters, and mussels. We knew PSP from our time in New England. There it arrived in episodic "red tides," concentrations of toxic algae high enough to actually turn sea water red. Red tides, while not common, were dreaded events, forcing the closure of clam flats in affected areas for months at a time and wreaking havoc on the commercial clamming, restaurant, and tourist industries.

We learned that PSP existed in Southeast Alaska, but was far more insidious. It did not come in waves of red tide, but was endemic—always present, everywhere, in concentrations varying from harmless to lethal. Shellfish from most areas, most of the time, contained at least some; most levels were below the threshold of toxicity in humans, but not all.

Exhibit A for demonstrating what PSP can do occurred in 1799 along a stretch of Peril Strait, which separates Baranof from Chichagof Islands. At least a hundred Aleuts, who had been impressed as sea otter hunters by the Russians, died of PSP after a mussel feast enjoyed at appropriately named Poison Cove and Deadman's Reach.

Because there was no commercial clamming industry in Southeast Alaska, the state lab in Juneau did not routinely monitor the innumerable flats for PSP. The State thus had no official stance on the consumption of clams from local beaches, other than that it was to be done at one's own risk. Recreational clamming in Southeast seemed, to us, a sort of Russian roulette.

Nonetheless, clamming, and the subsequent consumption of clams, was a rite of the big spring tides among a solid core of Juneauites. My surgical colleague, Gary Hedges was one, and I suspect that most were, like himself, lifelong locals without experience of the dreaded red tides of the Northeast. They always targeted the same select beaches "out the road," which they claimed were always safe, and as far as I know none ever got sick. An exception to the "locals" rule was our colorful anesthesiologist, John Taylor, a transplant from Southern California and an enthusiastic participant in these clamfests. You'll meet John in a later chapter. I suspected the crusty old buzzard was constitutionally impervious to the effects of PSP.

I'd hazard a guess that the indigenous peoples of Southeast had been harvesting and consuming clams and mussels for thousands of years. Unlike the conscripted Aleuts from afar, the local Tlingit and

Haida had learned from eons of experience which flats were safe and which weren't.

One local bit of advice was that when you came back with a bucket of clams, first feed one to your cat, as they are exquisitely sensitive to the toxin—sort of like a canary in a coal mine. If the cat lived, the clams were fine. The problem was that almost any Southeast clam would kill your cat; they were many times more sensitive to the effects of the toxin than humans. The locals also said that should your lips start to tingle, stop eating the clams (or drinking the margaritas).

Almost all who were admitted to our hospital with PSP were people from the lower 48 who were cruising the unfamiliar waters in their own boats. Ignorant of the PSP situation, they indiscriminately harvested clams from flats of opportunity. Some choices would be unfortunate. One not far from Juneau was Funter Bay on northwest Admiralty, whose flats were invitingly accessible but whose clams were regularly loaded with toxin.

The effects of PSP are dose-related—to the level of toxin present in the shellfish, and to the quantity of shellfish consumed. Symptoms could be mild, limited to the aforementioned tingling of the lips, or severe, up to and including paralysis of the respiratory muscles. As a surgeon I was not directly involved with these cases but my medical colleagues were, and I recall hearing of those who had to be intubated and placed on respirators in hopes that the toxin would eventually be cleared by the body. There was a death or two every few years, from respiratory failure.

One lesser effect was almost comical: partial paralysis of the extra-ocular muscles, those responsible for the coordinated movements of the eyeballs. The eyeballs of those patients could resemble pinballs in an arcade game until the effects of the toxin wore off.

Perhaps Linda and I, given our New England backgrounds, had too much knowledge. Despite our love of clams, we only indulged during our visits back East.

———

We were aware that shrimp inhabited Southeast waters and were available to recreational shrimpers. Some friends were into it, did pretty well on occasion, and were willing to share information, but we never spent much time in the supposed best shrimping areas and thus never learned the ropes. Until near the end of our time in Alaska the only shrimp we saw in the wild were two large specimens in the stomach of a just-caught coho that looked good enough to throw on the barbie. We didn't.

It wasn't until the late '90s, on a trip with Barb and Roy Greening aboard their boat, that we gave it a try. They had heard that good shrimping was to be found far up in Excursion Inlet, where we were headed, and they had along a shrimp pot they'd never used. We saw a number of buoys on the surface that told us where the spot was, put the pot down, and let it soak overnight. When we attempted to pull it we found it to be hung up on the bottom, and were able to free it only after an hour-plus of boat maneuvering and sweat. Our reward for all that labor: two shrimp. We cooked them, made up some cocktail sauce, and enjoyed half a shrimp apiece.

Southeast Alaska's Great Indoors: The Religion of Hoops

Among sports in Southeast basketball is king—and with good reason. Dr. Naismith might have invented it with Southeast Alaska in mind. As a sport that can be played indoors, it is immune to the whims of the region's wet and obstreperous weather. It doesn't require sizeable areas of flat land, as do baseball, football, and soccer. The number of players required is in line with the number of available bodies in even the smallest villages, and the minimal equipment in line with small budgets. Its popularity, from the largest communities right down to the tiniest outlying villages, indeed made hoops Southeast Alaska's great indoors.

While Southeast Alaska lagged some years behind the lower 48 in most areas—fashion and crime, to name two—it was actually some years ahead when it came to nurturing young basketball talent. As literally the only game in town, athletic youngsters were funneled into it and "specialized" from an early age, just as lower 48 youngsters with potential are into one of several popular sports today. Summer clinics featuring high-profile collegiate player-instructors were held in Juneau, and attracted attendees from all over Southeast. High school basketball was huge in communities large and small, and for a long time was the only sport played on the interscholastic level. The quality of play was surprisingly high, as was the level of coaching. Players making the Juneau-Douglas High varsity roster were expected to forego all other athletic and most other extracurricular activities. Juneau, as the largest community in Southeast, was and is a perennial powerhouse, and has sent a number of players to division I collegiate programs. One won a national championship with Duke, and went on to a long and distinguished career in the NBA. I recall going to a cafeteria-style seafood place one summer in the mid-1990s, and standing in line behind a guy whose elbow was at the level of my forehead—Carlos Boozer of Juneau and Duke University, soon to be of the NBA, home on summer vacation.

The larger communities like Juneau all had active recreational basketball programs for adults. In addition to providing open gyms for pickup games on the weekends, Juneau parks & rec provided leagues for both men and women with several divisions each, which kept every school gym in the community busy every night of the week during the winter. I became aware of it our first winter in Juneau, as one of the teams was sponsored by Bartlett Memorial Hospital—the Bartlett Bozos—and several of the medical staff and technicians were on the roster. I had been a fair player in high school, and an undistinguished one at a small college that did not offer athletic scholarships (if they had, I wouldn't have gotten one). It had been years since I'd last played competitive basketball, shot a few hoops, or even picked up a ball, and the rust showed when I first worked out with the Bozos. But everybody else had rust, too.

Our Bozo uniform shirts were classics—yellow, with a large image of Bozo the Clown on the front. Despite the klutzy shirts, the Bozos weren't all that klutzy. We weren't all that good, either. The roster varied from year to year, but we always had some height, and some who had played high school or even small-college ball and showed occasional flashes of their old skills. The perennial hub of the team was family practitioner Mike Franklin, a terrific athlete who stood a sinewy 6'3" and had a huge wingspan. He had a strong inside game, and despite atrocious eyesight a deadly midrange jumper. I was the oldest, and between that and a bum ankle from an old injury my jump shot had lost much of its jump, but the shot was still there—well, some nights anyway.

We opted to play in a mid-level division, never being good enough to compete at the top level. We shunned the lowest divisions too, in order to avoid the overweight, marginally coordinated, out-of-control specimens that could be hazardous to one's health on the court. Over the twelve or so seasons that I played, we won about as many games as we lost, and occasionally even advanced to the playoff finals in our division (we never won one). We survived by playing zone defense, and walking the ball up on offense. Many of our opponents played a similar style, since they were as old and slow as we were. As a spot-up or rhythm jump shooter, that was fine with me. The younger teams that ran and played man-to-man gave us fits.

Some of the wives came to watch, and one filmed a few of the games on a camcorder. I obtained a copy of one of those videos, had it converted to a VHS tape, and sometimes showed it to interested friends. One watched silently for about five minutes, then asked when the game was going to start.

This wasn't the NBA and most of the competition was amicable enough, but some of our opponents, both teams and individuals, got under our skin. A team composed of lawyers calling themselves the Loopholes couldn't stop whining. One individual, an attorney who played with a different team, carried a reputation as a pugnacious bully both professionally and on the court. Well past his prime as a player, his stock in trade was dirty tricks—undercutting, swinging high elbows, and throwing out knees and hips as opponents went by. I wasn't there for the game in question—must have been tied up at the hospital—but word of what happened got around the next day. Kim would probably call me on the details, but the gist of it was this: Having had enough of such abuse Bozo Kim Smith, of whom we'll hear more in a later chapter, lit the bully's fuse after the game by calling him a fat sack of some-thing-or-other, whereupon the bully took a swing at him. He missed, but Kim didn't. Juneau wasn't exactly sunglass country, but the bully was counselling clients from behind dark glasses for the next couple of weeks. I think Kim became a celebrity of sorts around the league for a time, as he'd done what just about every player wished he could have done—including, we suspect, a few of the bully's own teammates.

We often found ourselves in the same division as the team from the Lemon Creek Jail. This facility was Alaska's only maximum-security prison, so their roster was packed with veterans and they had a statewide talent pool. As you might expect, they played all their games at home, in a first-class gym with a regulation-size court, courtesy of the State of Alaska. Judging from appearances and the way they played, their players must have spent all day, every day, either pumping iron or pounding up and down the court. No pounding out license plates for them.

Neither we nor any of the other teams in that division ever felt really comfortable playing there. There was something about many of their players that suggested parts misassembled or missing upstairs, screws not properly tightened. They were like pressure cookers ready to explode at the slightest provocation, or even none. I knew this better than most, having served as a very much part-time jail physician for a few years after our arrival in Juneau in order to pay the rent while my surgical practice was growing.

Our son David, a good athlete put off by the high school basketball program's prohibition of participation in other sports and activities, oc-casionally played with the Bozos during his last years of high school. We had neglected to warn him before his first game at the jail, where he came out playing his typical style: hard-nosed, in-your-jockstrap de-fense with lots of pesky hands—and trash talk! He was pushing his op-ponents' buttons and we could see it was working—and also where it might take us. We called a hasty time-out to tell David to dial it down several notches, for the sake of his own health and ours.

During the final year of the Bozos' existence we played a heavily favored jail team in the double-elimination tournament that wound up each season, and lost in a cliff-hanger—our first loss. The jail's next opponent played them close, the game ending with a disputed foul call and a game-winning free throw by the visiting team—the jail's first loss. Another would eliminate them from the tournament—and their next opponent would be, again, us.

Lots of players in the league knew players from other teams, as well as the officials, and what happened in the aftermath of the jail's loss leaked out the next day. The jail players had gone ballistic, and the inmate spectators had stormed the court. The official whose call had spelled the difference was knocked down, punched out, and given a black eye. The terrified victors were hustled into the visitors' locker room by prison guards and kept under lockdown for over an hour while the riot was quelled. In the days following, not a word from Juneau parks & rec. Nothing was going to rain on their pet community relations project, and they put a lid on the entire incident. The official line was "What incident?" As the next gladiators to be fed to the lions, we were not happy about it; what would happen to us if we had the temerity to win? We elected to forfeit, and our punishment was banishment from league competition the following year. The Bozos' long run was coming to an end anyway.

———

It was only during the Gold Medal Tournament—Juneau's premier spring event—that us folks in the Big City got to appreciate just how pervasive basketball in Southeast Alaska was, reaching down to the smallest of outlying villages. The Gold Metal Tournament, sponsored by the Juneau Lions Club, was a week-long early March basketball-fest which attracted teams from every outpost in Southeast, competing in several divisions. The highest division even featured a team or two from Anchorage. The event provided a major boost to Juneau's economy, as not only players but also boosters and fans from everywhere filled up the hotels, motels, restaurants, and bars. Games at the J-D high school gym, which had a large seating capacity, went on all day every day for a week. Games were always well-attended, and the finals of each division were sellouts. All games were broadcast on local radio.

Even the smallest of villages had gyms, home to the local gym rats—"basketball Joneses"—which seemed to include every male inhabitant between the ages of 15 and 40-something. The quality of play coming out of these sparsely populated villages was amazing. The teams from predominantly native villages may have been lacking in size but made up for it in speed, playing an up-tempo game—and skills. Most of their guys were fine ball-handlers and adept passers; some were hot doggers who obviously got their game from watching the hotdogs of the NBA. Among them were some deadly shooters. And they never seemed to run out of gas.

Every team was allowed to pad their roster with a few ringers— really good players, a fair number from Juneau where the talent pool was largest. That also allowed some short teams to get a little taller. For several years Mike Franklin of the Bozos (never Gold Metal material as a team) was a sought-after ringer.

We occasionally attended Sonics games on weekend trips to Seattle, back when Seattle had that NBA franchise. We were having a late snack in our hotel lounge after returning from a game, and arrived at the same time as several members from that night's opposing team, which was obviously booked at our hotel. I got to chatting with one of those players, Scott Wedman, who would shortly become a good complementary player with the great Boston Celtic teams of the late 1980s featuring Larry Bird. I was surprised to learn that Scott knew of the Gold Metal Tournament, and had at one time or another played with or against some players who regularly appeared in it.

Our Marine Mammal Friends

The humpback whale is ubiquitous in Southeast waters; we seldom left the confines of Auke Bay without seeing at least one, and sometimes saw them within the Bay itself. While they traveled to distant Hawaiian waters in winter and early spring to calve and mate, not every humpback made the trip every year, as we saw them in local waters during every month of the year.

Humpbacks are baleen whales, whales without teeth that strain their food, mowing their way open-mouthed through concentrations of krill or schools of herring. Our penchant for anchoring up and fly-fishing the salt offered up the opportunity to view them at closer quarters than most. We didn't have to go to them; they would come to us. On two occasions we witnessed up close the rarely seen phenomenon of cooperative bubble-net feeding, whereby a group of several whales works together to concentrate a school of herring into a tight ball. They do so by circling beneath the school while exhaling streams of bubbles. Mission accomplished, they then shoot up open-mouthed through the school *en masse*. An awesome sight that most never even see once, and a phenomenon apparently limited to the humpbacks of Alaska (we learned later that bubble-net feeding by solitary whales occurs in many humpback populations worldwide).

When whales approached closely while we were anchored I'd start and idle one engine in hopes that the noise and vibrations would discourage them from getting *too* close. But sometimes they did. One surprised us, surfacing close by and heading straight for us amidships, like Moby Dick heading for the *Pequod*. When no more than ten feet away—close enough to make out individual barnacles adorning its head—it exhaled loudly and dove beneath our boat, somehow clearing the bottom. The deck was enveloped in a lingering vapor cloud of whale breath—world-class halitosis.

Another humpback almost floated into us while "logging." We were unaware of this behavior at the time, and as we watched for what seemed a very long time we thought that the animal was sick or even dead. It was actually just taking a nap, and at the last possible moment before colliding with us, awoke and lazily swam off.

On one of our trips to Glacier Bay we attended the annual meeting of the Alaska State Medical Association, held that year at the Bartlett Cove Lodge. Part of the official program was a day-trip to the face of one of the glaciers on the sizeable vessel that made the excursion daily out of Bartlett Cove. The guest expert aboard with us that day was Chuck Jurasz, a Juneau-Douglas high school biology teacher who had established a name for himself in the international whale research fraternity by pioneering the identification of individual whales by their distinctive fluke markings. Much of his research had been conducted in Glacier Bay.

As we drifted amongst the bergs near a glacier face he told us of how, on one early venture, he had been tipped out of his Zodiac inflatable by a whale that surfaced beneath him. Alone, it had been a near thing for him in waters not far above the freezing mark. He vowed to hypothermia-proof his body against future mishaps. His residence was a live-aboard in one of the Juneau boat harbors, and he began every day, twelve months a year, with a 6 A.M. "acclimating" plunge into the harbor waters. You can imagine the skepticism emanating from the physician audience, myself included. Acquired immunity to hypothermia? Pure hokum.

All the while Jurasz was holding forth on the after deck, he was doing a slow striptease; he was nothing if not a consummate showman. At length the lecture was over; now down to his briefs, he mounted the rail with a flourish and dove over the side, swimming about 100 yards to a growler which he proceeded to climb out on. He posed and gave us a big wave and smile before swimming back to the boat. We knew that the surface water temperature near the face of a glacier, even in summer, was no more than 39 degrees F.

All watched closely as he came aboard and calmly toweled off. No shivering. No flushing of the skin. No goosebumps. No teeth chattering. It was just as if he'd stepped out of the shower at home.

One early summer evening in the late 1980s I left the hospital to be accosted by an ungodly stench that pervaded the entire parking lot. Seems that a humpback whale carcass had washed up on a beach in Seymour Canal south of Juneau, and Chuck Jurasz, with a handful of his students, had been making daily flights to the site with the aim of removing all flesh so as to be able to reconstruct a complete skeleton. On the day in question he had brought one of the huge flippers into the parking lot, and arranged for our x-ray technicians to bring the portable machine outside and take a series of overlapping films in order to map out the complex skeletal anatomy—actually, much like that of a human hand. I don't know how the project eventually turned out, but the stench at the beach site must have been several orders of magnitude greater than that in the parking lot. I hope the student volunteers all received an A+.

———

Orcas, or killer whales, we saw less often, although they too were year round residents of Southeast waters. While occasionally solitary, they commonly traveled in packs, or pods, of up to a dozen or more. The high, curved dorsal fins of the females were impressive, but the huge, triangular "sails" of the less numerous adult males were in the neighborhood of six feet in height. Orcas are toothed whales, the largest members of the dolphin family, and an apex predator with no natural enemies.

Many of our sightings occurred when we were fishing. When a pod of orcas came through, you might as well forget fishing and watch, because you wouldn't catch anything then or for hours after. Every fish in the area would clear out, alerted by the orcas' echolocation sonar.

We once left Swanson Harbor in early morning to be greeted by a pea-soup fog that limited visibility to mere yards. The sea was mirror-flat. Running on radar at a speed of only a few knots, we suddenly found ourselves in the midst of, and traveling with, the largest assemblage of orcas we'd ever seen, two dozen or more animals. It appeared that they were keeping pace with us intentionally, some close enough alongside to reach out over the rail and touch. They seemingly ghosted along, the silence broken only by short, explosive blows. It was an eerie, otherworldly experience, and at the same time vaguely disuieting; while there have been no documented instances of attacks or predation upon humans by orcas in the wild, unsubstantiated tales of mariners having been snatched from their boats are out there…. We weren't frightened, but were too enthralled to even think of getting our camera out.

One morning Linda received a call at home from an excited friend who lived even closer to Auke Bay than we did. She had witnessed the cornering of a group of sea lions by a small pack of killer whales near the government float at the head of Auke Bay. Panicked 1000-lb. sea lions were clamoring onto the float and swamping the skiffs tied up to it in attempts to escape the carnage. The water around the float reportedly turned red; the entire show was over in a matter of minutes. Having heard about it on the phone from Linda, I stopped there on my way home from the hospital hours later—and indeed most of the skiffs tied to the float were half-swamped and barely afloat.

We'd also heard tell, second- or third-hand, of attacks in local waters by orcas on humpback and minke whales. Those of you conversant with orcas from perusing National Geographic or other scientific sources (as we were) may be thinking that Southeast must host two distinct and genetically different populations of orcas that don't intermingle: resident fish-eaters, and lesser numbers of far-ranging mammal-eaters. Likely true.

———

Southeast waters were home to large numbers of Stellar's sea lions. These creatures are far bulkier than the sleek California sea lions that frequent areas such as Monterrey Bay, and balance balls on their noses at circuses. Mature bulls easily top 1000 lbs. Again, we saw them mostly when we were fishing; like us, they went where the fish were. Apparently nobody ever taught them that you don't play with your food, as we'd sometimes see them surface with a salmon in their mouth that they would toss high into the air. We once encountered a huge carcass washed up on the beach on Shelter Island; the snout whiskers were each at least a foot long, and thick as soda straws.

Although we were never so burgled, friends told us of reeling in half a salmon when sea lions were in the area. They were more commonly a scourge of commercial fishermen, where they would pick off salmon one after the other from multi-hooked commercial troll gear. They didn't discriminate by nationality; special "seal grenades" were used aboard Japanese trawlers to discourage marauding seals and sea lions. I knew this because I'd had occasion to treat, at Mt. Edgecumbe, a Japanese fisherman whose hand had been mutilated by a grenade that went off before he threw it. Although protected by federal law, credible rumors circulated about how bad things sometimes happened to thieving sea lions, far from any witnesses.

Northern Southeast had four major sea lion rookeries and haul-out areas that we knew of, probably more that we didn't: Midway Island in

Stephens passage, Benjamin Island north of Juneau in Lynn Canal, the Inian Islands at the entrance to Icy Strait, and an island off the outer coast. These were noisy, smelly, and great fun to hang out near and watch.

A friend hunting Benjamin Island, attracted by the noise and commotion, came at the Island's haul-out area from the land side and was promptly driven back into the woods by a huge, angered bull. Those canines are not to be trifled with. Some scuba-diving friends recalled being approached to point-blank range by apparently curious sea lions. Although never threatened, they found it a discomfiting experience. I've seen a couple of Stellar's sea lion skulls, and had I not known better would have guessed they'd come from saber-toothed tigers.

———

Harbor seals were also common. We saw them in greatest concentration in the pup "nursery" at the face of the South Sawyer glacier in Tracy Arm, on our July 4 weekend trips there; this was actually at the very end of the birthing season, and we'd have seen far more a few months earlier. The same phenomenon occurred annually in Endicott Arm at the face of Dawes glacier, at the southern extreme of Holkham Bay. Years before, and of course well before the Marine Mammal Protection Act of 1972, the State of Alaska had placed a bounty on harbor seals, paying three dollars per scalp—as it viewed them as significant predators of commercially valuable salmon. More than a few homesteaders became seal bounty hunters in the early spring when the animals were concentrated, and Holcomb Bay was a productive area for them. In those days the price offered for sealskins by fur dealers was sometimes less than the bounty, and hunters might find it not worth their while to skin the animals, other than the scalp.

Among the Holkham Bay bounty hunters had been the three Short brothers of *The Cheechakoes*, part of a family homesteading at the southern tip of Admiralty Island circa 1950. It was sufficiently lucrative for each of them to have invested close to $500 in single-purpose, heavy-barreled custom rifles chambered for the flat-shooting .220 Swift cartridge, with high-magnification telescopic sights—a lot of money, and remarkably sophisticated equipment, for the time. They regularly made kills—head shots, as a wounded seal would dive and be lost—at ranges up to 400 yards. It was also of interest to me as a gun enthusiast that these homesteaders reloaded their own ammunition for these and their other rifles.

We regularly saw harbor seals, in lesser numbers, in the bays and estuaries we fished when salmon were in. Inquisitive, their round heads would pop up near the boat to have a look-see, sometimes with a salmon crosswise in their mouth. During our Alaskan years seals were hunted legally on a limited basis by Southeast Alaska Natives, in acknowledgement of their cultural heritage. When our children were young they had locally crafted sealskin slippers, and Linda a beautiful sealskin handbag. We never did indulge in the native delicacy of herring eggs fried in seal oil.

———

Porpoises—bottlenose dolphins—often accompanied us while cruising. While capable of bursts of speed, they preferred a more relaxed pace. We found that by throttling down to eight knots or less, they'd stay with us for miles on end, crisscrossing under the bow.

(above and L) The falls at Pavlov Harbor, and mountain backdrop

(below) The 43 lb. king salmon that wouldn't fight

(below) Linda, giving herself an ice-cream headache, below the falls at Pavlov Harbor

(R) David portages our inflatable through the reversing falls at Mitchell Bay

(below) Mike Franklin on the rocks at Mitchell Bay

(R) David lands a big Holkham Bay halibut

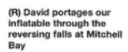

(below) Chrome-bright fly rod coho, close to 20 lbs., from Icy Strait

(R) Watson displays one of our trophy Japanese glass fishing balls

Images from Tracy Arm Fjord

(Above) Roy Greening (L) and the author marooned on the beach at Neka Bay, pondering our bear-trashed inflatable

(L) Whale researcher Chuck Juracz, showing off at Glacier Bay

The abandoned Chatham cannery at Sitkoh Bay, 1977

(below) Student and teacher, Mitchell Bay 1977

(R) Trout for dinner! A year later, David with a string of fly-caught cutthroat for the frying pan

A Glacier Bay Moonscape

(above) *Raccoon III,* anchored in Bartlett Cove

(above) Mountain goats
on talus slide, Mt.
Wright, Glacier Bay

(L) Sea lion rookery on
an islet off the outer
coast

(L) Hammer's Hole, just below tidewater on Petersburg Creek, from the deck of the cabin. Snow in May!

(below) Author with flyrod steelhead from Hammer's Hole

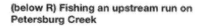

(below L) Jim Hammer beaches a steelhead for Tom Stengl

(below R) Fishing an upstream run on Petersburg Creek

(abover) 1974. Not every Alaska trophy is huge

(R) The height of fashion. David admires Mike Franklin's size 14 wading sneakers, with day-glo orange laces

(above) An Alaska Marine Highway ferry

(below) Gary Hedges, WGF, with 1971 Golden North Salmon Derby winner (Marg and Gary Hedges photo)

(L) hunting partner Hank Bryson

245

MESSING ABOUT IN BOATS:
(clockwise from top L) *Ginger*, Our Mt. Edgecumbe boat without a name, *Raccoon*,
Raccoon Iii, *Raccoon II*

"Happy Valley", Tracy Arm Fjord

(clockwise from R): *Raccoon III* crew, 1985; quartermaster and skipper dockside in Auke Bay, 1994; David at the helm on our last *Raccoon III* adventure in 2000

Hunting country: A high muskeg on Admiralty's Glass Peninsula, looking out over Stephens Passage to the Coast Range beyond

(above) Skana, our floating deer camp, at anchor inside Midway Point, Admiralty Island

(R) Author with a Sitka blacktail buck, 1978

248

The deer hunters: Clockwise from top: Kim Smith, Frank Rue, Eric Simpson, Alex Wertheimer, Larry DePute, mentor Tom Parke, Author, Randy Wiest (aka Dr. Rut). Center: Don Nash

The Deer Hunters

This is the longest chapter in this book. It deals with the longest, most difficult part of the journey, and the one that took me farthest from my roots.

———

The Sitka blacktail is the deer native to Southeast Alaska, and inhabits virtually every island of the Alexander Archipelago. They inhabit the mainland also in some areas, in lesser numbers. The blacktail is the *de facto* game animal among Southeast Alaskan hunters.

Because of its restricted range the Sitka blacktail is far less well known than the whitetail and mule deer, one or the other of which inhabits every state of the lower 48. It is the northernmost of the three blacktail variants that inhabit the Coast Range, and is closely enough related to the mule deer of the American West to interbreed in those few places where their ranges overlap. They look similar, but in general blacktails are smaller. An average blacktail buck will dress out at about 120-plus lbs., a real "honker" at 150; a buck of 200 lbs. will land you in the local newspaper. Does top out at around 100 lbs. dressed weight. To those familiar with mulies and whitetails, blacktail antlers are not as impressive—but they should properly be judged against specimens of their own kind.

Populations on the islands are generally high, but subject to the cyclic fluctuations so favored by nature. Weather is by far the most critical determinant: A succession of hard winters sends numbers plummeting, while a succession of easy ones can lead to overpopulation with over-browsing, stunting, and disease. Predation by wolves plays a significant role on the mainland and on the islands of central and southern Southeast Alaska, but there were no wolves on the ABC islands where we hunted. Despite the popularity of hunting, human predation plays a negligible role. There aren't nearly enough hunters, and much deer habitat is inaccessible. Coastal brown bear do prey on deer in the ABC islands, but the effect of such is no greater than that of humans.

The conditions described allowed for lengthy hunting seasons and liberal bag limits in most areas and most years. The game management areas we hunted out of both Sitka and Juneau had, ordinarily, a season limit of four and seasons that ran from August 1 through December 31, with the last three months open to the hunting of either sex. Such long seasons and liberal limits must seem mind-blowing to deer hunters the lower 48, other than in a few southern states. They were conducive to a better hunting experience, and a safer one; with hunting pressure spread out over time, not everyone was out there at the same time, and even in areas easily accessible from Juneau it was almost unheard of to encounter another hunter that was not from your party. And, no one was trigger-happy. If you didn't bag a deer this time out, there was always a next time.

Blacktail behavior differed from that of their whitetail and mule deer brethren, influenced by the unique terrain and habitat of a mountainous, temperate rainforest, and thus they were hunted differently. Blacktail had at their disposal altitudes of from sea level to over 3000 feet in places, all within a short horizontal distance, and they made use of it. Their preference for different altitudes at different times during the season divided hunters into three classes: First, the "iron men" who did early-season hunts in the alpine, above tree line. Many deer spent summers in this zone, away from the heat and taking advantage of the lush browse offered in the high country during summer's brief window. Hunters of the alpine glassed the open bowls above tree line, then stalked to within shooting distance. Given the vertical distances they covered first getting to their quarry and then getting back down with it, they truly earned their venison.

Last, the late-season hunters, whose goal was the most deer for the least expenditure of time and effort. They hunted the beaches, where deer were concentrated when snow and lack of forage drove them from higher elevations.

Most hunters, including myself and those I hunted with, favored the midseason. Not only were deer spread out from top to bottom, but it also coincided with the rut, or mating season, when they were more active in daylight hours and bucks less cautious. During the midseason deer were "still-hunted" at a variety of altitudes, the hunter working his way slowly through the forest and along the edges of muskegs, with frequent pauses. This was commonly combined with the periodic use of a deer call—which we will get to shortly. Midseason hunts were considered "quality hunts" by the Department of Fish and Game, as they maximized the challenge and the outdoor experience for the hunter.

Blacktail venison is delicious, several cuts above any other we've ever tasted. Lean but tender, and without a hint of gaminess. Grilled backstrap, venison steaks, or venison pot roast the way Linda does it is gourmet fare fit for royalty. Whether it's genetics, the diet available to the deer of Southeast, the fact that the meat remained in prime condition during the cool weather of our hunts, and that we took meticulous care of it from forest to freezer, I cannot say. Probably all contributed.

One late afternoon on arriving home from work, I caught all three children watching the conclusion of Walt Disney's *Bambi* on TV. There wasn't a dry eye between them, and the youngest two were bawling. I asked Linda what was for dinner, and when she said, "Venison," all three forgot their blubbering, perked up, and chirped in unison, "Yum, deer meat!"

Southeast Alaskan venison checked all the nutritional and eco-boxes before there were even boxes to check: organic, low cholesterol, sustainable, low carbon footprint, et cetera. Early on, we took our skinned and quartered carcasses to professionals for butchering and packaging—virtually every supermarket and butcher shop in Sitka and Juneau offered this service throughout the long deer season, most did a good job, and the charges were very reasonable. Later we would do this ourselves whenever I had the time. That way we were able to customize the cuts and portions to exactly the way we liked them.

———

Given lots of deer, lots of habitat, and low hunting pressure, one might be tempted to think that the hunting of blacktail deer in Southeast Alaska was hardly hunting at all, about as sporting as picking up your shrink-wrapped meat at the local supermarket. To this suburban cheechako newly arrived at Mt. Edgecumbe, nothing could have been further from the truth. And it remained just as far from the truth even years later, after I'd become a reasonably proficient hunter.

The mysteries of deer hunting remained largely unrevealed during my two seasons at Mt. Edgecumbe; curiously, none of the veteran members of the medical staff were into it, and as a clueless cheechako I was reluctant to impose myself on some others I knew to be veteran hunters. I hunted little the first season.

With the coming of our second year there arrived a few new staff members who did have interest—but who were every bit as clueless as I. We were together at the very bottom of the learning curve, trying to teach ourselves without tutor or textbook. Much time was spent in hunting all the wrong places: there was no one to tell us that logged-over terrain—clearcuts through which we trekked on logging roads—were devoid of game. Our outings were good exercise, but also exercises in futility. Up until the last day of my second and final deer season at Mt. Edgecumbe, I saw a grand total of one deer while hunting—its white rump, that is, with its raised tail literally giving me the finger as it bounced off and out of sight. Just as well we didn't shoot anything on those earliest hunts, as we would have had no idea of what to do next.

On the last day of that last season I finally shot not one but two deer, as related in an earlier chapter. Taking them on the beach in the late-season was actually no great accomplishment, although it seemed so to me at the time. The most significant impact of that experience was to affirm that I had made the right decision in choosing to become a hunter. I don't believe anyone can really answer that question until confronted with his personal moment of truth.

I did take away some other things of value from my low-yield two-year effort: comfort, familiarity, and a degree of competence with hunting firearms. Field-dressing game, a skill that came easily given my profession. An introduction to the making and use of deer calls. There was still so much to learn, and on leaving Mt. Edgecumbe I believed there might not be another opportunity (New England had whitetails, but it also had lots of hunters and short seasons, and my one Maine venture a year later made me imagine what it must be like to walk through a combat zone in the Vietnam jungle). There would be another opportunity—but it would have to wait for our move to Juneau two years hence, where this story really begins.

―――

The first two Juneau years were busy ones, occupied by the building of a practice as well as overseeing the building of our new home. But I watched, talked to people, and absorbed all I could in preparation for eventually launching an assault on the deer population. In the process I bonded with two kindred spirits, family practice physician Kim Smith and dentist Eric Simpson.

As aspiring but close to clueless deer hunters, we three had much in common. Both were eight years younger than I, but we had all landed in Juneau at about the same time—Kim from an upscale Detroit suburb, Eric from Texas. Like myself, neither had grown up in a hunting family, and both had hunted—a little. We would form the core of a group that would hunt together for the next several decades.

The three of us observed, compared notes, and plotted. We'd watched with envy as some of the larger boats coming into Juneau's harbors offloaded deer after deer in the wake of successful, extended hunts, and it was dawning on us that our odds of success could be increased by destination-hunting, getting as far away as possible and staying out as long as possible.

———

By 1976 Eric had acquired a boat, an aging 32-foot beater named the *Salty Dog* that seemed sizeable enough for a destination hunt, and we planned one. Our late fall one-week trip would take us first to Pavlov Harbor on Chichagof Island, then back across Chatham Strait to Hawk Inlet, on Admiralty. Off we went, in good spirits, with high hopes.

Our results wouldn't match our enthusiasm. We weren't helped by the fact that northern Southeast Alaska had just suffered through a series of heavy winters, and deer populations were down. In three days at Pavlov we saw a grand total of one doe, which I'd brought in with a deer call—my first successful use of a gadget I'd learned about at Mt. Edgecumbe. Eric had a hasty shot from close range and couldn't believe he'd missed, but miss he did. He thought it must have been his scope or rifle that was off, and when we emerged from the woods late that afternoon he set up an impromptu target on a tree to check it out. The rifle was spot-on. Most likely he'd fallen prey to "buck fever," a very real phenomenon. He would soon develop immunity, and become a cool and deadly shot.

———

We should digress for a moment and talk about deer calls. Most hunters of deer in the lower 48 have never heard of them; in Southeast Alaska, everyone has. They come in many forms, from the folded leaves used by some Alaska Natives to store-bought, and everything in between. When blown, they produce a plaintive bleat very much like that of the predator calls used by hunters in the lower 48 to lure in coyotes. In this case, it is intended to mimic a fawn in distress. The call is widely used and effective, but only within that specific time window when fawns are in the process of becoming independent from their mothers and often wander off. The bleat of a call triggers the maternal instinct, and does will come running to the aid of their errant offspring (who, at that point, don't need any help). This time happily coincides with the rut, when randy bucks were on the prowl for female companionship, and was at its peak from late October through the end of November. To the best of my knowledge pedophilia is unknown in the deer world, and bucks have not the slightest interest in fawns, but they know that where there's a fawn there's apt to be a doe.

Many hunters manufactured their own deer calls. I made mine from wooden yardsticks cut in 3" lengths, sandpapered to produce a sound chamber, with a thick rubber band for a diaphragm and thinner bands to hold the two pieces together. The product could be tuned to the precise bleat frequency and volume that the maker was certain worked best, but no two homemade calls ever sounded exactly alike. We would find that when the deer were in the proper frame of mind, they didn't seem to care.

Larry DePute, who we'll meet shortly, later presented me with a finely crafted carved wooden call that was less affected by the damp weather that sometimes wreaked havoc with yardstick calls. It worked as well as mine at their best, and became a favorite. Kim never got the hang of deer call manufacture. I likened blowing on calls he'd made to blowing into a baloney sandwich. He'd later buy his.

Deer, both bucks and does, responded to calls in various ways, from hesitant skulking to reckless charging. Rarely a charger would come to within a few feet, making shooting them a matter of self-defense. They could be called in from surprising distances, and a call might bring in a doe with an amorous buck butt-sniffing close behind.

There are few veteran deer callers that haven't been "snorted" at least a time or two. A snort is a violent, loud exhalation made by a doe when alarmed, possibly to alert her fawn(s) to danger, a fearsome sound totally out of keeping with the appearance of the animal. Hunters were prone to being snorted when they called up a doe on their blind side, and the animal approached undetected to within yards or even feet. Upon discovering the deception, her sudden snort at close range was enough to levitate the unsuspecting hunter and send his heart rate soaring (I know, I've been there). In my experience a snorter never stayed around long enough to get shot at.

The reader might be wondering: Might the sound of a bleating fawn also be of interest to a big fuzzy? Yes. The first time I heard about it was from the Native Alaskan at Mt. Edgecumbe who first told me about calling deer. He'd called in a fuzzy while deer hunting with a rifle chambered for the .22 hornet cartridge, fine for woodchucks at close range but downright wimpish for anything larger, including deer. Against a fuzzy, lawn darts might be a better choice. At any rate, our hunter spent an hour cowering in silence beneath a huge blown-down spruce, hardly daring to breathe, until he was sure the coast was clear. Since then I've heard of other instances, one of which was associated with a fatal predatory attack. Neither I, nor anyone I've hunted with, has ever called in a bear—at least we were never aware of having done so. How many might have been attracted to a call and silently departed upon discovering the fraud? Anyone's guess. Mine is at least a few. Maybe a lot.

I became by default, and by virtue of some early success, our merry band's Stradivarius of call making, and Paganini of deer calling. The "system" I adopted was first related to me at Mt. Edgecumbe, and I'd find it similar to that used by most veteran callers; it proved effective to where it needed no modification even as I gained more experience. Pick a spot that offers both a field of view and some degree of concealment, or at least a blending into the background. Wait five minutes before blowing a series of two or three bleats, and when you do, put some *soul* into it. Repeat about every five minutes for a total of three, and be sure and wait five minutes after the last sequence before moving cautiously on. If a deer materializes at any point in the sequence and appears hesitant, attempt to work it in closer with single, soft bleats. Don't overdo it. The call can also be effective in bringing closer, or at least stopping, a deer that you've spotted while still-hunting. Calling is unlikely to be effective when the sound has to compete with that of wind, or of running water. Calling very late in the season? Forget it. Fawns are out of the nest, and the rut's over. Deer of both sexes simply ignore it; I've watched them do so.

For a few years I basked in the reputation as the pied piper of deer, but it couldn't last. My mysterious "gift" wasn't so mysterious, and it was inevitable that the others in our growing group would get the hang of it, each making or buying their own calls and becoming (almost?) as effective with them as I was.

———

Back to the *Salty Dog* hunt. The following day Eric and I hunted together, this time ascending a dome-shaped knob of about 1000 feet on the opposite side of Pavlov Harbor. As the steep terrain leveled out near the top, we separated: Eric went one way and I the other, intending to meet up on the opposite side of the knob. We figured it might not take much more than 40 minutes to each hunt the half-circle and come together. Unbeknownst to us, what had appeared as a knob from our boat was actually the nose of a long ridge that headed directly away from the Harbor. Of course we never met up, he hunting along the front side of the ridge and I along the back side, both putting ever more distance between us and the beach we'd come in on.

It had been a clear day, but the light begins to fade early in these latitudes at that time of year. The sun was dipping low when it dawned that I was not about to encounter Eric, and it was way past time to make tracks back toward the boat. I made a rapid, very steep, sometimes scary descent as it got darker, arriving at the base of the knob with just enough light left to see that I had come down at the back of Pavlov Lake, which was above the falls and behind the Harbor. I was a long way from our boat but at least I knew where I was, and after an hour of crashing brush in the semi-darkness and then walking the beach, arrived opposite the anchored Salty Dog, where Kim was (of course) already aboard and wondering about us. He saw my flashlight, picked me up in the Zodiac, and off we went in search of Eric. We found him well down the beach outside the harbor, in Cedar Cove, a long way from the boat, 180 degrees and a *very* long way from where I had come out.

The lesson: Make use of topographical maps, if you have them, but most important, always take a compass bearing on the beach before you go into the woods, and *always rely on your compass rather than your instincts* when coming out. Doing so ensures that you'll come back out somewhere near where you went in.

When the hunt shifted from Pavlov to Hawk Inlet, it was with a rising sense of desperation; time was growing short, the sand was running out of the hourglass. On the next-to-last day the three of us stayed together as we worked our way higher and farther back than we'd ever gone before. We ultimately came out on a bench of broken muskegs with patchy snow, beneath a somber overcast. It was the first snow we'd encountered, and the deeriest place we'd seen yet. We took positions out of sight from one another, and the pied piper blew on his call. It was about 1:30 P.M.

Just as if it had been scripted, a forkhorn buck silently appeared at the edge of the small clearing I'd chosen to focus on. The suspense grew as I tried to cajole him into the open with subtle toots on the call. It worked, and as he started slowly across the narrow opening in the brush I had a clear broadside shot. The range? I later estimated it to have been about 40 yards, but distances can be deceiving under dark, overcast conditions. It might have been less. The sight picture looked good, the bark of the .44 magnum broke the silence, and I recall seeing the bright muzzle flash—good evidence that I'd not flinched on the shot.

The buck bolted at the shot and was lost from view in less than a second. I hastened over to where he had been when I shot, and was crestfallen to see neither deer nor any sign of blood. A lack of confidence in my shooting kept my search perfunctory, and I moved off a few hundred yards to wait and then blow again—but my heart wasn't in it. Some twenty minutes later I heard one of my partners playing a loud fanfare on his deer call. I followed the sound and found my two companions standing over my buck—stone dead, shot fairly through the lungs. It had fallen no more than fifty yards from where it had been shot, and had left a blood trail in the snow I could never have missed—had I just looked. Another lesson learned: Don't give up on an animal you think you might have hit. They don't always drop like the bad guys in a B movie. You owe it to the animal, if not to yourself, to look long and hard.

A moment of shared elation, one snapped photo, then back to reality. After field-dressing, a skill I'd learned, we faced the task of getting the buck from where it lay to the *Salty Dog*—one we discovered we were sadly unprepared for. Getting a downed game animal from A to B is an unglamorous part of hunting, glossed over or unmentioned in the hunting magazines. A pity. We were far from the beach, in daunting terrain.

We at first double-teamed the critter, one of us each grasping an antler and pulling, with one in reserve to take over when a puller pooped out—which was every few yards. It was also agonizingly hard on the hands. Over the rough terrain, with its brush, gullies, ridges, and deadfalls, it was much more of a project than it sounds, even as we headed generally downhill. We were fast learning that a 130 lb. deer can balloon to 600 lb. in a surprisingly short distance. At least we didn't make the cheechako mistake of trying to drag it by the hind legs. Tempting as those handles might be, dragging against the grain of the hair would have any sourdough rolling in hysterics. Might as well attach an anchor. Discouraged by our slow progress, Eric, the biggest and strongest of the three, hoisted the carcass crosswise on his shoulders and started off. So much for shouldering a deer like in the movies. After a few wobbly steps, he staggered and went down.

How much easier things would become when we learned to each pack along a short length of stout cord—a drag rope—together with a short wooden T-handle. With the cord looped around head or antlers, and adjusted to just the right length, the deer could be dragged with one or both hands while facing forward and marching straight ahead—the forequarters barely touching the ground to reduce resistance. It didn't make deadfalls, blowdowns, and creek beds disappear, but it did render them at least possible to negotiate. Going down steep slopes, we'd learn to use gravity and let the deer go first—getting out of the way before casting off, *and* being sure that the carcass was going to stop in a place where it could be retrieved.

We'd later learn that dragging was not the only way of getting deer out of the woods, although it remained the method of choice among all of the hunters I knew, or hunted with. There was the "Alaska pack": The fore and hind legs on each side could be fashioned into pack straps, and the carcass worn like a pack. It had been routinely used by the homesteading Short brothers of *The Cheechakoes*, who shot a *lot* of deer. It must have required great strength and stamina, and one wonders how their outerwear fared, given the inevitable saturation with gore and body fluids. Eric Simpson used it once, on a day hunt together early in our hunting careers, and as far as I know never used it again. And, in one of only two accidental shootings of a deer hunter that I know of, the packer was mistaken for a deer he was carrying in this fashion.

A second alternative was skinning and boning out the animal at the site of the kill, bringing back only the meat in a manageable load on a pack frame. A fresh-killed deer is incredibly easy to skin—it can be done in a matter of minutes—and the meat of even a large buck carried out in this manner would weigh less than 40 lbs. A favorite of alpine hunters, and occasionally used by some I hunted with when they chose to hunt at greater distances from the beach.

Four-wheelers or pack animals? Not in this country.

We manhandled my prize slowly, laboriously, and inefficiently down the mountain, and all the while the clock was running. Daylight was fading far more quickly than we were progressing. Following the path of least resistance, we dropped into a creek bed that promised easier going and a quicker descent. The sides became steeper, the ravine narrower, and we reached a point where we could neither proceed further nor get out of that creek bed with the deer. We had no choice but to leave the buck behind; it was hard enough to scale the sides without it, and when we reached the spine of the ridge above, the light was completely gone. Another lesson: Beware the siren song of ravines and creek beds. They lose you altitude quickly and may look to be the easiest, quickest way out, but they never are.

In total blackness we groped and staggered our way to the beach by flashlight. We'd just learned, the hard way, not to hunt any higher or farther back than we could get a deer out from with daylight to spare. At least we had learned days earlier to use and trust our compasses rather than our instincts, and we came out not far from our skiff. It didn't take that long; we'd been closer to the beach than we realized when we were forced to abandon the buck. The tide had gone, leaving our skiff with a long mud flat between it and the water's edge. We tried pulling it over the flat to the water, but were thwarted by soft, squishy mud that threatened to come up over the tops of our boots. The temperature had dropped, it had begun to snow, and we were exhausted, hungry, and now cold, but there was nothing for it but to get into our beached skiff and wait for the tide—which was still going out. Larry, Curley, and Moe shivered and shared a granola bar in the blackness, every so often shining a flashlight over the side in hopes of seeing water rather than mud. It must have been 10 P.M. by the time the Three Stooges made it back to the *Salty Dog*.

It had been our intention to retrace our steps the following morning and retrieve the deer. We knew it wouldn't take long if only we could find our way. In the morning, bad news. We awoke to 12" of fresh snow on the ground. In the woods, nothing looked familiar under this new blanket, and in minutes we were hopelessly disoriented. We had to give it up and head for home. Had we known to flag our way out with orange surveyor's tape, which of course we didn't have, we could have followed the flagging back and located the deer with plenty of daylight left to extricate it from the creek bed. Surveyor's tape would become a must-carry on future hunts—like breadcrumbs, only better. Not only was it a violation of the law to abandon a game animal in the woods, once taken: It was also a violation of a hunter's ethic. We felt awful, especially me.

We arrived back home with only a few empty Jim Beam bottles to show for our efforts, but we'd somehow survived, and the many lessons learned would be valuable and lasting. I still have the expended .44 magnum cartridge case as a reminder of that hunt, and all we didn't do right.

It could have been worse. At least we were properly dressed, had flashlights as well as some quick-energy snacks, and water (we'd later find that headlamps were as good as flashlights, and left our hands free). You might think that water need not be carried in a land where water seems to be everywhere. But as medical professionals, we already knew what some cheechakoes learn the hard way: Don't drink the water. Any fresh water you encounter in the Tongass is apt to harbor the *giardia* parasite, and produce in the consumer a truly nasty and long-lasting gastrointestinal affliction known as "beaver fever."

It remained extremely cold all week, and it snowed. I traded call the following weekend and chartered a float plane—not telling my partners, as I felt they had already done more than their fair share—in to Hawk Inlet, with a prearranged pickup time for later in the day. I had to salve my conscience by going back after that buck. If it was still there and somehow escaped the attention of ravens, otters, marten, or even bears, it would be frozen and the meat in good condition. It *was* a fool's errand. The snow, a foot deep last week, was now over two feet deep on the ground, and I got nowhere.

———

Two seasons later, in 1978, the three of us along with another kindred spirit, physician's assistant Larry DePute, made our first destination hunt with Juneau guide and charter skipper Tom Parke. Tom was a sourdough's sourdough. During a career with the State of Alaska, his job entailed making the rounds of Southeast towns and villages repeatedly, in his own boat. He learned the waters intimately and came to know every nook and cranny, how to stay out of harm's way, when and where to anchor under different conditions of wind and weather. He took the opportunity to learn all the best places both to fish and to hunt. Upon retirement he took to guiding and charter skippering in that same boat, the rugged, 42' wooden *Tiller Tramp*. I don't think he had to do this. Rather, he loved the outdoors of Southeast, enjoyed showing it to the people he took out, and enjoyed the people themselves.

Tom was advancing into his mid-seventies when we first chartered with him, and while his grizzled, weathered visage was in keeping with his age, he had the vigor and twinkling eyes of one far younger. We felt lucky to have been able to book him for our early November hunt; he was usually booked solid far ahead. We felt even luckier when we were able to do so season after season. If Tom didn't care for someone or some group, he wouldn't rebook them; we felt it a high compliment that Tom welcomed us back. We kept to his rules, cheerfully pitched in with the work, and were willing to learn. I think he found our group good company, and kind of funny.

The deal was this: We made up the menu, bought the food, cooked the meals, did the dishes, and did what we could to help him out and stay out of trouble ourselves. Tom chose the itinerary, ran the boat, and chauffeured us to and from the beaches every day in an outboard skiff. We relied on his judgment to keep us safe on the water and get us to places where the deer were. We paid for the boat fuel used; over and above that, Tom charged what seemed to us a pittance.

Tom's unvarying itinerary took us south down Stephens Passage on the Admiralty side, where we stopped for a half-day hunt at "first day bight" on outer Glass Peninsula. We hunted on down lower Glass, stopping inside Midway Point, then on to Last Chance and finally Church Bight and the North Arm of Gambier Bay. We seldom saw another boat, and never another hunter. Our hunts from dock to dock lasted seven days.

Mornings at breakfast, Tom prepped us on the topography and terrain to be hunted that day, with tips on how best to hunt it. We started for the beach at around 8 A.M.; in early November there would be "shooting light" in the woods by 8:30 or 9. We hunted ideal blacktail habitat: old-growth timber and the muskeg meadows contained within, terrain both steep and flat. There was much to be seen and marveled at: the temperate rainforest itself. Land otters scurrying along trails behind the beach fringe. Also in the beach fringe, the scattered bones of winter-killed deer from the season before. The occasional mink. A marten snarling over an appropriated gutpile. Saplings rubbed bare by rutting bucks. Bear poop, both old and disturbingly new. Antlers shed by bucks the previous winter. On steep pitches not far from the water, massive stumps left by handloggers as evidence of their work decades before. In the era before industrial-scale logging, handloggers— rugged men working alone or at most in pairs, using hand tools—felled massive spruce and yellow cedar to fill contracts made with sawmills for a given number of board feet of high-grade timber. Quality trees were selected on the basis of location, and felled such that they would fall downslope to the water's edge. From clearings at elevation, we had breathtaking views out over Stephens Passage to the snowy spires of the coast range beyond.

There were sounds, too; the mysteries of sound transmission brought the sea lions and humpback whales feeding offshore a mile or two away and far below us right next to us. The raucous scolding of Stellar's jays, telling every deer for hundreds of yards around of our presence. The croak of ravens low overhead, in keeping with the brooding, mist-shrouded landscape, right out of Edgar Allen Poe. When weather fronts brought wind, the sound of it gusting through the trees seemed amplified, as did the creaking and groaning of branches high above. There was never consistent wind direction, the gusts shifting constantly from quarter to quarter as they were affected by the extreme terrain. I found those days in the woods vaguely disquieting; the deer did too, as they bedded down and were seldom encountered.

We were expected back on the beach for pickup at a preordained hour, 3:00 or 3:30, as darkness was not far behind; this was a rule strictly enforced by Tom, and violation was a cardinal sin. We had no trouble with this, having learned our painful lesson on the *Salty Dog*.

Evenings Tom told stories, of which he had an inexhaustible supply. These he interspersed with pearls of deer-hunting wisdom, of which he also had an inexhaustible supply. His hunts were a weeklong tutorial, and we didn't even realize we were in school.

When at a sheltered and secure anchorage such as Last Chance, Tom would occasionally take the skiff ashore after dropping off the last of us, and get in an hour or two of hunting himself. One afternoon when all of us returned, exhausted, to the *Tiller Tramp* after having been skunked across the board, we were confronted with the sight of a fine buck hanging over the side from a davit. Tom had gone ashore, popped it just in back of the beach fringe, and had no difficulty getting it back to the beach, into the skiff, and onto the *Tiller Tramp*, his newly installed hip notwithstanding. It's easy when you know how.

Tom had a droll humor that was never far beneath the surface. Departure time from Juneau on day one, and on day-hunts, was 5:00 A.M. sharp, and all hands were expected to be aboard. If a straggler showed up at 5:02, Tom would be waiting at the pilothouse door with a big smile and a hearty "Good morning! What's left of it."

Once when Larry and I were working the deer call at the base of a knoll in Last Chance, a sudden roaring and crashing of brush immediately above and behind us literally set our hair on end. We didn't stay around to investigate, but double-timed to the beach back-to-back with adrenaline flowing and guns at the ready. We were about two hours early, but Tom saw us come out on the beach and picked us up. We didn't mention the reason for our early and deerless appearance, and Tom didn't ask. Larry and I gave it our best imitation of nonchalance. Once back aboard the *Tiller Tramp*, though, he studied us a moment. His face was deadpan but his eyes were smiling: "Seen a bear, did ya?"

Tom's eyesight was legendary. He could pick out a deer on the beach, tell us if it was a doe or a buck, and if a buck how many points it had, before any of the rest of us could even make out a deer. And he was always right. On a later hunt, running up Glass Peninsula at some distance from shore he spotted two bucks sparring with one another on the beach. None of us would have seen them had he not pointed them out. The water was calm, and he left the *Tiller Tramp* idling while he ferried Larry and I in to the next beach down, hidden from the contestants by a point of rocks. We stalked unseen to within shooting range. Sure enough, a forkhorn was jousting with, and bullying, a much smaller buck with mere spike antlers. From a steady sitting position about sixty yards away, I drew down on the larger one, squeezed the trigger of the .44, and down he went at the feet of his 97-pound weakling opponent. The little guy just stood there, looking down at the prostrate bully with what seemed a quizzical "Holy cow. Did I just do that?" expression.

Everyone came back with a deer from that first hunt with Tom. I got two, including the trip's biggest buck, both coming to the call and taken with my iron-sighted S&W .44 magnum revolver. I took another, even larger, buck with the revolver on a day hunt late the same season. You may have gathered that from the very beginning in Juneau, I had opted to hunt with a handgun. I'd taken a deer with one at Mt. Edge-cumbe, and during my two years away from Alaska had continued to practice with it at great length despite not knowing whether I would ever put my hard-earned proficiency to use. You may also have gathered, from my embrace of fly-fishing, that I had a penchant for doing things assbackwards—the hardest way possible, even before mastering the easier way. Guilty as charged.

Such early success with the handgun produced the illusion I could hunt on an equal footing with my rifle-hunting companions—but the worm was about to turn. It proved more delusion than illusion, as henceforth I would be regularly outscored by my cohorts. I wasn't regressing; I was actually becoming a better hunter, but so was everyone else. What was happening was the unmasking of the limitations of the handgun as a hunting arm *in comparison with the rifle*, and the laws of probability manifesting themselves over time, as they always do.

The heavy timber we hunted was ideal for the handgun hunter, given that encounters with the quarry were often at close range. Still, given hunters of comparable skills, the rifleman will be presented with perhaps four times the number of high-percentage shots on deer as the handgunner, and I wasn't good enough to overcome those odds. If a handgun hunter and a rifle hunter are hunting together, the rifleman will most often have a good shot first. Sizeable blacktail bucks in Southeast are neither smarter nor more wily than lesser deer, especially during the rut, but are far less plentiful; thus my early success on bucks was more a statistical aberration than a demonstration of superior hunting skills. From then on I would still take a decent buck with my revolver now and again, but mostly brought home does and knuckleheads (Tom's term for young bucks with nubbin antlers), which, in keeping with the probabilities, came under my sights more often. Not brag-worthy, but superb eating.

Even after the truth became obvious I would stay with the iron-sighted revolver for twenty years. It became frustrating at times, but the choice of weapons had always been mine. Truth is, I liked hunting with it. And the rare taking of a "honker"—a really big buck with impressive headgear—was all the sweeter. The late Col. Jeff Cooper, arguably the foremost authority on pistolcraft and the handgun to this day, wrote that *any* game animal taken with a handgun merits a gold star in the hunter's private book of trophies.

I must confess to my own susceptibility to buck fever—the adrenaline surge that can confound everything one ever learned about the discipline of shooting. It was always lurking, and I hated when it happened. Strangely, it reared its ugly head only on the closest, easiest shots. Even stranger, had I ever been completely cured of the propensity for this dread affliction, I might well have been cured of hunting. Looking back, the hunting accomplishment in which I took most pride was the ability to keep that evil genie corked in its bottle as often as I did.

Tom passed away suddenly, shortly after the 1983 (I think) season, while vacationing in Hawaii. Our sorrow was tempered by the gratitude we felt at having known him, and hunted with him for as many years as we had.

Our hunts with Tom had schooled us well. We'd built on what we'd learned from the *Salty Dog* experience, and cheechako pratfalls were largely behind us. With more time logged in the woods we were seeing more deer, and bringing more of them home. We were coming of age as hunters.

———

In the meantime Eric Simpson had acquired a 46-foot trawler he named *Skana*. He'd fitted it out with a dental suite, and was already doing itinerant dental clinics in the outlying villages of northern Southeast. *Skana* became our new floating deer camp.

Eric's humble beginnings as a neophyte Alaska deer hunter would lead him into new territory as a successful hunter of trophy big game all over North America, including the coveted grand slam of North American sheep—although his enthusiasm for hunting blacktails never flagged. He would also accumulate an eclectic collection of fine rifles. It seemed that every year he would show up on the hunt with a different custom rifle (or two) in some exotic wildcat (nonstandard) caliber. In his spare time, he restored classic pickup trucks from the 1930s and '40s.

Kim Smith and wife Ethel were an outdoorsy couple, into things like ocean kayak-camping, marathon hikes, cross-country skiing, and jogging. With regard to firearms Kim was the antithesis of Eric. From the beginning he hunted with the same 30/06 that was eventually dubbed "Old Rustworthy." He had little use for Eric's and my discussions on esoteria like the finer points of the Mauser action—it was the mouser action to him, just another mousetrap. But Old Rustworthy somehow worked just fine, despite its owner's willful ignorance, and consistently brought home the venison. It still does.

We plied the same waters, and hunted the same places, that we now knew well from our hunts in the *Tiller Tramp*, and went by the same procedures. We generally started into the woods each morning in pairs. We might either stay together, or separate as we worked our way in. I remained paired with Larry Depute; we were the oldest by a considerable margin, and hunted a little lower and slower. We dubbed ourselves B-team, but we did okay (Larry, with a rifle, did better than I did).

Larry was a renaissance man and our "Mr. Fixit," the turn-to guy when something didn't work. He had built his own home and most of the furniture in it. He would build a rowing skiff and an iceboat in the home workshop that he also built. He was an accomplished private pilot with several advanced ratings who eventually built and flew his own high-performance aircraft. In his spare time he and wife Connie were avid birders and fossil-hunters. On a not-long-ago road trip during which they visited us at our Idaho home, they attempted to pass off a large sugar beet they'd found along the side of a southern Idaho highway as fossilized dinosaur poop.

B-team was, despite general competence, subject to the occasional comic regression. While hunting an area in North Arm we'd dubbed "confusion meadows," I called up a doe that came in from an unanticipated direction. Surprised, Larry got off a hasty shot. The doe bolted, but left at the scene a moderate-sized splotch of blood on the snow. Off we Sherlocks went on a blood trail that was easy enough to follow at first, but which soon became more and more sparse. After an hour of intrepid sleuthing the trail petered out altogether, and we found ourselves…right back where we had started. The doe had led us in a wide, complete circle. Looking down, we both saw something we'd completely overlooked in our haste to follow that blood trail: a small, furry object, unquestionably half of an ear (on a later hunt out of Elfin Cove, Frank Rue returned disappointed one afternoon after missing a shot at a truly impressive buck. The following day, hunting the same area, he called up and shot a truly impressive buck—the best of that season's hunt. The animal had a perfectly drilled 30-caliber hole through one ear).

On another hunt Larry shot at a doe standing at the base of a giant spruce; the animal dropped like it had been poleaxed, seemingly dead before it hit the ground. But when we reached the spot, no deer—and neither blood nor hair. Long minutes later and on the verge of giving up, one of us noticed a previously overlooked hole in the mossy earth at the base of the trunk, between two massive diverging roots. It seemed inconsequential, too small, and looking into it revealed only blackness—but we were out of ideas. Larry reached in to what proved a cavernous void in the root system, one that would doubtless be the undoing of this giant at some time in the future. He was in up to his shoulder as far as it would go before he felt something that didn't belong there. Larry's doe, like Alice, had gone down the rabbit-hole. He was able to grasp a hind leg and extricate his prize from the clutches of the Mad Hatter.

Skana was more spacious than *Tiller Tramp* had been, and our group would expand to fill the space; some were already veterans of the later Tom Parke hunts. Fisheries biologist Alex Wertheimer. Frank Rue, who would later become Alaska's commissioner of fish and game. Schoolteacher Dave Haas. A pair of fisheries research biologists we dubbed the Goofy Brothers. They weren't brothers, but they were goofy. All were wonderful companions, already skilled hunters and outdoorsmen when they came aboard, and people you could count on if you needed to. Not everyone was able to make the trip every year, and we averaged seven or eight.

And then, in a class by himself, was family practice physician Randy Wiest, aka Dr. Rut.

Randy was a small, neat, fastidiously groomed individual who looked like he'd just stepped out of an L.L. Bean ad even as he stepped out of the woods after a hard day's hunting. Unlike many in our group he had grown up hunting—whitetail in rural Pennsylvania—and when he came to Juneau the skills he had so obviously acquired traveled with him. Also unlike the rest of us he would not deign to shoot does, but was still somehow near the top every year when it came to number of deer taken. He also often ran neck-and-neck with Eric when it came to the trip's biggest buck.

But his extraordinary success came, like major-league home run records, with an asterisk: Just as Lon Chaney morphed into a werewolf at every full of the moon, every time he went into the woods with a rifle mild-mannered Randy transformed into that intrepid predator of the northern rainforest, Dr. Rut. He hunted alone, high up and far back, and all would suppress a groan when we heard the distant crack of a rifle at 3:00 P.M., when the rest of us were close too or on the beach, awaiting pickup.

Randy was chronically late to the beach, and not just by a little. We sometimes had to put our plans for moving on to a safer anchorage for the night on hold while we waited. All got familiar with sitting in a skiff just off the beach in total darkness (with a strong flashlight at the ready) waiting for Randy to materialize with his buck. I don't think anyone believed he was doing this intentionally any more than poor Lon Chaney, but when Dr. Rut was in control it just happened. Nonetheless, this behavior was putting us all at risk. We entreated and cajoled, even threatened banishment from future hunts, but nothing helped. Had he gone over to the dark side in the earlier hunts with Tom Parke, Tom *would* have banished him. Things got a little better when we began carrying handheld VHF radios with us. At least Randy could tell us back aboard the *Skana* when he was in the process of screwing the pooch.

It was hard to stay mad at Randy, much as he deserved it. Once back aboard he left the rasty Dr. Rut deep in the woods where he belonged, and became once again the affable, funny Randy Wiest, wide open to having his chops busted but also full of pontificating horse pucky about how he owed his extraordinary hunting prowess ("it's but expected skill, boys") to paying homage to the spirits of the deer he killed, and how we'd do better if we emulated his example. Of course the only one who bought his bullshit was Randy himself, but it was fun to listen to.

Dr. Rut's most outrageous caper was—well, outrageous. We—the rest of us—had been back aboard the Skana for well over an hour, awaiting Rut's inevitable VHF transmission. When it came crackling through we learned that yes, he was on his way down the mountain with a big buck, but was still far from the beach and the going was difficult. He would call in every twenty minutes with a progress report. As we watched out the *Skana*'s windows, a heavy cloud layer brought the ceiling down to under 500 feet, and darkness was closing in.

At length, the next report: He was coming down through a steep creek bed (of the sort one should never get into), the going was getting tougher, and he was still up in the clouds. Between that and the fading daylight, he was having difficulty making out where he was going. He'd left his buck behind so he could scout the route ahead unencumbered.

And next: He'd gone back for his buck—and it wasn't there. In going back for it he'd left his rifle behind, resting against a tree—and when he returned to the tree, deerless, his rifle wasn't there either.

It was long after dark and well into the evening when we plucked him, deerless and rifleless, off the beach. At least he still had his pants. The next morning Randy led Eric and Kim back to the scene of the crime. They found his rifle, leaning against the tree where he'd left it; he'd obviously not been able to relocate the right tree in the dark. Of the deer there was no trace. A big fuzzy had probably been stalking him as he descended with his kill, and appropriated it as soon as he turned his back on it. This was not the first deer Randy had lost to a bear.

———

The nature of Autumn weather in Southeast Alaska was such that our hunts were always embarked upon with the knowledge that we might not make it back when planned. We were lucky to have made it back on schedule for ten straight years. But luck eventually runs out, as ours did, to the best of my recollection in 1988. We were forced to hole up in Gambier Bay for two days as gale-force winds from the southeast whipped up Stephens Passage; such weather systems were not uncommon at that time of year. We didn't lack for either comfort or food and were well-prepared for this eventuality, but families and work were waiting and we all wanted to get home. The marine forecast for the following day suggested that the winds would slack off just enough for us to make a run for home, and we went for it.

The wind from the southeast was strong on our stern, and the seas lumpy, as we made our way northward. But all was progressing on schedule and we figured to be approaching Taku Inlet, only a dozen miles from the boat harbor in Juneau, at about 3:00 P.M.

The wheels came off the wagon when we hit the southern edge of Taku Inlet. Without warning, we were slammed by a wall of wind and frothing water coming out of Taku and taking us beam-on. Within minutes we were beyond the point of safe turnaround.

The next three hours were a living nightmare. The mouth of Taku Inlet is little more than three miles across, but the force of wind and water abruptly brought our speed down to one knot, even with the engines straining at full power. Darkness soon enveloped us; in the blackness we monitored our position and progress on the radar, which miraculously continued to function. Eric kept *Skana* quartering into the maelstrom, necessary to counteract the sideways crabbing that was carrying us at right angles to our desired course. Nonetheless, every prolonged gust heeled her almost on her beam ends. The starboard prop cavitated as it came clear of the water, and the starboard engine began to overheat as it starved for coolant—the saltwater intake often out of water for a minute at a time. I don't know to what degree Skana was heeling, but it was far more than I'd ever encountered in any vessel, and when it went over it stayed there for what seemed an eternity before righting. We all believed that with the next roll it might just keep going. The anemometer on the bridge had pegged at 80 knots before being torn away.

Eric in the wheelhouse was fighting the helm and juggling the throttles. With him were two of our number—I don't recall who they were—who periodically ventured outside, secured by lifelines, to scrape accumulating ice off the windshield. The temperature had dropped and ice was building up on *Skana*'s topsides, raising her center of gravity and making a dire situation worse. Eric and the other two up forward were doubtless too busy to be frightened. For those of us back in the salon, saliva dried up and there was nothing to do but ponder just how close to death we might be. I've never felt that way in a boat before or since.

Added to this was the physical pummeling. We were thrown about the salon like toys. So was everything not nailed down, and heavy doors were alternately being thrown open and slammed shut. No bones were broken, but some suffered bruises that would be sore for weeks. No thought was given to donning life vests.

Eric ultimately put out a MAYDAY call on the VHF. A Mayday call is serious shit in the maritime world, and false alarms are not taken lightly by the Coast Guard, but this was no false alarm. We believed were close to being *in extremis*, and probably were. Coast Guard Juneau replied that they were sending a boat down the channel toward us ASAP.

Then, perhaps twenty minutes later, it was over. The wind died and the seas abated, like flicking off a light switch. We had reached the lee of Point Bishop at the entrance to Gastineau Channel, and not a moment too soon. I don't believe that *Skana* could have lived in the winds and seas of Taku for much longer.

The lights of the approaching Coast Guard vessel shortly appeared, and it escorted us up the channel and into Harris Harbor. After docking, we were boarded for routine questioning and inspection. Eric received a citation for not having the required number of PFDs aboard. All of our life jackets had been tied to the railing of the bridge ladder outside the salon door, and had been ripped away to disappear into the maelstrom.

The wives were waiting at the dock, but there wasn't much talk. That would come later.

We rode the tiger, and survived. Not one of us will ever forget the experience. But now for the postmortem review: We had blundered into something we hadn't seen coming. We were experienced in these waters, knew very well the perils of Taku when it was out of sorts, so why hadn't we? Tom Parke had told us years before, and had complained to NOAA, the Coast Guard, and anyone else who would listen, that the weather-sensing apparatus intended to monitor Taku Inlet conditions had been installed in the wrong place—that Taku could be a roaring hell while nearby Point Bishop, where the instruments were, was reporting "southeast winds at fifteen knots." Tom's entreaties had fallen on deaf ears, and thus there had been no warning on the marine weather channel we were monitoring.

Tom had also foretold the precise conditions we encountered that day: A strong southeasterly wind coming up Stephens Passage, abruptly confronting high pressure air coming out of the Yukon and spilling off the Juneau icefield, accelerating as it funneled through the slot of Taku Inlet. The cold, dense Taku air, forced down on the deck and further compressed beneath the prevailing warmer wind from the southeast, accelerated yet more. As we now knew from experience, the transition from a lumpy but manageable southeast sea to the hell we ran into was almost instantaneous. A phenomenon observed aboard larger vessels under these conditions, those the size of the Alaska state ferries, was that frigid temperatures and 90-knot winds screaming out of Taku might be experienced on the lower deck, while at the same time milder winds blowing opposite from the southeast prevailed on the bridge.

We got back on the horse that threw us. Not a one of us bailed on the hunt the following year, and the *Skana* hunts continued for another decade until Eric's retirement near the end of the millennium, when he sold his boat.

———

During the Juneau years my hunting was not limited to the annual destination hunt. I loved being out there, seemed I always had tags to fill, and on many weekend days during the season when I was not on call and the weather permitted, I day-hunted out of Auke Bay with a number of different friends, and did occasional long-weekend trips. In Juneau the day hunt was the hunt for Everyman, well suited to the small, fast craft owned by so many. Destinations were Shelter, the back side of Douglas, Lincoln, and Benjamin Islands, as well as north Admiralty. These day hunts, and occasional extended hunts a bit further afield, were actually about as productive per day in the woods, for me anyway, as our annual destination hunt.

A frequent day-hunting partner was lifelong Juneauite Hank Bryson. After quitting early on a frigid and fruitless December hunt of Lincoln Island, Hank suggested a quick drive of tiny Ralston Island just to the north before heading home; he recalled his father having seen deer cross over from Lincoln to Ralston at extreme low tides. Ralston seemed an unlikely place. It was flat, little over a mile in length, and about 300 yards wide at the widest—timbered, with a band of impenetrable, thick brush running down the center. Hank would walk to one side of the brush band, I the other. The ground was covered with frozen, crunchy snow, stealth was impossible, and neither of us harbored much hope. We were just going through the motions, figuring on being back at Hank's open skiff in under an hour and ready for a chilling ride home.

I walked my side with pauses after every few noisy steps. Less than halfway up the island I began hearing the faint crunch of snow on my backtrail during every pause, almost like a delayed echo. I knew it couldn't be Hank—he should be somewhere abreast of me on the other side of the brush. I finally looked back during a pause, and there came a large buck deliberately walking up my tracks; he didn't stop until he was within 20 feet of me. Although a forkhorn he was big-bodied, with a high, wide, heavy-beamed rack that now looks down from our wall.

For one of the extended hunts we took the *Raccoon III* to Hawk Inlet, of *Salty Dog* fame. Hank Bryson was along, and the first afternoon came back with a fine buck that looked like it had been bagged in a gay bar. One ear was festooned with bright fluorescent ribbon, and it sported a heavy collar about its neck that looked to us like S & M paraphernalia.

The following day we saw, as we hunted high above the inlet, a small plane come in from the direction of Juneau and circle above our boat for several minutes before departing in the direction from which it had come.

After we'd arrived back home, Hank took the collar in to fish & game headquarters. They were not happy to see it. It contained a radio transmitter, as Hank's buck had been an unwitting participant in a long-term study being conducted by Alaska Fish & Game into the movement patterns, habits, and other features of Sitka blacktail behavior. Until Hank brought it in, the entire office had been puzzling over what deer #___ had been doing smack in the middle of the basin at the head of Hawk Inlet, and why it had not been spotted by the observer in the plane tracking the collar transmissions. The only thing down there was somebody's boat. We had hung the buck from the rail at the bow, apparently out of sight of the observer.

Hank's kill had been perfectly legal—and, he claimed he never saw the ear flag or the collar until after the deer was down (quite reasonable. In such instances you see what you need to see.). A summary of the blacktail study was subsequently published as a booklet, and Hank got copies for both of us. It was fascinating, well done, and comprehensive; it confirmed much of what we knew, and revealed much more of what we didn't. Included was an analysis of the effectiveness of various hunting modalities—calling, still-hunting, stand hunting—in terms of number of deer seen per unit time hunting. The guys who accumulated the data must have had a ball.

———

An era had come to an end with the sale of the *Skana*, but life, and hunting, would go on. Our crew needed a white knight, and one came along in the person of Don Nash.

Don had come from Oregon to Alaska as a young man to commercial fish. Legend had it that he brought his boat up from Seattle using as his sole navigation chart a placemat from a Seattle restaurant. The story remains unconfirmed, but Don has never denied it.

He pursued a career as a commercial fisherman, power-trolling for salmon in the Gulf of Alaska summers and longlining for black cod winters, while living first in Pelican in later in Haines, where his growing children had access to better schools. Any time during the season when he wasn't out on the water, he was hunting Chichagof and Yakobi Islands on the outer coast and along outer Icy Strait. He came to know the waters, and the country, like the back of his hand, and frequently hunted the high alpine in the early season. As a hunter he was in that elite "predator" category, and in additional to innumerable blacktails had taken at least one of every big game species that Alaska has to offer, including several moose with a bow.

In the year 2001 he became owner-operator of Cross Sound Lodge, one of several relatively recent sportfishing lodges at Elfin Cove, which Linda and I had briefly visited on our trip with Ben Forbes 30 years before—a tiny hole-in-the-wall with a sheltered harbor on Chichagof Island near the entrance to Icy Strait, and close to 90 miles by water from Juneau. The lodges' seasons ended around Labor Day, when they were closed up for the winter. Don proposed reopening his lodge in November and using it as the base of operations for our hunt. One of his lodge's sportfishing boats, with skiff(s) in tow, would get us out every day to the areas to be hunted. Several of our group, myself included, knew Don and had hunted with him before. We couldn't have been happier with the arrangement.

In spite of the ten-or-so modern sportfishing lodges, which were spread out and concealed within enveloping spruce and hemlock, Elfin Cove looked much as it had 30 years before. In summer a frenetic hub of the salmon and halibut fisheries of the Northern Gulf, and with sportfishing lodges filled to capacity, in autumn and winter it morphed into a virtual ghost town. The winter population census varied somewhere between one and eight, usually closer to the former, and visitors were few and far between. Someone needed to be there to tend the town's diesel generator, for the occasional fuel dock customer, and to generally look after things. These were hats that one person could wear without difficulty. Not counted among the residents was the occasional lone fisherman who overwintered with his boat, tending to maintenance at a leisurely pace. Such folk generally preferred their own company.

The *Skana*'s accommodations had been comfy enough, but it was still a boat. Don's lodge catered to an affluent crowd, as did all the lodges, and so had all the amenities. Suites with soft beds and real bedding rather than bunks and sleeping bags. Hot water, with daily showers, and the chance to do laundry and dry outerwear when needed. A big chef's kitchen (some of the guys actually knew how to take advantage of it. I stuck to dishes.).

The format was a familiar one: Don, who had the lodge, the boat, and knew the territory, would assume the role of Tom Parke—but Don would not only be leader but also an equal participant, hunting alongside us every day. With the exception of Don, who of course rated a pass, all shared the cost of food, boat fuel, electricity for the lodge, and transit to and from Elfin Cove (never done the same way twice, and sometimes as much of an adventure as the hunting). It was a good deal for all concerned.

Nothing remains the same over time, and a few of our Juneau hunters, including Larry and eventually Eric, fell away over the years, their places taken by friends of Don's from Haines. All proved good hunters and good companions. Among the Juneau folk we now tended to rotate hunting partners, and I also paired on occasion with Bruce Smith, the director of the Haines DPW (department of public works. In Haines, that meant not only giving the orders but also driving the heavy equipment.).

The territory we hunted was every bit as expansive and remote as that of our Stephens Passage trips—maybe more. The terrain was not different from what we knew, other than that the tree line dropped to around 1800 feet—a consequence of the harsher weather of the outer coast. The views from elevation were, on clear days, even more spectacular than those of the Stephens Pasage hunts—out over Icy Strait to the face of Brady Glacier and the towering Fairweather Range beyond. Where we hunted on any particular day was entirely dependent on the weather, as we were at the edge of Cross Sound and the wide open Gulf of Alaska. Sloppy, blowing weather meant Idaho Inlet, the Inian Islands, or Port Althorp; on calmer days we went further outside to Bird Rock, Column Point, Lisianski Strait, Soapstone Harbor, and even Cape Bingham on the Gulf itself.

Because of the often higher beach surf, getting on and off the beaches was more of an adventure than it had been on the Stevens Passage hunts. Each day, we went into the woods prepared for the possibility that we might have to spend a night on the beach if the weather kicked up during the day. In all the years we hunted, it is little short of miraculous that it never once happened to any of us.

We came close once. On returning from a day's hunt at Cape Bingham, we discovered Don's 40' boat to have dragged anchor in Bingham Harbor and grounded out on the beach. The receding tide had swamped it and left it careened on its side, damaging both shafts and props and flooding the engine room. Fortuitously, a friend of Don's had come down from Haines in his own smaller boat and arrived at Elfin Cove earlier that day; he arrived at Bingham hours later and took aboard Don and a skeleton crew of hunters to stay on-site to right and pump out the boat when it floated on that night's tide. We were doubly lucky in that a commercial fisherman was passing by northbound along the outer coast at the time; Don was able to contact him, and he took the rest of our hunters (myself included) aboard and in to Elfin Cove. Our rescuer was the *Jenny*, a vintage wooden commercial salmon troller I had first encountered at Angoon 35 years before; its present owner-skipper turned out to be the son of an Angoon health aide and former surgical patient I had known from my Mt. Edgecumbe days. Don had a sat phone, but had not these two boats been where they were, when they were, all would have spent at least a night and probably more on the beach, in survival mode.

Don's boat was towed back to Elfin Cove the following day, and ultimately to Sitka, where Don spent the winter repairing and reconditioning it.

Don, 13 years younger than I, had long ago attained sourdough status. Wiry and youthful-looking, he must have shared some genes with the Energizer Bunny. He never seemed to tire, and even though every day he was last into the woods and first out on account of his ferrying duties, he regularly out-hunted us—even when he brought his bow and left his rifle back at the boat. Don usually hunted alone, but on those occasions when he did hunt with someone, that someone would mysteriously get lucky.

The first time I hunted with Don, years before, he watched over my shoulder while I field-dressed a large doe I'd shot. This I'd done many times before, and, as Don knew, was a surgeon to boot. I considered my skills more than adequate, but Don kept yanking my chain with one critical but good-natured comment after another. Finally, enough was enough: "Don, any klutz can disassemble a critter. Why don't you try putting one back together some time?" Don would repeat that story for years after.

He arrived from Haines every year with a fistful of proxy tags—the deer tags of Haines residents who were entitled to take deer but unable to hunt because of advanced age or disability. It was legal for such people to designate a "proxy hunter" to harvest their deer for them, and Don was in great demand. He always implored us with a pitch that went something like "Guys, help me out here and shoot more deer! Think of the old people who'll go hungry this winter if you don't." It wasn't strictly kosher, and anyway I usually had my hands full getting enough deer for myself.

One afternoon we arrived back at the boat to find a fresh, rolled-up bear hide, with skull, on the deck. Don had been hunting alone up near tree line when he saw a good-sized brown bear with a fine pelt, perhaps heading for hibernation. He had a brown bear tag he'd been saving for just the right bear, and this had been it. He dropped it with a single shot, then skinned the huge beast and packed the heavy hide and skull back to the beach, arriving there in time to pick everyone else up on schedule, and seemingly without having broken a sweat.

Don's concept of acceptable risk always seemed just a little outside the margins of my own—perhaps shaped of necessity by a life spent out of doors and on the water in one of the world's least forgiving environments. I don't know how the other guys felt. But this was his turf, and given that his capabilities and level of experience were far beyond my own, I never questioned his judgment. Neither did anyone else, and we never had reason to be sorry.

———

Even before the Elfin Cove hunts began, I had retired and we were living in ski country, the Central Idaho Rockies. I commuted for the hunts; it was a means of staying connected to a place, to people, and a pursuit that I loved. Now restricted to just the one destination hunt per season, I needed to increase the odds for putting venison in the freezer. I did so by switching to a rifle—something my aging eyes (and maybe common sense) told me I should have done years before. I had the .375 H&H magnum beachcombing rifle that had stood sentinel duty for our family for so many years fitted with a peep, or aperture, rear sight (never gave in to a scope). I had restocked it myself shortly after buying it in the mid-'70s; almost as much by accident as design it came out light for its great power, beautifully balanced, fast-handling, and pointed naturally. The stock design helped mitigate the hefty recoil. It was many times more gun than needed for deer but I shot well with it, and it was a comforting security blanket in the domain of the big fuzzies. Contrary to what you might suppose, the big .375 doesn't ruin any more meat than lesser calibers. It became my regular companion on the last Skana hunts, and on all the hunts out of Elfin Cove.

As a non-resident I now had to buy my deer tags (formerly free), and they weren't cheap, so I settled for two per season. At the same time, hunting with a rifle allowed me to become selective. The first tag was earmarked for a sizeable buck, and I passed on a number of deer I would have taken in previous years waiting for one to come along. In each of the years I hunted out of Elfin Cove, one did. Some ranked among my best ever. The second tag was for any good deer that presented itself, but not wanting to fill this last tag too early in the hunt, I again passed on some shootable animals. As a result, there were a few years when the clock ran out and I didn't fill it at all. Our family missed the additional venison, but strangely, passing up deer now bothered me not at all.

I had always been our group's oldest hunter, and the age disparity had widened with the Elfin Cove hunts. And, as the Elfin Cove years passed I increasingly felt the toll the years had taken. Toward the end of a day, especially when dragging out a deer, fatigue became an oppressive weight. Everything ached, and I'd have to concentrate on just putting one foot in front of the other to make it back to the beach. I sometimes took an off-day so that my body could regroup, reading in the lodge or strolling about Elfin Cove, taking in the funkiness. Between 1978 and the last *Skana* hunt I had not missed a season, but I missed three between 2001 and 2010. I was all too aware that I was no longer able to pull my oar when it came to sharing in the heavy-duty chores that were part and parcel of these hunts, that I was gradually being marginalized by diminished abilities. I didn't like being that guy. 2010 would be my last hunt.

Why did we do it? None of us would have gone hungry had we not harvested deer, but we all shared the predator gene, the one that had kept our ancestors of millennia ago alive, and which now seems in danger of being bred out of the population. We loved the venison and the satisfaction that came with bringing it home ourselves. There was also a parallel satisfaction, at least for me, that came with having acquired the hard-earned skills that allowed me to do it.

We weren't hunting for trophies. That said, everyone preferred to bring back their meat in the form of bucks, the bigger the better (Larry DePute oft claimed that he preferred to shoot does, but he was lying). The hunting was never competitive, even though every year we each threw a few dollars into a pot that went to the bagger of the buck with the biggest headgear. Our skills weren't all at the same level but we were all competent hunters, and recognized that taking the biggest buck in any given season was as much a matter of chance as anything else. The winner's glory was transient, over the years the honor was spread around, and few could remember who had won from one year to the next (I do remember taking the pot one year, but Don gave my win an asterisk because Dr. Rut hadn't been on that hunt. The following season I led almost wire to wire, but Dr. Rut was along and beat me out on the last day, by a fraction of an inch—with a buck that got back to the boat late, naturally.).

I'm not much for the touchy-feely, new-age psychobabble about the male bonding that goes on in groups of guys who go hunting together, but there's no denying that the camaraderie was there, and a vital part of the experience. So was being out of doors in one of nature's most magnificent venues, whatever the weather. But at the end of the day, the hunt was about hunting. A philosopher whose name I can't remember said something to the effect that hunting wasn't really about killing, but that one must kill to have truly hunted. Work that one out for yourself, but I think he was on to something.

I don't have many photos from our hunts. I think we were too busy living in the moment. Over the years I took close to fifty deer, and we have in our Idaho home, on walls and shelves, the racks of numerous blacktail bucks. Some are fairly impressive, given the species and the locale from where they were taken, others run-of-the-mill. Personal trophies, I suppose, but that's not why they're there: Each one triggers a memory, allowing me to live all over again a treasured moment from a treasured time. I look at them often.

———

The Elfin Cove hunt continues on today. Only Kim Smith is left from those who first hunted with Tom Parke all those years ago, and from the *Skana* hunts. We keep in touch, and I'm always eager to hear the lowdown on the latest adventures. Don is still in charge; like Peter Pan, he never seems to grow old.

More on Hunting:
The Unexperienced Experiences

My hunting experience in Alaska began and ended with blacktail deer. Any interest I may have had in expanding my hunting horizons to Alaska's many other big game animals was tempered by the constraints of time: outside of what I did for a living, which took a lot, there was only so much to spread around between family and the outdoor pursuits that I loved. Priorities were sorted, choices made. When it was time, I hung up my hunting handguns and rifles with few regrets.

Bear we've already touched upon. Several areas on the Southeast Alaskan mainland harbored good populations of mountain goats, beautiful animals and great trophies for those willing and able to seek them out on the high, steep crags where they resided. Several friends did so on one or more occasions, and their trophies were well-earned. If there was one trophy I wished I'd pursued, this would be it.

A few friends did do-it-yourself caribou hunts in the Alaskan interior, being dropped off by bush pilots to camp along caribou migration routes, and being picked up on a prearranged date. Some others did guided trophy hunts in Southcentral Alaska's Chugach and Wrangell Mountains for dall sheep and other game. But for game other than deer, moose topped the list.

Moose hunting ranked among the significant rites of fall in Southeast Alaska, and many that I knew partook. The Alaska-Yukon moose is the largest of the three moose variants found in North America, mature bulls weighing in at 1500 lbs. on the hoof and standing almost seven feet at the shoulder. Their habitat in Southeast Alaska is confined to the mainland, along the drainages of largest river systems—the Taku, Chilkat, Stikine—and the rivers draining into Berners Bay. Also the Yakutat forelands, lowlands through which run the Situk, Italio, and Alsek rivers, flanked on either end by the Fairweather and St. Elias ranges. Because we spent little time in moose country, the only Alaskan moose Linda and I saw were in the lower reaches of Glacier Bay, once—although I had some fleeting glimpses on Yakutat steelhead trips.

Unless one lived in Haines or Yakutat, day-hunting for moose was out of the question. For everyone else, the logistic hurdles could be formidable, and limited the hunter pool to a relative few who really, really wanted to do it. Also limiting was the fact that the harvest in all hunts was carefully monitored and controlled, and some were by lottery permit (Berners Bay). The Haines and Yakutat hunts limited the total number of moose that could be harvested in a given season, as determined by population estimates. The numbers were sometimes no more than 25, the hunts cut off when that number had been reached (the game management official charged with overseeing the hunt became the area's least popular person; for the Haines hunt in recent years, it has been Kim Smith's son-in-law). The Taku hunt was that closest to Juneau, but access wasn't easy despite its proximity. The prime moose habitat straddled the Canadian border, and more than a few American hunters had been tempted by targets on the wrong side of the line. Every few years one got busted by the Mounties, who came out of the wilderness woodwork during the Taku moose season.

What follows is a description of a typical Southeast Alaskan moose hunt, cobbled together from the recollections of several friends who had been there and done that. Despite the fact that moose meat is delicious, it goes far in explaining why I chose to use my limited leisure time doing other things.

A group of hunters, two to several, set up camp in the area to be hunted. Each day they fan out over the area, each selecting a tree that offered a panoramic view over endless acres of sodden meadow that moose prefer. The hunters' days are spent aloft scanning the vistas for a legal bull, all the while fighting stiffness, cramps, cold, and boredom. Days may pass without any of the hunters spotting one. Eventually, one of three things happens: 1) The group's allotted fun time expires before a legal moose is seen and bagged, and everybody has to get back to work. 2) The harvest quota reached, the hunt is halted with our hunters still up in their trees. 3) At long last, one of the party spots a legal bull. He shoots and brings his quarry down. With one pull of the trigger, by one hunter, the hunt has ended for all—and yet it is where the hunt really begins.

In the event of outcome number three, the entire party gathers at the kill. All too often the moose has chosen to expire in an impenetrable bog, or a deep pothole with only a nose or hoof showing above the surface. Getting such a massive creature out to where it can be skinned and quartered is a group effort; it can take ingenuity, sometimes a float or raft of some sort, or a come-along—but mostly just lots of old-fashioned blood, sweat, and tears. The sweat and tears keep flowing as the huge quarters are transported back to camp, often a considerable distance away. Is everybody having fun yet? At the end of the hunt the meat is distributed among the participants. They've earned it.

Docs Tom Stengl and John Gove, while at Mt. Edgecumbe, did a Yakutat moose hunt together. Tom downed a moose early, and as they were marking time awaiting pickup at an airstrip in the bush, a moose walked out in front of them with the apparent intention of committing seppuku-by-hunter. Tom, ever the predator, obliged (on Joh's moose tag). Poor John. As he eyed the huge carcass he must have felt like Sisyphus, agonized at the prospect of having to roll that ball back up the hill all over again. A quiet guy with deadpan humor, all he could bring himself to say was, "Tom, I'm not so sure I'm glad you did that."

The only truly easy moose hunt I ever heard of is related here, as told by a friend of the hunter. Moose from the Haines herd sometimes made their way south to St. James Bay, and much more rarely to the tip of the Chilkat peninsula at Pt. Couverden and Swanson Harbor. Swanson Harbor had a couple of cabins around its margin, one owned by a commercial crab fisherman who, when in residence, moored his crab boat out in front of it. He so happened to be there during the course of one moose opening when a legal bull walked out on the flats in front of his cabin. Bracing his rifle against the porch railing, he decked it—it fell at the high tide line. After field-dressing and skinning the critter, he left it where it lay and waited for the tide to come in. With the moose now at water's edge, he brought his boat in close to the beach and used its power-hoist to winch it aboard. He put the boat in gear and made straight for Juneau. Arriving at Harris Harbor down-town, he used the hoist at the dock to transfer his moose directly to the bed of his waiting pickup. Thence to Jerry's Meats for butchering, pack-aging, and freezing. Maybe the only bloodless, sweatless, tearless moose hunt ever.

Some Alaskan Originals

Dr. Gary Hedges was born and raised in Juneau, put himself through school hand-trolling for salmon during summers, and returned to his hometown after residency to open a solo practice of general surgery. Among his patients were more than a few to whom he had delivered newspapers on his paper route as a boy. A few years older than I, he had been in practice there for about five years prior to my arrival. During that time he had won the Golden North Salmon Derby, Juneau's *el primo* summer event, with a king salmon of 59-plus lbs. (ask Gary, he'll tell you to the ounce), still the largest king ever caught in the 74-year history of the Derby. Since then he has billed himself "Gary Hedges, WGF"—Worlds's Greatest Fisherman. It's printed on his cards, and he'll gladly tell you even if you don't ask.

When called in to the hospital on weekends to see E.R. or admitted patients for surgical consultations, he usually arrived wearing B.F. Goodrich rubber pacs (trademark Southeast footware among locals) or ancient carpet slippers, bib overalls, and a worn flannel shirt. Gruff and heavyset, with a perpetual five-o'clock shadow and a set of trophy eyebrows, he was an intimidating sight to tourists off the cruise ships who were accustomed to physicians being white-coated, silver-haired, and silver-tongued. He looked more like Beelzebub. As his appearance suggested he might have had about him a whiff of brimstone, from all the time logged soaking in the sulfurous waters of the Tenakee bath (see below). Gary scared the crap out of them, he knew it, and I think he thought it was funny. We all did. He even scared my wife the first time she met him.

Gary was a fine surgeon in addition to a good friend. Our families would have socialized more but for the fact that when one of us was free, the other was likely on call. "Thumbs" and "Sausage Fingers" regularly insulted and assisted one another at surgery.

One can't talk about Gary without talking about Tenakee. The small burg of Tenakee Hot Springs, located on the sheltered waters of Tenakee Inlet on Chichagof Island, attained notoriety during the Yukon gold rush of 1898, as a winter resort for those miners who neither struck it rich nor struck out. Those who struck it rich could afford to winter in San Francisco, where they gambled, drank, and whored their newly acquired wealth away. Those who struck out were forced to overwinter in the frozen north, where they gambled, drank, and whored away whatever pittance they had, or cadged freebies. Everyone else hauled off to Tenakee.

Tenakee, about 65 miles from Juneau by water, is a shorter hop by floatplane (no airport). In the '70s the village consisted of small, ramshackle buildings lined up along both sides of an unpaved street that ran parallel and close to the shoreline. Vehicular traffic was limited to bicycles and hand-carts. The dwellings on the water side were built out on pilings, and had a clear advantage in the waste disposal department, at least at high tide. Where the road ended at the eastern end was a small boat harbor. Near the center of town were located a small general store that sold everything, a diner that was sometimes open, the float plane and fuel docks—and, at the center of everything, the bath.

The Tenakee bath was quite different from those previously described for Baranof Warm Springs. The outlet from the geothermal spring was housed within a building containing a changing room and a second room with a single, concrete-lined, sunken "bath" of sufficient size to hold several people at a time. The constant inflow from the spring was balanced by overflow exiting drain holes in the floor around the bath. The hot, steamy enclosure indeed smelled of brimstone, and was dimly lit by a couple of naked lightbulbs hanging from the ceiling.

The bath was the social center of town; all the latest gossip was exchanged there. As no bathing apparel was permitted, there were regularly scheduled men's and women's hours throughout the day (and night).

I had no problem with the Tenakee bath. Linda thought it was gross.

I don't remember what the year-round population of Tenakee was in the '70s. It may have been 100, maybe more, probably less. But it was the nature of its residents, rather than the quantity, that made Tenakee special. Almost to a person they could have been clones of Mammy and Pappy Yokum, ancient characters in the vintage Al Capp comic strip *Lil' Abner*. I came to think of the Tenakee of that time as Dogpatch North. For those readers too young to remember this iconic comic strip—which may be most—I urge you to take the time to google it. You won't be sorry.

Gary Hedges had two loves in his life: his wife, and Tenakee Springs. Marg knew before she married him that Tenakee was Gary's vision of an island paradise. She married him anyway. Gary owned one of those decrepit shacks along main street, going back and forth between Juneau and Tenakee every chance he got to fish, crab, hunt deer, hit the bath, and just hang out with the locals. As Tenakee had no doctor or other source of medical care, he became the community's *de facto* physician, managing the chronic ailments of the aged population, making sure they got their medications, and coaxing them into the hospital in Juneau when necessary. I don't think he ever charged for his services, but often received tokens of gratitude in the form of local specialties, such as pickled deer brains.

Tenakee underwent a transformation through the 1980s as the aged denizens of Dogpatch North died off, to be replaced by comparatively upscale second-home owners from Juneau. The ramshackle dwellings were improved or replaced with bigger and better ones, one of which was built by Gary. Four-wheelers replaced hand-carts on main street. As his surgical practice wound down into retirement, Gary spent as many as 100 days a year there—much of the summer with Marg and visiting family, and a month in the fall with deer-hunting cronies (in these later years his mode of hunting was to reach a favorite spot by water, pull his skiff up on the beach, walk a short ways into the fringe timber wearing his toasty orange Mustang flotation work suit, set down under a tree with a good book, and wait for a deer to come along. Sometimes one actually did). Tenakee Springs somehow managed to retain its essential funkiness through the transformation, a consequence, I suspect, of Gary and the other physicians, attorneys, teachers, etc., slowly morphing into Al Capp characters themselves. Gary didn't have far to go.

———

Dr. John Taylor came late to Southeast Alaska. A transplant from Southern California, he was short, bandy-legged, gruff, and grizzled with a grey crew-cut. I don't think anyone knew his age for sure, but I'd guess it to have been late fifties or even sixty when he first arrived. Long-divorced, he led a bachelor life in Juneau, sometimes visited by a girl friend from down south. John was great company and never lacked for a social life. He was a regular at liar's club, the impromptu daily noon gathering of medical staff otherwise unengaged, in the hospital cafeteria, where he was the natural raconteur-in-chief.

John loved to fish, and on his arrival wasted no time getting into it. A few days into his new life in Southeast, armed with light spinning tackle and no local knowledge (and maybe no license), he was casting a small lure from the bank at Tee Harbor, with absolutely no idea of what he might be fishing for. As related at liar's club, he hooked onto something that felt like a snag. The "snag" eventually came to the surface and revealed itself as a huge, silvery slab. It rolled once, then proceeded to run him completely out of line, which of course then snapped. John had hooked into a really big king salmon, something many try to do for seasons on end without succeeding.

My mother could be something of a snob when it came to "my son, the doctor." She didn't mean to but she couldn't help it. After telling her of a recent fishing foray with the local gas-passer, she went on about how nice it was that I would associate socially with a gas station attendant. I had to explain that John was neither a pump jockey nor particularly flatulent, but an anesthesiologist.

He accompanied Mike Franklin and myself on one of our annual spring steelhead safaris to Petersburg, where we would stay at Jim Hammer's cabin on Petersburg Creek for several days of concentrated fishing. On our final day John, whose knees were none too good, opted to stay at the cabin rather than make another long trek upstream. When we returned in late afternoon we found him sitting on the cabin steps in his long johns, with two nice steelhead lying on the grass nearby. His story went something like this: He put a watermelon, which he had impulse-bought before we headed off from Petersburg, in the shallow tributary stream in front of the cabin to cool, while he alternated fishing the deep hole just down from the cabin (with spawn bags. To John, flyfishing was an incomprehensible affectation.) with basking in the unseasonably pleasant weather. As the day wore on, unbeknownst to John the incoming tide lifted his melon off the tributary bed and it began its journey out into, and then down, the creek proper. From his perch on the cabin steps, John was horrified at the sight of his precious melon accelerating past him and escaping. Saving it would require an heroic effort, but he was up to it: stripping to his birthday suit, he charged ass-deep into the creek's forty-something degree water in hot pursuit of the fleeing melon. Success! As he was returning to

297

shore with his prize, a couple in a skiff coming up the creek on the tide went by and gave him a cheery wave. John reciprocated the gesture. What else could he do?

The couple in the skiff probably still talks about the elderly gent they encountered that day, emerging from the frigid creek in his all-togethers, clutching a watermelon.

We gave John holy hell for keeping those steelhead, as it put him over his limit. All he could do was grump about "what's the use of catching fish if you can't keep 'em?" The catch-and-release ethic had not yet reached him.

After returning to Juneau and work as usual, we were concerned when John turned up missing. He was actually in Seattle, undergoing a double coronary bypass. He had never mentioned to us the chest pain induced by his aquatic caper.

John was once pulled over by JPD for a broken tail light or some such thing, and flunked the routine field sobriety test in spectacular fashion. He seldom touched alcohol, and related at liar's club that he couldn't have passed that test on the best day he ever had. He'd never been able to get beyond "Y" when asked to repeat the alphabet backwards, and his bad knees and marginal balance made it impossible for him to walk a straight line. Anyway, he was packed off in the paddy wagon and booked on suspicion of DUI. He demanded, and was given, a test for blood alcohol level—but the damage had been done. The result wouldn't be back for days, by which time his name had appeared in the police blotter of the local paper. He was justifiably incensed, and demanded a retraction from the newspaper when ultimately cleared by a zero blood alcohol. A retraction was duly printed in a subsequent issue. But who reads small-print retractions on the back page, anyway?

John's small skiff swamped and capsized while he was tending his crab pot alone in Lena Cove. Fortunately someone on shore had seen it happen, came to the rescue, and pulled him out of the drink. On arrival at the hospital he was hypothermic and not in the best of shape, and would spend several days recuperating and being monitored in the ICU. He gave the ICU nurses fits. He'd sneak out of bed and double-time up and down a back staircase in his hospital johnnie—the silly gown that leaves one's butt hanging out in the back—all the while monitoring his own pulse and oxygen saturation in response to exercise.

John's time on the Alaskan scene was short—not much more than a half-dozen years—but he made up in quality what he lacked in quantity. He easily merits a place in the pantheon of characters that contributed to making Alaska what it was.

———

Dr. Mike Franklin arrived in Juneau about four months ahead of me, he and his wife running their 24-foot boat up from Seattle through the inside passage. A family practitioner several years younger than I, he, Kim Smith, and another doc similar in age and experience would establish a group practice in family medicine, the Juneau Family Practice Clinic.

My first impression was that Mike would probably not last a year in family medicine. He had none of the warm-and-fuzzy about him, with a brusque, no-nonsense, cut-to-the chase manner. He didn't seem that much of a people-person, didn't suffer fools lightly, and his rich but wry sense of humor went right over the heads of those without one. Add to that an Ichabod Crane-like physique (on second thought, more like a young Abe Lincoln) with eyes magnified behind thick glasses, and you have what seemed one more cut out for a career in pathology or radiology—but I could not have been more wrong. Over time he proved to be highly popular with his patients, a capable and caring physician, willing and able to step out of his comfort zone when it was in the best interest of his patients.

We bonded over our love of fishing, and in particular, flyfishing. A natural athlete—see the chapter on basketball—Mike was a graceful and efficient fly caster. We would share many outdoor experiences together, more than a few of which Mike turned into real adventures.

Mike was one of the smartest people I have ever known, and had the gift of finding humor in almost any situation. His was the business mind that kept the Family Practice Clinic on the rails. He largely designed his family home. He had played baseball at a high level, and when his son began showing signs of similar aptitude and interest, he almost singlehandedly brought Juneau's first youth and high school baseball programs into existence.

But there was another aspect to Mike: He was prone to one unintentional comic pratfall after another, often sucking innocents like myself into their vortex. If a complete list were compiled it would fill a book in itself, and the antidotes related here barely scratch the surface.

My first exposure came early. Mike had borrowed another friend's garage for assembling a trailer for his boat, but the 4WD vehicle he had ordered to tow it with had not arrived by the time he wanted to haul the boat out for the winter. Since we had just gotten our 4WD International Scout and it had a trailer hitch, he recruited me.

I should have known we were in trouble when I hooked the trailer to the Scout and started to move it out of the garage. The trailer turned out to be just a smidgeon too wide, and the wheels popped the wooden framing off both sides of the garage door opening (how that happened I don't know, as the trailer was supposed to be the same width as an automobile. But happen it did).

We got downtown and hauled his boat out at the Harris Harbor launching ramp, and things were looking good. But as we motored along Egan Drive I saw disaster unfold, first in the side view mirror and then out the side window. A trailer wheel was overtaking us on its own, eventually veering across the oncoming lane and coming to rest on the opposite shoulder.

Most fortunately it was a tandem trailer, and could withstand one set of untightened lug nuts. I pulled onto the shoulder and Mike went to retrieve the errant wheel. What luck—our pull-over site just happened to be right in front of the Juneau state trooper detachment headquarters. Just as Mike returned with the wheel, the head honcho came out to see what was going on. He spotted Mike and started chatting while I slunk down as low as possible, knowing full well that Mike's trailer lacked not only the mandatory tail and brake lights but also a license plate and registration.

I could hardly believe it when the trooper walked back to the building without even a glance at me. Seems that Mike had recently delivered the latest addition to the trooper's family, and he was out there to let Mike know that mother and infant were doing fine at home.

Once Mike and wife Beatrice chartered a floatplane to take them, a small inflatable, a cooler, and some fishing gear to a spot on the Taku River, from where they would take a leisurely day-float down to a designated pick-up spot. The Taku, one of Southeast's longest and largest rivers, flows out of Canada to emerge at the coast just south of Juneau, and its banks exhibit no signs of human habitation for miles on end save for a few getaway cabins owned by a group of Juneauites calling themselves the "River Rats." Long stretches of river are not likely to see a soul for days on end, and those who get into trouble are on their own.

Mike and Beatrice got into trouble. Curious about a wooden structure hard against a bank—it proved to be an old fish trap—they pulled closer, unaware of the jagged metal protruding outward just beneath surface and rendered invisible by the glacial, silty water, which was also quite deep. Poof! The mortally punctured gasbag went down from under them. The cooler and all their gear were gone, leaving the couple clinging to the wooden structure in deep, frigid water with a strong current running. I don't recall how long they were marooned in this precarious fix, but luck would be with them. River Rat Jerry Adams happened by in his jet sled, the standard mode of transportation for those negotiating the opaque, snag-filled river. He saw them, pulled them out, and took them to safety (Jerry Adams was the founder and proprietor of Jerry's Meats in Juneau. The business is now in its third generation of family ownership, and offers a variety of Southeast Alaskan seafood products both at their retail outlet and on the internet. Their smoked salmon is right up there in a class with Linda's; give it a try.).

The following spring when Mike and I first arrived on Petersberg creek, I noticed that his fly rod container appeared the worse for wear. He explained that he'd received a call over the winter from a hunter who had found the case washed up a beach on Admiralty Island, across Stephens Passage from the mouth of Taku Inlet and River; Mike's name and contact info were still legible on the case. Of course Mike had never bothered to open the case since he got it back, and when he did so now the reel seat fell out first, followed by a rod with disintegrated guide wrappings and a moldy cork grip. It was the only rod he had brought, but luckily I had brought a spare.

Mike was repeatedly confounded by loose ends of his own making. He once brought his boat alongside ours with the intent of tying up to us, and threw us a line—both ends of it. Pulling up to anchor near us on another occasion, he tossed his anchor off the bow and watched in consternation as it and the 20 feet of chain to which it was attached disappeared into the depths, unencumbered by an anchor line. At Petersburg Creek a big steelhead took him into his backing—or would have, had his backing been attached to his fly line. The following morning while walking the trail alongside the stream he spotted a sizeable fish washed up on a gravel bar, his fly embedded in its jaw and the length of his fly line trailing off into the current. The steelhead had apparently played itself to exhaustion against the resistance of the line. All of these things actually happened.

In his professional life, bizarre cases seemed drawn to him as if by some mysterious tropism. On one of the days he was on call to admit patients who had no physician, a young man turned up in the emergency room with nasty second-degree burns involving the pubic area and genitals, along with some shallow puncture wounds in the same area. Afflicted in the worst way with crabs—pubic lice—he had taken matters into his own hands with an ingenious home solution: He first shaved off precisely one-half of his pubic hair, then saturated the remaining half with lighter fluid and set it ablaze. Any lice surviving the inferno he stabbed to death with an ice pick as they fled into the clearcut.

Did this really happen? The story as related is the abridged and embellished version that emerged in the course of multiple retellings at liar's club—but the first half of the story is true. Mike never lied or exaggerated, even at liar's club. But the embellished version that became ensconced in hospital—and Mike Franklin's—lore and legend, is the way I prefer to remember it.

Mike was afflicted with colon cancer at about age 30, a particularly aggressive form associated with a bad gene. Given less than a year to live, he lived for twenty. He wanted to watch his infant son grow up, and in doing so endured treatments that would have broken both the will and the constitution of most mere mortals. He was able to continue, with periodic interruptions, an active and fulfilling personal and professional life. He passed in 1998, and I still miss him.

———

Each of those profiled in this chapter—indeed, any more briefly profiled or even mentioned in this book—could have written this book, or one like it. All have a story to tell, of their own Southeast Alaskan odyssey. All are, or were, exceptional people, drawn to an exceptional place by some common thread.

Epilogue

Two roads diverged in a wood, and I - I took the one less traveled by, And that has made all the difference.

—Robert Frost, from **The Road Not Taken**

Chance and choice. How different but how closely intertwined they were, coming together not once but several times as between them they determined the trajectory of our lives. Chance ultimately created choice, and we chose the road less traveled by.

The journey we embarked upon along that less-traveled road began more than half a century ago. During its course our children grew to adulthood; one had been born in Southeast Alaska. Almost the entirety of my career in surgery was spent there. We had embraced the lifestyle, made lifelong friends, learned and exercised new skills, saw and experienced the country with an intimacy accessible to few others. I lived out my teenage fantasies. Linda and I were approaching our mid-50s, still productive and in good health, when we opted to pull the plug, to bring it to a close. Why would we do that?

We had reached another fork in the road. Early in my residency, my mother-in-law once asked how I was able to handle the oft-ungodly hours and the workload. My answer to her had been that it beat working. Indeed, beginning with residency and for years thereafter, surgery had been fun—even exhilarating at times. Now there were all too many days when I arrived home angry, tired, or both. I had long felt that, for any physician, when the practice of medicine became a chore, just another job, it was time to go. And by 1990, I knew it was time for me. I still loved to operate and was still good at it, still enjoyed the satisfaction that came from seeing patients get well and jobs well done, but I was tired—tired of and from all the night call, tired of watching reimbursements shrink while overhead and paperwork soared, tired of low-level gum-snappers at insurance companies telling me how to manage my patients, tired of watching as colleagues were harassed by ambulance-chasing lawyers and of wondering if I would be next.

I was also watching as quantum changes in treatments and technology were, bit by bit, rendering my procedural repertory obsolete. Recent personnel additions to the medical community were also eliminating some of the extra hats the general surgeons wore, making our skills in those areas redundant and reducing our economic base. I was not alone; every general surgeon of my generation had to face one, the other, or both of these issues, and I wasn't going to be one that stayed too long at the ball. One thing that made it easier to let go was that I had never allowed what I did to become who I was.

Southeast Alaska was, by its nature and by virtue of its isolation, an intense but narrow experience. We also realized that Southeast Alaska was not likely to treat us kindly as we aged; with notable exceptions the likes of Ben Forbes, Tom Parke, and Don Nash, it was a young person's country. There were places and things we still wished to see and do, and we'd seen all too often in the course of my practice what happened when people waited too long. Our children were educated and out of the nest, the life we looked forward to down the road required more good health and vitality than it did wealth, and we'd saved enough to make a go of it. We knew full well that we would sorely miss what we were leaving behind, but it was time to turn the page and move on.

And so it was that we retired to the Central Idaho Rockies and became ski bums. We've now lived more years there than we had in Alaska—but in some ways it feels as though we never left. We phased out gradually: We kept our boat for several years, spending some of each summer living aboard. I did a number of locum tenens stints for friend and colleague Gary Hedges, covering his surgical practice while he took time off. We came up to spend time and boat with friends, and I returned to hunt every fall for many years. Even now we return periodically to renew ties with old friends and old, beloved places, and we remain in touch with other friends who, like ourselves, had spent their careers in Alaska and eventually moved on (many of those who did, like ourselves, retain deep connections to Southeast). I think—feel—that when we left we took some of Southeast Alaska with us, and at the same time left some of ourselves behind.

How would things have turned out had we taken the conventional and more-traveled fork? It's not something we can know, and not something we think about. And how do we feel now about choosing the less-traveled road all those years ago, not knowing all that was in store around the bend where the road was lost from view? Robert Frost's traveler summed it up in fewer words, and far more eloquently, than I could ever hope to do.